Sex Positive Now

AN ANTHOLOGY OF MOVERS AND
SHAKERS IN THE WORLD OF SEXUALITY

Allena Gabosch & Jeremy Shub

Published by Sexy Activist Publishing
Jeremy Shub and Allena Gabosch

Copyright © 2019
First printing 2019 All rights reserved.

No part of this publication may be reproduced, distributed, or transmitted in any form or by any means, including photocopying, recording, or other electronic or mechanical methods, without the prior written permission of the publisher, except in the case of brief quotations embodied in critical reviews and certain other noncommercial uses permitted by copyright law.

For permission requests, write to the publisher.
jeremy@shub.info

ISBN 978-0-6487021-2-2

Cover Design by Ann Roberts Creative
www.annrobertsgraphics.info
Cover image @lauradesign at Unsplash

Illustrations by Jing JingWang
Instragram: @jingshiwang01
jingshiwang01@outlook.com

Printed by IngramSpark Austraila

 A catalogue record for this book is available from the National Library of Australia

Some names and identifying details have been changed to protect the privacy of individuals. Although the authors and publisher have made every effort to ensure that the information in this book was correct at press time, the authors and publisher do not assume and hereby disclaim any liability to any party for any loss, damage, or disruption caused by errors or omissions, whether such errors or omissions result from negligence, accident, or any other cause. This book is not intended as a substitute for the medical advice of physicians. The reader should regularly consult a physician in matters relating to their health and particularly with respect to any symptoms that may require diagnosis or medical attention.

Sex Positive Now

Allena Gabosch & Jeremy Shub

Published by Sexy Activist Publishing House

CONTENTS

Holy Body Poem – Captain Snowden — 8
Introduction – Allena Gabosch and Jeremy Shub — 10
Sex is a lifelong component of my personhood: my sex positive journey – Allena Gabosch — 11
My sex positive life – Jeremy Shub — 14

1. CULTURE AND DEFINITIONS — 19

The principles of sex positivity – Charlies Glickman — 21
Sex positive, sex negative or sex critical – Meg-John Barker and John Hancock — 24
Sex positivity for a more positive world – Tamara Pincus — 27

2. SEX NEGATIVITY — 31

The negative in sex positive – Kim Loliya — 32
Sexual shame: How to become sexually empowered (and live longer while boosting your creativity!) – Veronica Monet — 38
Sex negative culture is a threat to civilisation – Gloria Brame — 41
Surviving sexual assault – Jimanekia Ebor — 47
Sex positivity and asexuality – Shay McCombs — 49

3. SEX WORK AND PORN — 55

A nice girl like me – Eva Sless — 56
Sex positive can't be whore negative – Maggie McNeill — 57
Peep show pedagogy: Lessons from the Lusty Lady – Ron Richardson — 60
The birth of the blue movie critic – Susie Bright — 62
How to edit lesbian porn – Sui Yao — 68
How porn (yoga) changed my (sex) life – Yuri Kotke — 70

4. DISABILITY — 75

The reality of working as a queer cripple and the inaccessibility of sex positivity to the disabled community – Andrew Gurza — 76
Twisted bodies, kinky minds – Jordan Bouray — 78

5. PLEASURE AND JOY — 83

Openess, energy, expansive orgasms, oh my – Mac McGregor and Dawn Celeste McGregor — 84
DDF/UB2**: on being sex positive in a shame based, insensitive culture – Joel Davis — 87
I'm not washed up on the beach yet: sex, relationships and ageing – Linda Kirkman — 90
My first girlfriend – Buck Angel — 94
A size queen solution – IM Jae — 95
Learn a new orgasm: How to upgrade your orgasm technique – Betty Dodson — 98

6. GENDER — 103

Meaningful support: How to be an ally to trans people – Sara Blaze — 104
Power, pleasure and justice: Towards an anti-oppressive sex positivity – Tai Fenix Kulystin — 109
Two spirits – Beau Black — 113

7. EDUCATION — 117

Sex positive education – An interview with Uma Ayelet Furman and Deej Juventin by Jeremy Shub — 118
My sex positive journey – Nekole Shapiro — 129
To love free of chains – Lasara Firefox — 132
Five things I learnt from twelve years of sex positive podcasting – Cunning Minx — 134
Sex positive parenting – Taryn De Vere — 137
Extending knowledge and solving problems: The creation of the journal of positive sexuality – DJ Williams and Emily E Prior — 139

8. RELATIONSHIPS — 145

Ten tips for fulfilling relationships (of all types!) – Eri Kardos — 146
Switching speeds – Kevin Patterson — 150
Claiming your power with no – Kris Lovestone — 152

9. KINK — 155

Spinning the wheel of destiny – Mark A. Michaels and Patricia Johnson — 156
Sex in the dungeon (yes really) – Janet W Hardy — 159
Intimacy and the D/S relationship – Jay Wiseman — 161
When your erotic identity is damaged – Race Bannon — 164

10. SPIRITUALITY — 169

Spirituality and sex – Interview by Jeremy Shub with Kenneth Ray Stubbs — 170
Circles of love, sex and spirit – Erfahrungskreis: Verena Neuenschwander and Remigius Wagner — 180
Has Judeo-Christian culture ever been sex positive, or has it always been an incubator for sexual shame? – Tina Schermer Sellers — 184

11. ECOSEXUALITY — 193

Eco sex – Interview with Jaz Papadopoulos with pioneers Annie Sprinkle and Beth Stephens — 194
From roots to shoots: The sex positive foundations of the ecosexuality movement – Teri Ciacci — 198

12 POLITICS AND COMMUNITY — 211

Polyamory and the black feminist – Ruby Johnson — 212
The politics of sex positive – Dawn Serra — 214

13 OUR SEX POSITIVE FUTURE — 219

How death taught me that great sex can change the world – Liz Powell
Sex positivity, eh? – Jaz Papadopolous — 220
How I came to be sex positive as an asian woman who is also a sexologist, and how you can be too – Martha Lee — 228

Sex is boring in parts poem – Captain Snowden — 231

HOLY BODY POEM
Captain Snowdon 2014

Air
I need to feel you
suck you from my lovers mouth
and fill them up again with you

Air
suspire away my shame as I contain you
until it is almost to late
then release

Air to re-spirit Let's
Let's gasp gulp and giggle
Let's to snore, sneeze snort and sniffle

air with you I pant, whisper and heave

Guardians of the watchtowers of the east
feel our body prayers of bliss and resistance
know we conspire to re-spire with you
help me catch my breath

Fire

I need you
to feel my heat
friction of bark on skin- sand on skin- fur on skin

Fire lets's snap, crackle   and   pop my desire
before breakfast
at the rest area
with a hot being in my mouth
in this room right now

Fire teach me of your ways to burn   and fuck
spark -   flame-   embers -   ashes

Guardians of the watchtowers of the South
feel our body prayers a blaze with glitter and irreverence
know we alight to insurrection
with you

Water

I need
you in all of your forms of dripping
dis ambiguation

Water let's drool
splash and spray
steam and sprinkle

Water let's run off together
Dam it
drop by drop by drip by drip
I am learning your preciousness

Guardians of the watchtowers of the west
feel our salivating, lactating squirting prayers for you
we are becoming clear in our protection of you
with you

Earth

I need to feel you
under me, on top of me an in me
To stick things in you and to stick your things in me
I surrender to the weight of you sometimes

Earth I need your mud in the folds of me
the taste of berries in my mouth and your poison oak on my ass

This body needs to be soiled, muddied and casted in the evening sun
Earth my beloved finds you in petrified form and you fuck us apart together

Guardians of the watchtowers of the North
Feel us listen for you and to you
Feel us touch with you

Spirit-

feel our bodies call to your bodies which are your body and our body our body our
body you are
we are our body are you your body our body
we are you

INTRODUCTION

Allena and Jeremy have a grand vision. That one day we can live in a world where sex and sexuality is celebrated. Both long for people's experience of sexuality with themselves and others to be positive.

Our goal is to create a new sex-positive world. To support the change of cultural norms around sexuality and relationships. In the world of Sex Positive Now people have the freedom and permission to be the sexual beings that they already are. Pleasure and joy are vital to our well-being. Sexual shame is a thing of the past.

People are celebrated for their sexuality, gender, who or how they love.

Consensual sexuality in all of its forms is healthy and life affirming.

People can make conscious choices about their sexuality and relationships, such as celibacy, asexuality, kink, polyamory, fetish and other forms of sexual and relationship expression that are outside of what is now considered the norm. We are frolicking playfully with ourselves and each other.

Why did we write this book? We desire future generations to experience sex as pleasurable, healthy, and natural. It is possible for change to come to this area of human experience. In our vision we include a wish to see a shift in the global perspective. Our goal is to influence the whole planet. We believe that by writing this book together and allowing diverse people to read it, that transformation is possible. The book has been designed for a wide audience including friends, family, community, politicians, doctors, parents, teachers, police and health professionals. This book contains a variety of voices and a variety of styles from people all over the planet.

Allena's biography

Allena Gabosch, was the executive director of both the *Center For Sex Positive Culture* and *Foundation for Sex Positive Culture* from their creation until retiring January 1, 2015. She has been active in the sex positive movement practically from its inception; producing educational and social events for the sex-positive community since 1990. She was the development director for the center until full retirement in January 2017 and was a board member of the *National Coalition for Sexual Freedom* (ncsfreedom.org).

Allena worked for Seattle *SWOP (Sex Workers Outreach Project)* and is also a relationship coach. She is a frequent speaker on many sexuality related subjects at colleges and conferences around the US, Canada and Europe with an emphasis on sexuality, relationships, BDSM and polyamory. She is a frequent guest on local and national radio and television as an expert on sexuality and has been in numerous documentaries.

She is a former Producer of the *Seattle Erotic Art Festival* and a former commissioner with the *Seattle Commission for Sexual Minorities*. Allena is currently working on a book about navigating relationships. She is a kinky, mix-raced, cisgendered, sapiosexual, polyamorous switch and considers herself extremely blessed as she has a rich and full life, with many amazing and loving people in her "polycule".

Allena's personal mission statement
To bring joy to sexuality and to make a difference in the world.

Jeremy's biography

Jeremy currently works as a sex therapist, sex educator, and sex coach. He lives in Melbourne Australia. He identifies as polyamorous, kinky, and queer. He has two teenage kids that teach him about millennials, patience, and authenticity. Jeremy has university degrees in education, science, sexual health and creative art.

Jeremy's personal mission statement
To lovingly serve people with healing, supporting the journey back to self.
To allow love to flow with myself, family, friends, and community.

SEX IS A LIFELONG COMPONENT OF PERSONHOOD: MY SEX-POSITIVE JOURNEY
by Allena Gabosch

We are born sexual beings. From the time we are born to the day we die, erotic energy and sexuality are a part of our life. Even the absence of sex and erotic energy, they are still a part of our life. When we're young, if we're lucky and live in a sex-positive world, we have the freedom to explore our bodies and our erotic energy as soon as we discover that certain things make us feel good. I remember my first conscious orgasm. I was in the fourth grade on the playground climbing a rope. When I got to the top, this amazing intense pleasurable feeling almost knocked me off of that rope.

When I went home that night I used my hands to replay that feeling. I masturbated almost nightly until I realized that I was probably committing a sin (I was raised fundamentalist) because touching myself "down there" was wrong.

My celibacy lasted about a month before I was right back at it. I shared a room with my little sister and brother, so I instinctively knew to be quiet. Sadly, that quiet colored my sexuality for years. It wasn't until a partner asked me if I was enjoying myself that I realized that sexuality also could be loud—and I have made up for it ever since.

Being a young hippie girl in the early seventies meant I embraced the "free love" movement with a vengeance. I've never looked back. I have explored and played with and made love to and just fucked many amazing (and some not so amazing) people over the forty-five plus years that I've been sexually active. When I found this kinky sex-positive community it got even better. I was able to explore new things that had always been in the back of my mind, like bondage and SM.

While I've always been sexually adventurous, I didn't really start my journey to sex positivity until I met my former husband, Steve. Prior to meeting Steve, I was just starting to experiment with kinky sex with my then partner, Jake. Oh, I'd done a few kinky things prior to Jake (that's for another story), however, he was my first conscious kinky partner and we explored many things. (That, looking back, were not always the safest or the most thoughtful). However, it's what got me to meet Steve and that's huge.

Jake and I were looking for others to explore our kink with and back in the late eighties, that was usually done by answering ads in magazines (yes, paper magazines, not online). There was a local swinger magazine that had a few ads looking for couples to join them in kinky sex. We answered a few and didn't hear back from any for awhile. We had one response from a couple who turned out to be rather unpleasant and we kind of gave up. At the same time, our relationship was strained, and we ended the romance to save the cafe we owned together (Back Alley Jake's, in Auburn WA). And that's when, a few months after we'd placed the ad, Steve contacted me. He and his then girlfriend were looking for another couple and since Jake and I weren't a couple anymore, it meant no play. However, it turned out Steve worked for Boeing in Auburn and he came by the cafe to at least meet us. And a friendship was born. He was a fount of knowledge and answered my silly beginner questions with patience and what eventually became love. In the midst of our burgeoning friendship, he and his girlfriend parted ways (not because of me, thankfully) and this opened the door for what would eventually become my longest marriage and my introduction to a whole new world of what I now consider Sex Positive Culture.

For a couple years, prior to our meeting, Steve and his girlfriend had been renting a local swinger club and holding parties called Kinky Couples. This were originally under the umbrella of the National Leather Alliance (NLA), which started in Seattle and of which Steve was a huge part of. I'd heard of the NLA and their yearly conferences, Living in Leather (LIL). In fact, the year before Steve and I became a couple, another kinky friend of mine invited me to LIL-IV in Portland, which I chickened out on. Just like I had chickened out on attending a Kinky Couples party when Steve and his girlfriend were running it. This time, I was an item with Steve and couldn't chicken out again. (of which I'm very thankful).

When Steve took me to Living in Leather V, my mind was blown. They were doing some things that at that time were pretty groundbreaking. The NLA was started by a bunch of queer kinksters and their parties were usually segregated by gender. However a few straight folk, like Steve, wanted to be involved and they adjusted their parties and events to accommodate and welcome the "pansexual" crowd as they soon became known. The 10,000 square foot dungeon had a women's area, a men's area, and a place called Any Which Way area. I remember walking into the dungeon, terrified and then I heard the sounds. There were people crying, cumming, screaming, and laughing and all of a sudden I felt totally at home. I'd found my people. Needless to say, this event changed how I looked at kink and my life. It was transformative.

Then there was Kinky Couples. That took my transformation to a whole new level. I started helping Steve with the parties, shortly after LIL-V. We took over a local swing club called New Horizons and turned it into a two- or three-day kinky party four to six times a year. We opened our arms to the swing community as long as they played by our rules (we had few: attend as a couple or moresome, practice safer sex in public play, be respectful of the people and the space, ask before touching, and listen to the dungeon monitors) and we also created space for our ageplay community (we had a room with adult sized playpen, crib, and highchair), the pony community, and other niches within the kink/fetish world. This kind of melding was unheard of at the time, yet for us it was important. We attracted people from all over North America. We were creating sex-positive culture and didn't even know it. We just thought we were throwing great parties.

If it wasn't for the NLA, Kinky Couples, New Horizon, and, of course, Steve, there wouldn't be such a strong sex-positive community in the Northwest. Because of this early journey, in the mid-nineties we eventually created The Center for Sex Positive Culture (aka The Wet Spot) and the Foundation for Sex Positive Culture. We also inspired several other organizations to take off and we created a community of people who work together, play together and love together. A sex-positive community. It's been an incredible adventure.

Now I'm 65. With age comes a whole new approach to sex and erotic energy. I'm not as instantly ready to play as I used to be. Not only has my desire waned some, so have my abilities. My body aches in areas it never ached before. There's the wonderful dryness that comes with menopause. And I just don't bend the way I used to. While I haven't stopped, I've learned to adapt. My sexuality has become more thoughtful and a bit less crazy, and it's still fulfilling and amazing.

People my age and older are staying more sexually active than ever before due to healthier lifestyles, advances in medication (i.e. Viagra and vaginal lubricants) and the realization that we don't have to stop being sexual. In fact, sex can be enjoyed much later in life than we'd ever imagined. And when you add kinky sex to the mix it is even easier to continue, since many of the kinky things we do don't require body parts fitting into other body parts.

Up until a few years ago, when he passed away his mid-nineties, my friend Walt used BDSM to stay sexually active. He was an amazing guy who loved to cross-dress, and he played up until a few years before he passed. I fondly remember the last time I saw him play. He had on a sexy lacy bra and panties (and men's sneakers because his feet hurt) and was joyfully receiving a spanking from a sexy younger dominant woman. He was in his element and it made me so happy to see him so happy.

For many of us sex and erotic energy are critical to our health and well-being and the longer we can keep going the better for us!

There's a lot more to this story and I'll tell it another day. However, I wanted to share with you where I got my start and why I'm writing this book, *Sex Positive Now* with Jeremy Shub. It's because I want to create a sex-positive world and this is how it starts, with a few people, creating space and community and realizing that sex is a lifelong component to personhood.

MY SEX POSITIVE LIFE
by Jeremy Shub

In 2014 I went to a talk by Janet Hardy in Melbourne, at the Society of Australian Sexologists, where she was talking about sexuality, her book and her life. At one point she threw out the expression sex positive without an explanation as to what it was, and continued talking. I'd never heard the term before, so asked her immediately what she meant by it, to which another person in the room responded, "oh, everyone knows what that is!" Without an answer in hand, I left the talk and surveyed some friends about the term, but no one was totally clear about what it meant, even though we all had an intuitive sense about what it meant and that it was important…

So the journey began.

I have always had a great interest in and desire for sex. However, my earliest memories of sexual experiences were often associated with guilt and shame.

I work as a sex therapist, relationship counsellor, sacred intimate, sexological bodyworker, and sex educator. Strangely I have ended up in this field because of the culmination of many years of distress and upset that my desire has caused me. I've been in so many relationships where I fumbled my way through sex and intimacy, often not knowing that they were different things, and had to learn about sexuality and relationships so that I could be healthy. I am now in a position to support other people as they become aware of old wounds and walk the path towards wholeness.

That's not to say that I don't still get tripped up by my desire. I still get frustrated and act out in childish ways. I still fuck up in relationships. However rather than to be crippled by this, as I might have before, I now think it's liberating for an "expert" to still make a mess of such interactions. Sometimes my inner child is still in the driver's seat, even though he can't see properly over the wheel. This little boy has wounds and needs that my adult self can't understand, and as an adult, though I know many theories and "understand" how people can relate in healthy ways, my child self struggles to trust this adult self to look after us properly.

The child is still caught in the stories and the nervous system of the past. The struggle to survive when I felt neglected or ignored, or worse, abused. The child that didn't have any tools or resources to express that I wanted attention or hugs.

Somehow as an adult I need to hold myself and trust that I'll be held safely by others. I need to trust that I can stand alone or reach out for another. These are the fundamental lessons for all people to grow and thrive as adults. For me personally this gets complicated by the weave of stories about touch, sex, and intimacy.

It might be more clear to you if I explain the childhood abuse I referred to earlier. This is hard to talk about. In 2009 intense bushfires surrounded my home. My family had evacuated and I stayed. Not from some "save the house" heroic illusion. I had a deeper unconscious sense of wanting to stay with the land. One morning at five am I woke up abruptly with a clear sense that I had been sexually abused as a child and the person was known to me. I immediately called The

Centre Against Sexual Abuse and told them my story. After speaking with the worker, who suggested that I come in for an interview that week, I arrived at their service and met Deb for a session. In the session, though I became aware that I didn't have distinct memories of any abuse, Deb told me that she would take my case and we worked together for three years. They were painful years of exploration and healing. We trawled through all my childhood, all the stories of a little boy not feeling loved.

How does this relate to sex positivity you may ask? What I saw from these sessions was that I really wanted intimacy. I was starving for touch and play—sometimes wanting a skin-to-skin sensation and sometimes just loving touch. This was an important part of my healing journey towards healthy sexuality. As an adult I still get confused about what sensation I want to feel. Sex can be an experience of intimacy or it can be just raw pleasure and desire. Sex can be a sacred experience of joining another person in a profound expansion. Overall sex can be many things for each person.

As an adult, and what I'd also like to talk about, is whether or not I became a sex addict. When I was married to a person with a significantly different libido style, it was easy for me to see, well now at least, how I thought I was an addict. Many therapists now question if sex addiction is a real diagnosis. I know that I would not call myself that now. Not because I have changed but because my beliefs and landscape have shifted. I now have delicious intimacy with people that see the world through a sex-positive lens, so my sexual desire is now welcomed and matched by others. There are adult conversations about wants, consent, agreements, and boundaries. I identify as slutty, poly, kinky, queer—these titles are fluid and generally suggest a passion for sex positivity rather than sex addictivity.

The places that I am starting to find such sex positivity is play parties. Play parties are social events for adults to have sex. I have been to a few different versions of these events. Often there will be a moment when my awareness shifts from my personal experience of pleasure into sensing the freedom for sex. At the parties people enter a space where the expectation is that sex is on offer. Sex is normalized and becomes natural. Once such experience happened to me last week at a swinger night, at a "sex on premises venue." For a second I glimpsed 100 people being naked, playing and having sex, and it struck me how these events are still seen with discrimination from the outside. There are so many taboos about how adults should play. Somehow in our history we developed a cultural view that sex has very specific constraints. It should only be done with certain people (monogamous partners), in certain places (privacy of the bedroom) in certain ways (heterosexual, genital, vanilla). There is still so much stigma about how we can play with each other and have pleasure. How we can share pleasure with each other. Whereas actually, adults can have sex in many ways, wherever and however they want. When people consent to play, explore, pleasure, and get turned on, then everything is possible.

I feel that in my little bubble of friends that there is a growing movement of sex positivity around Self Pleasure. Some people call this masturbation or wanking. I prefer to call it self-pleasure, or solo sex, to emphasize the healthy element of the experience. Solo sex is the most practiced form of sexuality on the planet. My personal experience of this is growing from something I did with shame and haste (fear of being caught) to a healthy pleasure time. It feels really wonderful to have this lover (me!) who is always with me, always up for sex, always giving and consensual. This self-lover is sometimes kinky and doesn't shame me for my fetishes. I'm generous with sexy times, then sometimes up for just a quickie.

I believe that our journey from the sex-negative world, into the sex-positive lands of bliss, must pass through this area of self-pleasure. It is our first place of embodiment. Like when a baby first touches itself and feels joy—which I have had the honor of witnessing—and discovers itself. The way they explore, then test their skin, their fingers and toes, it's quite magical. As adults we can have this experience again by slowing down and trusting ourselves. I occasionally set up a quiet time for myself to indulge in myself. This is not usually a "candles, oils and worship my inner goddess" affair. It is simply when I close the bedroom door and give myself permission to enjoy the pleasure of my touch.

It still seems radical to enjoy these times, a rebellious act in the face of the dominant society. I'm aware of how I needed to be taught this practice by others. Not literally how to touch myself but that there are creative nourishing ways to be with me. Even writing this now I am remembering a session of erotic play from today. Though it feels treacherous to say that I'm my best lover at the moment, I realize I don't need to feel shy with myself when I want something. I can just know exactly what I want to feel.

Our sex-negative society, the shaming, the taboo, and the stigma, these things all motivate me to collaborate on this book. I dream of a sex-positive world where sex can be seen as healthy, natural, pleasurable, and fun. Currently, everything seems to be covered in shame and guilt. Even when I tell people my profession, there seems nervousness. It's a stigma faced by sex workers every day, where our culture is extremely prejudiced against the profession of exchanging sex for money. Maybe one day in the future sex therapy and sex education will be as normal as hairdressing or office work. I hope that one day sex workers, and this career type, will be accepted and valued for its service. I have recently started paying for sex and found it one of the most liberating experiences of my life. When I go to a brothel and pay a person for the experience I want I feel extremely satisfied. I am able to fully receive pleasure without needing to give. This to me is like the experience of receiving a massage. When I pay for this service I don't need to massage the practitioner back; they get the money and I get the massage. When I pay a sex worker I get to choose the experience I want.

Thanks for being on this journey with us. We are activists asking for change in the world. Thanks for being part of the Sex Positive Movement.

CHAPTER 1

WHAT IS SEX POSITIVITY? CULTURE AND DEFINITIONS

According to Wikipedia

The **sex-positive movement** is a social movement and philosophical movement that promotes and embraces sexuality and sexual expression, with an emphasis on safe and consensual sex. **Sex positivity** is "an attitude toward human sexuality that regards all consensual sexual activities as fundamentally healthy and pleasurable, encouraging sexual pleasure and experimentation."[1] The sex-positive movement also advocates for comprehensive sex education and safe sex as part of its campaign." The movement generally makes no moral distinctions among types of sexual activities, regarding these choices as matters of personal preference.[2]

Although the usage of *sex positive* goes back to the 1920s, it has only been in the last two decades that it has become a popular cultural and more mainstream movement.

THE PRINCIPLES OF SEX POSITIVITY?
by Charlie Glickman

Talking about sex positivity can be tricky because the concept is slippery and hard to define. The term was originally coined by Dr. Roger Libby in 1976—though Dr. Libby credits Wilhelm Reich's writings from the 1940's as his inspiration. In Dr. Libby's own words,

> Being sex positive means affirming sexual open, joyous sexual freedom and consensual, lusty pleasure. It means supporting rather than stifling sexually free and uplifting choices and offering sex education that is pro-sexual rather than antisexual (as with the current emphasis on abstinence).[3]

While this is a good starting point, it can have some unintended consequences. A lot of people fall into the trap of equating enthusiasm for sex with sex positivity. Others assume that having wild sexual adventures, or lots of partners, or being into BDSM automatically makes you sex positive.

Equating sex positivity with certain sexual behaviors would imply that people who don't do those things are sex negative, which simply isn't true. Sure, plenty of folks refrain from sexual exploration or from engaging in specific sexual acts because of internalized sex negativity or sexual shame. But there are many others who have tried a variety of sexual activities but decided that those pursuits aren't the kinds of things they enjoy. There are people who simply have no interest in them, and there are people who don't engage in various sexual acts because of previous experiences of discomfort, pain, or trauma. None of this makes a person sex negative, and we do them a disservice when we forget that.

I know some people who are asexual and incredibly sex positive. They can celebrate other people's joys and pleasures while also being quite clear that they have no interest in participating in the same activities. And I know some people who have wild and crazy sex with lots of people but who are still sex negative. These people carry a lot of negative judgments about people whose sex lives look different than theirs, and they aren't shy about shaming folks for it. The sex that you do or don't have and the attitudes you have about people whose sex lives are unlike yours are two distinct things; it's a mistake to assume that one implies anything about the other.

In my view, sex positivity is the perspective that the only measure of a sexual act or practice is the consent, pleasure, and well-being of the people who do it—and the people who are affected by it. Any other judgments, attitudes, or feelings that one might have about it are likely to be reflections one's own perspective, rather than anything about that sexual act or practice. Having said that, each of these ingredients is far more complex than they might first appear.

---

[1] Gabocsh, "A Sex Positive Renaissance," https://allenagabosch.wordpress.com/2014/12/08/a-sex-positive-renaissance.

[2] Ivanski, C., & Kohut, T. (2017) Exploring definitions of sex positivity through thematic analysis. The Canadian Journal of Human Sexuality, 26(3), 216-225. https://dx.doi.org/10.3138/cjhs.2017-0017

[3] "Interview with Dr. Roger Libby on Sex Positivity." Simplysxy, September 2, 2014, http://simplysxy.com/articles/2014/09/02/interview-with-dr-roger-libby-creator-of-the-term-sex-positivity/

Consent is a surprisingly complicated thing that goes far beyond the question of whether someone says yes or no. Somatic sex educator Betty Martin points out that a lot of people comply with or endure touch that they don't want because of early childhood experiences. When we were infants, people needed to do things to take care of us that we didn't like. This means that, when our nervous systems are wide open and learning to adapt to the world around us, we got the message that there are times when our desire to not be touched will be set aside. We learned to expect and tolerate unwanted touch, and we learned that this is simply how things will sometimes happen.

Of course, many of us have plenty of other experiences that reinforce this early life lesson. Some of us go through sexual intrusion, assault, and trauma. Some of us are explicitly taught that we don't get to say no. Some of us are shamed into not even being aware of where our no is. There are trends that relate to gender, race, social class, physical ability, and other aspects of our lives that impact how often our "no" is ignored and therefore, how intensely we are trained away from using it. But even without those added factors, every single one of us has learned that there are times when we don't get to say no to unwanted touch; we learn that we have to comply with it. This is simply a part of the human experience, and it shapes everything we do as sexual beings as we get older.

Learning how to move out of compliance and endurance and into empowered consent can be a surprisingly complex and multifaceted process. When we talk about whether the participants of a sexual interaction consented to it, we're really talking about whether they each had the awareness, the capacity, the skills and tools, and the freedom to speak their needs and desires. The question of whether an individual is able to provide meaningful consent goes far beyond the superficial issue of whether they each said yes or no.

Pleasure can be difficult to pin down because there are so many different ways to assess it. What makes something feel good to one person and unpleasant to someone else? What makes a sensation feel good one day and not another day? What makes an experience feel good with one partner and not with a different person? Each of us moves through the world with a unique body, a unique nervous system, and an individual set of emotional responses. There are plenty of things that you enjoy that someone else finds unpleasant, and plenty of things you dislike that someone else loves.

There are also different kinds of pleasure. In her book The Pleasure Zone, psychotherapist Stella Resnick identifies eight different categories of pleasure, each of which has many variations. They include,

- primal pleasure (letting go and "just being")
- pain relief (releasing and resolving old hurts)
- elemental pleasures (play, humor, movement, and sound)
- mental pleasures (curiosity, learning, and positive thinking)
- emotional pleasures (gratitude, love, courage, and enthusiasm)
- sensual pleasures (taking delight in the senses)
- sexual pleasures (arousal, desire, romance, and abandon)
- spiritual pleasures (feeling a part of something good)

An erotic experience can include any of these in a variety of combinations. So how do we assess, for example, a situation in which someone might not experience a lot of sexual pleasure but where the emotional or elemental pleasure they feel makes it worthwhile?

Well-being has multiple definitions, making it a particularly difficult concept to pin down. At its most basic, well-being describes feeling good or positive about one's life. But even this definition gets tricky because we each have our own ways of experiencing the positive. When I apply this definition to the concept of sex positivity, I see it as asking the question: does this experience or practice support my life, my relationships, and my sense of self? Or does it limit or hinder them?

We also need to consider at the time frame that we're using. A sexual experience might feel incredibly positive and supportive in the moment, but if it's followed by a shame reaction or health consequences, what does that mean? Who gets to decide how to weigh each of these considerations? I might view the injuries that a marathon runner has as hindering their well-being, while they might feel that the overall benefit outweighs the pain. Similarly, one person might have nothing but positive thoughts about being bruised from an intense spanking while another person might find it unpleasant or upsetting.

Ultimately, consent, pleasure, and well-being all need to be defined by each person based on their own experiences, feelings, and beliefs. If you're going to judge someone else's sexual practices without asking them how they feel about them, your assessment almost certainly says more about you than it does about them.

The people who are affected by it also need to be considered. My original definition of sex positivity only looked at the people involved in a sexual experience, but I later came to see our action's effect on others also needs to be taken into account. If you get turned on by having someone watch you during sex, there's nothing wrong with inviting a friend over, going to a sex party, or finding someone to watch a video. But if you have sex in public without the consent of the people who see you, that's a different story.

While each of these elements are difficult to pin down or make generalizations from, I think this is a feature rather than a bug. The complexity of the problem highlights how often our judgments about a sexual act reflect our personal experiences, and discomforts rather than anything about the sex itself. It creates room to take a look at our attitudes and ideas and to ask ourselves where they come from. It invites us to listen to someone's story about their sexual experiences and hear it from their perspective, instead of assuming anything about their story. But perhaps more important than that, it requires us to shift our attention away from what people do and attend to how people feel.

However you express your personal sexuality, and however you experience it, the core of sex positivity can be distilled down to the question of how you feel about people whose sexualities are different from yours. Can you celebrate and honor them? Or is there a part of you that holds back from that because you think that there's something wrong about them? If it's the latter, is that because there's something about the consent, pleasure, and well-being of the participants or the people affected by it? Or is it because you feel discomfort? And if you feel uncomfortable with it, can you own that and take care of it? Or do you distance yourself from it through shame, anger, or judgment?

In the end, sex positivity is difficult to operationalize because a set of principles more than rules. But then, the things that make for the best sex are the same way. Great sex is much more about the connection between the participants than the specific kinds of stimulation and sensation. Sex positivity is much the same, and that is both its greatest challenge and its greatest strength.

SEX POSITIVE, SEX NEGATIVE, OR SEX CRITICAL
by Meg-John Barker & Justin Hancock

We're a couple of British sex advisors who aim to provide inclusive, accessible sex advice through our book *Enjoy Sex (How, When and If You Want To)*, the accompanying website, megjohnandjustin.com, and our regular podcast. We were stoked to be asked to contribute to this book project, but also a little bit surprised because we don't actually see ourselves as being sex positive.

That might seem strange to you. I mean we have written a book called *Enjoy Sex* which sounds pretty positive right? And we're certainly not negative about sex, which is the alternative to being positive.

In this chapter we want to dig into a bit of the history of sex positivity, and the different kinds of sex positivity there are, before explaining why we prefer to follow a third way beyond the sex negative/positive binary, which we call being sex critical.

Sex negativity

The reason sex positivity exists as an idea is because, for a long time, western society was highly sex negative. We needed a reaction away from that. Back in medieval times, European society only allowed certain kinds of procreative sex, and you were only supposed to have sex at certain times or on certain days. The wrong kind of sex, or sex at the wrong time, was viewed very negatively. Things were still pretty sex negative by the late nineteenth century. Early sexological texts were all about listing every single "deviation" from "normal and natural" sex, i.e. penis-in-vagina sex leading to procreation.

In the early twentieth century Freud shifted the prevailing view to be that sex was for pleasure rather than procreation, and middle-class people started seeing sex as an important leisure pursuit. That might sound less sex negative, but still only penis-in-vagina heterosexual sex counted, and women weren't really supposed to want sex and should "lie back and think of England" (or whichever country they were in!) while their husband got the pleasure.

Only after the sexual revolution in the 1960s did the dominant sex-negative view start to shift, thanks to the invention of the contraceptive pill, the decriminalization and depathologization of homosexuality, second-wave feminism and women's consciousness raising groups (which emphasized female sexual pleasure), and the free love movement, which questioned monogamy as the only way of doing relationships.

Mainstream sex positivity

Sex negativity wasn't completely replaced by sex positivity. We still have a strong set of sex-negative ideas in our culture alongside more sex-positive ones.

Also, there are actually *two* kinds of sex positivity, which overlap somewhat. There's the mainstream kind of sex positivity that's out there in wider culture—in sex advice books, Hollywood movies, and magazines. There's also a more alternative form of sex positivity, which is what we're all talking about in this book or when we speak of the sex-positive movement.

Starting with mainstream sex positivity, this is the common idea that people should work at having a great sex life, and show how much they're enjoying themselves, but still in the context of a monogamous, coupled, long-term relationship. Meg-John has worked with academics Rosalind Gill and Laura Harvey to analyze how mainstream sex advice pressures people to keep having sex of a certain kind in long-term relationships, otherwise they're seen as a failure. The anxiety around sex in mainstream culture serves the purpose of keeping people buying sex toys and other products, as well as sex advice that promises to teach them the techniques and skills they need for a hot sex life.

There's definitely more of a focus on pleasure in mainstream sex positivity than in sex negativity, but it's a very pressured kind of pleasure that is more about *demonstrating* how much we're enjoying sex than tuning in to what we really want and going for it consensually. Mainstream sex positivity also includes a very limited range of sexual practices: still mostly heterosexual penis-in-vagina sex, but in lots of different positions, and perhaps with the occasional addition of fluffy handcuffs to keep things spicy.

The sex-positive movement

In the context of this book, what we all mean by *sex positive* isn't that mainstream version, but rather the *sex-positive movement*, which views all consensual activities as fundamentally healthy and pleasurable and encourages sexual openness and experimentation. The sex-positive movement helpfully shifts the focus from a narrow range of activities to anything potentially counting as sex. It understands that sex can happen in many different relationship contexts (monogamous, nonmonogamous, recreational, solo, sex work, etc.). And it rightly puts the focus on defining good sex by whether it's consensual or not, rather than whether it's "normal" or not.

However, sex-positive communities and spaces can end up feeling as pressured as mainstream sex positivity. For example, there's often an implicit sense that because people *can* be sexual in all these ways, they *should* be sexual in all these ways. The "shoulds" and "oughts" easily sneak back in there. Instead of the pressure to have penis-in-vagina sex and show how much you're enjoying it, now there's a pressure to do a range of sexual things and show that you're enjoying them. In other words, there's still a sex hierarchy with one form of sex being seen as better than another. As soon as we have any kind of hierarchy—with one kind of sex as the ideal—some people are going to be excluded and stigmatized, and some people are going to feel pressured to have that kind of sex.

The brilliant zines *Fucked*, and *2 Fucked 2 Furious* explain how many groups are implicitly excluded from the culture of sex-positive spaces. This includes people who struggle with sex, who've experienced sexual trauma, who're on the asexual spectrum, who don't fit the body ideals present there, or who don't enjoy the kinds of environments they're often in (e.g. social, noisy, often with drink and/or drugs). There's often an expectation in sex-positive spaces that people will find sex simple, will easily experience pleasure, will know what they're into, and will be up for trying new things.

Also, as Elisabeth Sheff and Corie Hammers point out, sex-positive spaces are often overwhelmingly white and middle-class. Many sex-positive organizers have questioned norms around sex, gender, and relationships that affect those organizers directly, but often not around race, class, and disability—if these don't apply to them. This means that people of color, working-class people, and disabled people may well not feel welcome in these spaces.

Finally, any space with a set of implicit "shoulds" and "oughts" around sex makes consent difficult. Just like sex negativity and mainstream sex positivity, if people have a sense of the kind of sex they should be having in sex-positive spaces, then it'll be hard to tune in to what they actually want—if they want anything at all. There can also be a lot pressure involved in going to a sex-positive event. After you've spent money on a ticket, time on dressing up, and energy on getting excited about it, you can easily feel like you should end up having certain kinds of sex. That can mean you behave in less consensual ways with yourself and others.

The consent-culture movement in kink communities has been all about pointing out these kinds of problems. In fact, the assumption in kink communities that everything will be consensual has often meant that people feel unable to speak about nonconsensual things that *do* happen, and that people who speak about those things get shunned because nobody wants to hear that sex-positive spaces or people can be nonconsensual or behave in nonconsensual ways. In some cases, people took advantage of this and engaged in abusive behavior which nobody called them out on.

Sex critical

So instead of being sex negative or sex positive, in our advice we aim to be sex critical. Basically, this is about moving away from the negative/positive binary and instead taking a critical perspective on all forms of sex. So, we'd be just as critical of sex advice as we were of porn, for example, or just as critical of kink as we were of heteronormative sex.

Being sex critical means that we can ask who is being included and excluded in any form of sex, event, or piece of writing. For us, it also means being really aware of power dynamics that might cause people to feel pressured, or struggle to give informed consent.

Perhaps this doesn't make sex-critical sex sound like much fun! In our book we suggest that a sex-critical perspective can actually lead to more enjoyment. For example,

- If we're aware of all the cultural—and/or subcultural—messages about sex, and the problems with them, then we're more able to figure out where we're at sexually.
- If we know we don't have to have sex we don't want to have, then we're less likely to have unenjoyable sex, which means we'll probably enjoy both sexy and non-sexy times more.
- If we know that no kinds of consensual sex are intrinsically better or worse than any others, then we're more likely to be able tune in to what we enjoy and do those things—and we are more likely to find other people who enjoy those activities too.

We hope this chapter has given you a sense of the value of moving beyond the negative/positive binary and embracing a *more* sex-critical way of approaching sex.

SEX POSITIVITY FOR A MORE POSITIVE WORLD
by Tamara Pincus

For me, sex positivity means accepting sex as a source of healing and joy. Sex positivity allows us to build connection in a disconnected world, and sexuality needs to be embraced and nurtured, not squashed and hidden. I use this philosophy in my work as a kink- and poly-friendly sex therapist every day.

Sex negativity keeps us apart from everyone. If we are in a relationship, or if we perceive someone else as being in a relationship, then we shut ourselves down. If there is someone who we feel a spark with, someone who makes us feel alive on the inside, we try to not get too close. We talk about the weather, or anything else that will keep things on the surface, to avoid making ourselves and the people around us uncomfortable. Over time, this shuts down large parts of our own expression. We learn not to let people see the parts of ourselves that are really alive and passionate. This leads to a great sense of isolation both for those of us in relationships and those of us who are not.

When we are open to sexual expression, we allow people to see our passion. We allow them to see the way we light up when we talk about the things in the world that bring us joy. We can use sexuality as a tool for sharing that joy and pleasure with others. I'm not just talking about physical interaction but also talking, flirting, cuddling, and other activities that make us feel alive.

Sex negativity also prevents us from accessing physical touch. Outside the United States, it is commonplace for people to hug and kiss their friends. Here, we are remarkably starved for touch. We consider it wrong or uncomfortable to hug people we aren't in a romantic relationship with. We rarely hug or cuddle our friends. This lack of touch has huge impacts on our mental and emotional health.

When we are open to sexual expression, we have the chance to connect on a profound level. We allow people into the deepest parts of ourselves, both literally and figuratively. We work through issues in our subconscious in ways that allow to grow and let go of past traumas. We let people really see us, and we really see them.

Sexuality can be used to work through our feelings about past situations through the use of pleasure, role-play, and other forms of sexual expression. Pleasure can help us learn that we are lovable and beautiful in a way that just hearing those words cannot, and sexual pleasure can help us heal wounds around our feelings about our bodies. Role-play can be used to recreate negative situations from the past in a way that gives us control of how things turn out, allowing us to rewrite the story.

I truly believe that sex positivity can change us and change the world, and my work is devoted to that purpose. I want everyone to know how sexuality can be a positive force in their lives. In my practice,

I encourage people to use all the tools available to them, including their sexuality, to enhance their well-being and better connect to pleasure and joy.

In my practice, I help people connect with, or reconnect with, the idea of sex positivity; I help people overcome their sexual shame and get in touch with pleasure; I help people develop their own sense of sexual pleasure and ethics—one that isn't built around societal ideas of what sexuality should look like.

To practice my craft, I have to hold my personal sexuality back. I believe that sexuality can be a force for healing and good in the world, and yet the kind of healing I work with my clients is more boundaried than that. It's those boundaries that allow clients to figure out what they really want, since in most cases what they desire has been clouded not only by society's messages about sex but also by the agendas of their partners and friends. Partners are invested in getting what they want out of the sexual relationship, while friends often enforce sexual norms to make themselves feel less alone, and for a variety of other reasons.

There's a part of me which would like to tell you more. I'd like to tell you about my sexual journey and my experiences in the polyamorous and BDSM worlds, but I know that having that information in print would not serve me well. The world is still a pretty sex-negative place, and I'm already at the edge for a lot of therapists. I am pretty sure reading about my sex life wouldn't be helpful for my clients, if they found the information, and I'm fairly certain my clinical supervisors would frown on it too. So, for now I stay professional. I hold a little bit of distance. And I hope one day we are all comfortable enough that we can really be ourselves with each other.

Going forward, I will keep working for a sex-positive world. This means continuing to educate and work with people around helping them embrace their sexuality in an ethical way. This means raising kids who understand consent and can teach that to the other children around them. This also means continuing to promote relationship choice and loving communication between sexual partners, no matter the length of their relationship. Above all I want myself, the people around me, and future generations to be able to harness the power of sexuality to promote healing, connection, love, and acceptance.

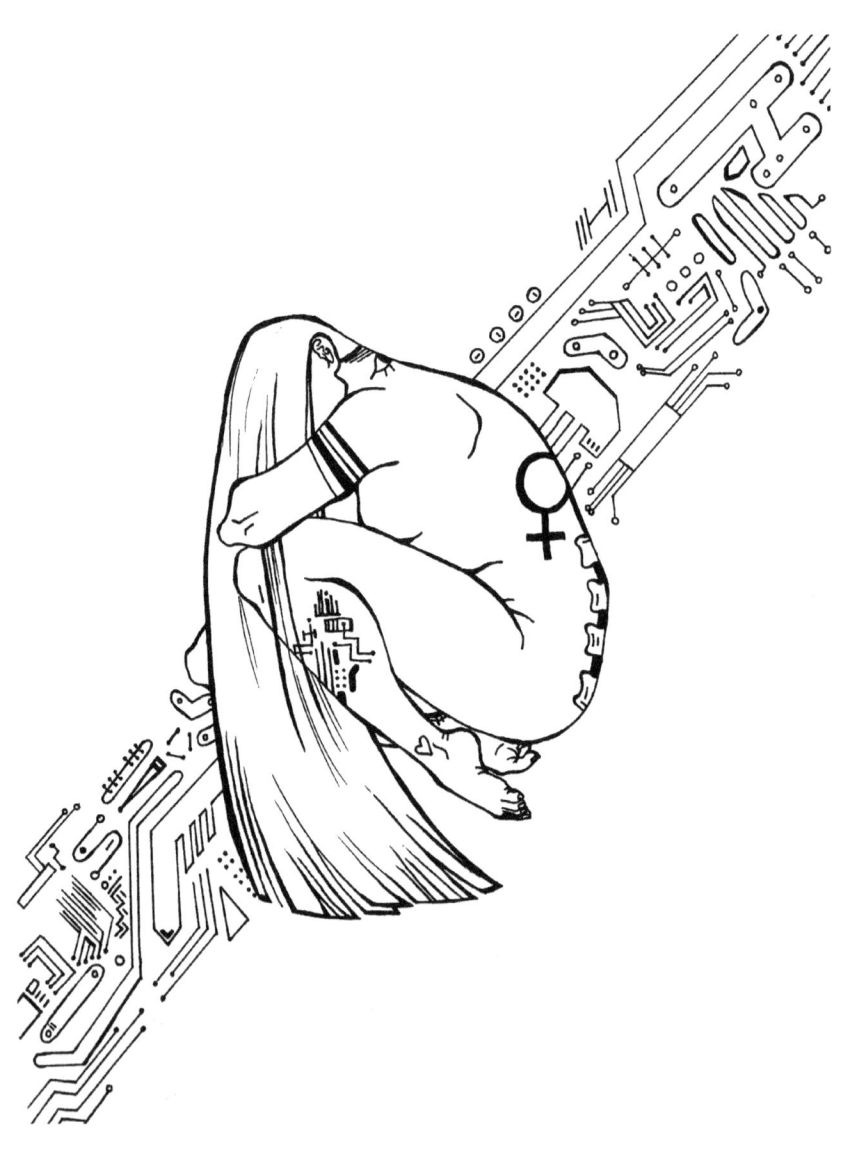

CHAPTER 2
SEX NEGATIVITY

We can't talk about sex positivity without addressing sex negativity. Sexual shame permeates our world. Most of us are not raised to embrace our sexual selves or celebrate sexuality in anyway.

THE NEGATIVE IN SEX POSITIVE
by Kim Loliya

Why is negative necessary?

Sex-positive culture has a lot to offer, including the potential for empowerment, freedom, and different paradigms of living and relating, as well as more integrated ways of coexisting and contributing to a better world. This is all wonderful and life altering for many, yet there are less positive aspects to sex positivity that are often overlooked or glossed over in favor of a more romanticized view. It is perfectly understandable to want to see sex positivity in the best possible light; many wish to avoid being unnecessarily critical in a world that often misunderstands and condemns different lifestyles.

Nevertheless, critical considerations can lead to greater awareness and growth and a deeper understanding of our humanity and why we do what we do. In this essay, my aim is to bring to light some uncomfortable truths so that remedial practices can be found and to support more balanced discussions that bring growth and longevity to sex-positive communities, movements, and pioneers worldwide.

How is negativity defined?

Within the context of this discussion, *negative* is defined as thoughts, feelings, and behaviors that disempower, cause harm or suffering, restrict choice or agency, and generally remove us from our more optimal states of being. Often this negativity can be brought about by our own conditioning, as well as by input from others, and acknowledging both is important when considering how this phenomenon manifests. These thoughts, feelings, and behaviors may conflict with our values, causing discomfort and shame. Over time, they may grow and occupy disowned or shadow aspects of our psyche, which brings even more suffering on a larger scale. In some new-age communities negativity has such a bad rap that it doesn't even get a mention; the shadow aspects are seen as gifts or teachers. This is undoubtedly true, yet it seems important to acknowledge that which is causing pain as real, and a part of our experience, if we are to move through and experience all that it can offer.

How does negativity manifest?

Disempowering behaviors can be broadly grouped into three different dimensions: the internal, the interpersonal, and the group/community. There is a huge overlap between these dimensions, as they operate simultaneously in many contexts, and it is virtually impossible to keep them separate—but it's helpful to consider impact through different lenses to see it more clearly.

Internal: Unlearning

Let's begin with ourselves. For many, the journey into sex positivity means leaving sex-negative beliefs behind and unlearning deep-rooted patterns that we have internalized from a very young age. This process of unlearning is nonlinear, takes time, and will inevitably bring about many situations that test progress.

Sometimes, we may catch ourselves shaming ourselves or others, not listening to our inner voice, or acting out harmful behaviors that we don't even recognize as such because they have been normalized for so long; though it is possible to avoid these pitfalls through self-awareness and positive decision making.

Our internal world is also imbued with social constructs (heightened by the postliberal times we live in), such as racism, homophobia, ableism, classism etc., which are particularly uncomfortable for left-wing/liberal identifying people to admit to. Without examination and discussion, these unconscious -isms and -phobias can dominate in the background and lead to suffering. Similarly, certain sex-positive spheres overlap with new-age communities where the emphasis on positive psychology is so strong that -isms or -phobias don't even get acknowledged and are left buried under a veneer of "love and light."

Internal: Enthusiasm/Self-Care

Due to the comparative freedom found in sex-positive communities, stepping into this world is exciting and enthusiasm can abound, especially at the very beginning of exploration. This can lead to diving in head first, taking risks, and overriding any fears or limits because the urge to immerse in a myriad of activities is strong. Under these conditions, self-care can become an afterthought, and this can lead to various degrees of harm. Again, self-awareness, education, and questioning are needed, along with a healthy dose of self-compassion, kindness, and self-love. Over time it is possible to hone skills and find boundaries that allow u to dive in and experience fun.

Interpersonal

Navigating the interpersonal realm can be a minefield, to put it mildly! We experience situations subjectively and see all experiences (including negative ones) through our own eyes only; which is worth bearing in mind when navigating interpersonal difficulties. In sex-positive communities, we have the opportunity to meet with others who are also going through processes of unlearning, healing, and becoming vulnerable. Relating to others magnifies wounds and serves as an, often uncompromising, mirror to the patterns and conditioning we have absorbed.

For this reason, relationships with other sex-positive people (whether romantic, platonic, or somewhere in between) can be beautiful and fraught at the same time. Immersing oneself into sex-positive community may require leaving old friends, communities, religious groups, and even family members behind because they are unable to support, understand, or tolerate this new version of ourselves. This can be a long and painful process of deeply questioning our changing needs and feeling isolated and confused is pretty normal.

Sexual relationships (whether monogamous, polyamorous, relationship anarchist, or other) have the potential to cause severe physical or emotional harm when safer-sex practices are not adhered to, when consent is violated (which can take many forms), or when sex is weaponized or experienced under manipulation or explicit or implicit duress. On a more subtle level, unawareness of power and privilege that leads to microaggressions can, over time, cause the erasure of self and disempowerment for those in target groups. In some polyamorous relationships gaslighting occurs, which brings disorientation and self-doubt to the person suffering it, especially if the relationship isolates that person from communities and support networks.

Group/Community

All the disempowering behaviors common to interpersonal relationships appear at, and are magnified on, the group/community level when multiple individuals behave in the same way, causing those behaviors to become normalized. Some group-specific behaviors create an additional layer: for example, in-group biases and the tendency toward groupthink are just as likely in sex-positive communities, if not more so, given how small and alternative these communities are in the sea of mainstream culture. These group behaviors can give rise to cult dynamics spearheaded by a charismatic leader. All hierarchical structures have the potential for abuse of power, gurufication, and bullying, and can perpetuate an impenetrable culture of silence and fear where it is so difficult to speak out that survivors choose to leave instead.

While abuse of power is often sexual within this context, financial abuse (e.g. exercising pressure and power to sell expensive courses) and emotional abuse (e.g. promising unrealistic results if something is purchased) are equally real and damaging forces. Communities that lack effective processes to deal with abuse of power are likely to inflict trauma and retraumatization on a considerable scale, creating a culture that undermines the progress and freedom that underpins the very spirit of sex positivity.

Remedial measures

In the same way that disempowering behaviors are multidimensional in their impact, remedial measures are also multidimensional, with a lot of overlap between the internal, interpersonal, and group/community spheres. Due to systemic oppression, it is not possible for everyone to partake in remedial measures equally and receive the same benefit and healing. Therefore, these suggestions are possibilities only for those with the privilege to engage with these processes.

Internal

The internal sphere revolves around actions we can take for the benefit of ourselves. First of all, removing ourselves from a dangerous or uncomfortable situation, person/people, or community—in whatever way that may mean—is a perfectly valid option: the health and well-being of the survivor must be paramount. Likewise, maintaining the status quo (i.e. doing nothing) may be necessary, and vital in many circumstances, for emotional and physical safety. It may be necessary to rely on conventional justice systems by calling the police or contacting a lawyer. This decision is valid, appropriate, and necessary in certain circumstances, despite any concerns that sex positivity may be misunderstood or misrepresented in court. Seeking support from friends, peers, or (ideally, sex positive) therapeutic professionals can also make a big difference in feeling heard and supported, both in the short- and long-term.

Self-care comes up again as a vital remedial measure for the internal world. This is based on self-trust and self-determinism, i.e. that each one of us knows what's best for ourselves and what we need to heal and feel better. Engaging in cathartic practices around what happened, such as writing, sharing stories, or taking part in other creative processes, can be helpful internally and may provide inspiration for others who have experienced or are experiencing something similar. For some people, education or research of the themes surrounding a transgressive act or acts provides an added dimension through which remediation can occur.

Engaging in "calling out" (speaking about the behavior on a bigger and more public scale) and the often-criticized alternative of calling-in (following less public, prescribed processes to inform the person of their wrongdoing) can serve as a more outward-looking alternative. Both of these approaches have the potential for using up a lot of energy and should only be used if it's deemed necessary and right for the person doing the calling out/calling in.

If you are the author of the behavior that has caused harm (or are complicit in any way) then seeking supervision (if applicable), therapeutic support, education, and peer support are all equally important to ensure the behavior doesn't repeat itself.[4]

Interpersonal

There is no "right way" or "right remedial measure" in interpersonal relationships because every relationship (and every person) is different. As with the internal sphere, doing nothing, or removing ourselves from the unhealthy situation, are perfectly valid options. For those who have capacity, and who feel safe enough to engage with other types of remedial measures, there are many types of mediation processes available—often involving a trained neutral third party who can ensure that both people feel heard and acknowledged. For those who can't, or who don't want to, involve a mediator there are alternative communication practices that get to the root issues without blame or judgment, such as focusing, circling, and empathic listening or NVC-based communication. Not all of these approaches work for everyone, and it is possible that none may work, as each practice has its limitations and individual flavor.

Group/Community (Accountability in Theory)

A series of robust community accountability processes have been outlined in the 2004 *Report from INCITE! Women of Color Against Violence* and summarized as follows:

- **Understand impact of unequal power** – Communities must understand and seek to minimize unequal power dynamics in the accountability process.

- **Prioritize survivor safety** – They must create safe spaces that are confidential and focused on supporting the survivors.

- **Prioritize survivor self-determination** – They must also consistently offer self-determination and choice over the accountability process (e.g. what information does the survivor want to receive, how do they want to receive it and how often, are they still engaged with the process or do they want to remove themselves?)

---

[4] Lyubansky, Mikhail, and Barter, "A Restorative Approach to Interpersonal Racial Conflict'," Peace Review 23, no. 1 (January 2011) 37 —44

- **Collective responsibility and action** - Direct perpetrators and community members alike must take responsibility for violence taking place on an individual level, as well as acts which happen on a broader, systemic/community level. This should lead to collective work toward ensuring these events don't happen again in the future. This must happen under the understanding that accountability isn't limited to individuals but stretches to entire communities and leads to building community accountability processes to end oppression.
- **Collective accountability for oppressive, abusive, and violence organizational culture and conditions** – All parties must take responsibility for the organizational (i.e. community) culture, structures, and practices that led toward perpetrating, tolerating, condoning, or encouraging abuse. Then, they must take action to change the culture and practices.
- **Abuser accountability for oppressive, abusive, and violent attitudes and behaviors** – Individuals and communities need to acknowledge the abuse, create an accountability process that acknowledges the abuse "without excuses, disclaimers, denials, minimizations, or victim blaming." Communities need to create processes where "the oppressor/abuser fully understands and acknowledges the impact and consequences upon the survivor/victim, their friends and family, the organization, and the community." Once this has taken place, the abuser needs to make "sincere and meaningful reparations which can include a full public apology, payment for damage, payment of debts, behavioral changes, counseling, leaving the organization, political education for self and toward others, etc." Any reparations must be survivor-led, meaning that apologies are not appropriate if the survivor does not want to see their abuser again. In order to create "long-term, permanent change," communities need to "create an accountability process where the oppressor/abuser can receive and take action toward meaningful and long-term personal and political education regarding his or her attitudes and actions, alternatives to abusive attitudes and actions, and is held accountable to a plan for long-term follow-up and monitoring including consequences if conditions are not met."
- **Transformation toward liberation** - The main goal for "community accountability is to transform all individuals and collective groups" and processes should allow "for the transformation of victims/survivors from victimization from oppression, abuse and violence to safety, healing, and self-determination…[the] transformation of abusers/oppressors from perpetrators…to responsibility, accountability, and advocacy and…the transformation of organizations and communities from those tolerating, condoning, encouraging, and perpetuating oppression, abuse, and violence toward those upholding in principle and practice" freedom, equality and respect.

Group/Community (Accountability in Practice)

The specifics of what sex-positive accountability will look like may vary depending on the specific community and its aims, as well as the wider culture/country the community is in and who the community represents. There is no one-size-fits-all approach, but if more sex-positive communities do this work and share best practices (and challenges) with other groups worldwide, it will be easier and quicker to build a knowledge base of processes and systems that act as a foundation and can be built upon. Inviting other communities to offer critique and perspectives will ensure accountability becomes a living process that is dynamic and effective.

Group/Community (Processes and Procedures)

Crafting accountability processes involves, at the most basic level, agreeing on a simple complaints procedure where complaints are dealt with by parties who are not connected to community interests or the individuals in question. If everyone in the community crafts these processes, they are more likely to be followed in times of conflict or difficulty. When complaints procedures explicitly invite community members to raise issues about leaders, and there are measures in place to manage this eventuality, the entire system becomes more robust in the acknowledgment of power and privilege.

It is vital to understand that a system only works if people feel safe and able to use it—and that some work might be necessary to ensure that this sense of safety exists. Ensuring that communities have an independent welfare team (ideally formed by individuals who specialize in therapeutic support or pastoral care) that can provide listening, referrals to other services, and also trigger accountability processes (if that is desired) can also support a successful accountability and complaints-management system. As with accountability systems, welfare teams are only effective if people feel safe enough to use them. It may need to be necessary to do outreach work and find out what supportive measures are needed to ensure these services can be accessed.

Other Remedial Measures

Since the dawn of time, circles have been used as a way of meeting and managing issues, and there are many types of circles available to communities (and many variations that you can invent yourself). There are restorative circles created by Dominic Barter, #MeToo circles, and circles for minority groups or survivors to speak about issues that are affecting them. Members of these circles can exclude those not in those groups or request that they sit in an outer circle at the back and just listen. Long table or roundtable discussions can also be used to craft or implement remedial measures in an inclusive and accessible manner with the potential for more creative solutions.

The future of sex positivity

The sex-positive movement holds a lot of promise and potential and will undoubtedly continue to provide new opportunities, sweet solace, acceptance, and love for many people in the future. As communities grow and are impacted by global shifts such as the #MeToo movement, we need to find the courage to spend more time understanding negativity and integrating it. This process won't be without problems or pain, but it's necessary and worthwhile to allow movement toward something greater. Facing these issues on all levels (internal, interpersonal, and community), while looking after ourselves and each other, will be key to bringing healing, integration, and collective liberation for us all.

SEXUAL SHAME: HOW TO BECOME SEXUALLY EMPOWERED (AND LIVE LONGER WHILE BOOSTING YOUR CREATIVITY!)

by Veronica Monet

It makes sense that sex would be a life-restoring force. After all, it is a life-giving energy. Without sex, there is no life as we know it, but unfortunately, we live in a world where the procreative sex is promoted as the only valid form of sexual expression. When we are given permission to experience sexual pleasure, we are rarely informed about all the other life-affirming properties of sex.

But sex is WAY more than we are led to believe. Sex is the central organizing principle of the Universe, and as such, sex isn't just a part of your spiritual and creative journey—sex is the very source of your spiritual and creative self. Sex sits at the core of your being, informing everything you do. When you are your most alive, you are connected to your sexual core.

All our creative and spiritual inspirations derive from our sexual center. This is true whether you look at it from the Tantric perspective, which teaches that sexual energy is the creatively charged kundalini coiled at the base of our spines or if you examine the religions of ancient human history, which were steeped in sexual awe and ritual.

Today, these assertions can create more confusion than clarity. That's understandable. Thousands of years of rewriting human history has separated us from the truth of who we are, but as recent technological advances have allowed us to peer into that first human environment, the womb, we are learning that sexual expression predates our first breath of air and our first sip of mother's milk. Yes, fetuses masturbate—and they do so to the point of sexual release. So, if sex is that primal, that central to your being, why have you been convinced that it resides in a place separate from all the other parts of your life?

We can find clues in the process of domestication. Anyone who handles livestock knows they are far more docile when castrated. With this one sexual control in place, procreation can also be controlled because those who own livestock can decide what sperm will fertilize the next generation of animals. Likewise, our human institutions, such as religion and government, gain a great deal of control over large groups of people by controlling sexuality. No, we are not being subjected to castration and forced pregnancies like livestock, but we are controlled through one deadly emotion: shame.

Shame is different from conscience. To live in a moral world, one defined by healthy boundaries and respect for the rights of others, we need to have a conscience. Otherwise, we risk building a society based upon selfish acquisition of resources and power. While the world might seem more rife with those darker qualities than ever, if you study history it becomes apparent that we have been on a trajectory of increasing generosity and caring and, not coincidentally, that trend toward altruism is accompanied with an increase in freedom of sexual expression.

This is why conservatives make sexual repression the centerpiece of their agenda. The central role sex plays in our psyches is the precise reason that laws curtailing reproductive freedoms and sexual liberties are a defining feature of movements to "restore" us to a "better" time. Really, this is code for restoring power to those who want to domesticate the masses for their own agendas—and shaming us around our sexuality is their biggest weapon.

You see, we are handed sexual shame with the warning that, if we allow ourselves to connect with our inborn sexual desires, we will engage in harmful sexual behaviors such as pedophilia and rape. We are told that the human animal is inherently evil and that, when we lack sexual shame, we will hurt ourselves and others.

But the opposite is true. It is sexual shame that produces the sex crimes that make the headlines. Sexual shame tells us that pleasure is suspect and sex should be controlled. This shaming destroys the creative and spiritual nature of our sexual core; once sexual shame infects our sense of self, we have in effect become chemically castrated. This can leave us feeling desperation, shame, and hate for our sexual selves. When we are not connected to ourselves and our sexuality in a loving and accepting way, that disconnect can lead to sexual perpetrations and acting out.

Rape is not a natural sexual expression for humans. Rape isn't about sexual pleasure. Rape is an act of violence—and I believe it is an extension of sexual shame. Because sexual shame tends to produce sexual expression that is infused with hatred for self, hatred for the object of one's sexual desire, and hatred for sex in general; sex sourced in the rejection of our core sexual nature can lead to violence.

Sexual shame demands that we approach sex as an obligatory act of procreation, proof of our love for that one special person, or a dark force from which we must abstain. Given such mandates, it is inevitable that sex will translate to sexual perpetrations, as is all too apparent in the numerous instances of pedophilic priests and incestuous Bible thumpers.

So what can we do to reclaim our sexuality? What are the steps we can take toward total sexual empowerment?

First, it is crucial that we distinguish between fantasy and fact. If you have rape fantasies, good for you. You can play those out with a consenting adult partner. But if you confuse your fantasies with fact, and give yourself permission to perpetrate actual rape, then you have abandoned your sexual self. Actual rape is not sexual. Actual rape is violence.

To liberate ourselves we must see sex in a human context, apart from the sexual-shame induced belief that sex is violence. Our closest living relatives, bonobo chimpanzees, do not engage in rape. Quite the contrary, bonobos use sex to diminish violence. And that, I believe, is one of the functions of shameless sexual expression for humans. We can connect with our true sexual selves, devoid of sexual shame, and begin to see how consensual sexual behavior actually creates more stable and respectful community—and beautiful things happen for us personally as well. Our health improves. Our enjoyment of life is multiplied. Our creativity soars, and we become alive and vital.

The crucial second step toward sexual empowerment is building a working knowledge of consent and healthy boundaries. Expressing authentic desire without trying to manipulate or pressure another person can feel awkward and vulnerable, but our quest for full expression of our sexual selves must be sourced in healthy boundaries and assertion skills, as well as mutual respect. Not only do we need to honor the no of others, we need to know how to assert our own no—something that a lot of us have trouble with. We probably don't want to hurt the feelings of the person inviting us to have sex, and we might be afraid of looking uptight, inexperienced, or of being called any number of derogatory terms that can be applied to someone who refuses sex. But as I often say, your yes has no validity if you don't also know how to say no.

Consent can be tricky terrain. There is a lot of confusion on the topic, but it is really very simple. Only an adult can give their consent to engage in sex—and only a sober adult at that. Moving away from manipulation and toward sexual empowerment means we have no desire for sex with an unwilling, or even unenthusiastic, partner. Interestingly, even bonobos get this. They will end a sexual encounter at the first sign of disinterest from their sexual partner. Sex is readily available in the world of bonobos, so if their partner is bored or disconnected they just move on to a partner who is genuinely interested in sex at that moment.

Of course I am not suggesting that humans emulate everything that bonobos do. For instance, although bonobos have an incest taboo, they also engage in intergenerational sex that I, as an incest survivor, find particularly problematic. What I am suggesting is that we humans look to bonobo culture for clues to how we might evolve our human culture to be less shame based and more peaceful, less patriarchal and more egalitarian. There is so much we can learn from bonobo culture, but our cultural evolution will be uniquely human.

So healthy boundaries and healthy assertion skills and mutual respect and a solid understanding of consent are essential to freeing yourself from sexual shame and achieving your sexual empowerment.

Does that mean you won't encounter moments of confusion and frustration? No. Any time we try something new, we are likely to be confused and frustrated at times. But if we are patient and kind with ourselves, and if we interject a sense of humor, we can experience freedom and joy, even in the face of those other emotions.

This brings us to the third step toward sexual empowerment: developing a sense of humor around sex. We don't often associate sex and humor. So many of us are inclined to approach sex as if it were a deadly serious matter, but all that rigidity doesn't bode well for our sexual physiology. Sometimes the best thing we can do is laugh; if we allow sex to involve humor, laughter and play, we can come closer to our sexual core than at any other time. After all, our sexuality is innocent. We can give ourselves permission to be childlike when we are sexual, and that childlike innocence is a very potent way to heal sexual shame.

About now, you may be wondering how your sexual empowerment can extend your life and boost your creativity. Research has linked a satisfying sex life with longevity. Some have argued that people who have lots of sex might just be healthier to begin with, but when all other health factors are equal, it's clear that sex itself extends our lifespans. If you want to live a long (and hopefully healthy and happy) life, sex should be a regular part of your health regime.

The research on creativity and sex is less clear. In scientific experiments, thoughts of love are far more conducive of creativity while thoughts of "lust" seem to boost analytical powers. Obviously, experiments that feature a polarized view of sex and love highlight how pervasive sexual shame is, even in scientific circles. A more empowered perspective might look at sex and love as complementary concepts that exist on a continuum and are not always easy to distinguish. After all, love is a very subjective experience and the less sexual shame one has, the more love one can experience in a variety of sexual situations including those with total strangers, and BDSM scenes that might look less than loving to an outsider. So, I don't really trust the researchers' conclusions because their premise seems to be based upon very traditional interpretations of love and sex.

But, we can still derive an important takeaway from this research. Given that most people feel less shame when they think about love, it could explain why thoughts of love boost creativity. It is likely that an empowered view of sex, one unencumbered by sexual shame, could produce the same increase in creativity.

More to the point, whether you are having vanilla sex with your life partner or taking a riding crop to a stranger's bottom at a play party, if your view of sex is free of shame and fully empowered, your heart will be full of love for yourself and the innocent appreciation of your core essence, which is after all, sexual.

SEX-NEGATIVE CULTURE IS A THREAT TO CIVILIZATION
by Gloria Brame

We often hear about the so-called dangers of progressive attitudes toward sex. Certain shady elements, who shall go unnamed (but many of whom write and blog for conservative sites), are wailing that our society is too sexy, too hedonistic, too sensitive to minority voices, and that our permissiveness will somehow bring an end to civilization. They spin every new civil right and humanitarian gesture toward minority cultures as the slippery slope to immorality. The hysteria is spread so wide it even extends to future sex, with some academics now trying to prepare for the day sex robots turn against their human overlords. It would all be hilarious if it wasn't so painfully real that these biases and ignorances dominate public opinion. The truth is that the real danger comes from sex negativity. It's sex-negative culture that is dragging society down, destroying lives, ruining sexual health, and treating people like widgets instead of flesh-and-blood humans.

In today's America, a backlash against LGB people and gender minorities is rising, fueled in part by volumes of anti-sex propaganda that are being cranked out on "wrong-wing" sites in an effort to defend anti-humanitarian discrimination. They claim that a sexually freer world is a dangerous place and constantly reinforce ideas as old and patriarchal as Freud's theory of penis envy.

Even the #MeToo movement is under attack, as if victims of sexual assault should all shut up now because we've heard enough. The anti-sex contingents want their good old days back—the days when you could abuse women and get away with it. In the United States, violence against women historically went unpunished; until the 1920s, it was legal for husbands to rape and beat their wives [5]. It then took US courts another fifty years to finally treat domestic abuse as a crime instead of a private problem. It still hasn't brought an end to violence against women, and that's what #MeToo is really about. It's about how women have historically been treated as male property, how women have been abused and sexually exploited by men, and how it's still going on behind closed doors from Hollywood to Hyderabad. If you want to stop the violence, the first step is talking about it. If you censor that speech, what you're really fighting for is a return to the days when women held no agency over their own welfare.

This is the dark side of anti-sex dogma. Nothing they are fighting for is moral or good on any rational level. It's all about oppression, suppression, fear, and prejudice. It's why, in 2018, we're still fighting many of the same fights our great-grandparents fought. We are still fighting for basic sexual freedoms. We are still fighting for prenatal and reproductive health rights. We are still fighting for abortion rights. We are still fighting for the right to live without abuse.

In the 21st century, most people choose to remain willfully ignorant about sex and gender diversity. They never learn the simple civilized rules that rightly should apply to how we treat other human beings, regardless of their race, gender, orientation, or ability. It's an entrenched ignorance that is mainly promoted by people who don't understand human biology and don't really care enough about human life to get educated.

Anti-sex = anti-life

Anti-sex people are anti-life at heart. They embrace an elitist and ideological bias that often poisons life for themselves, their partners, their children, and people who don't accept their ideology. They don't like the living as much as they like their version of how humans should live. People who don't conform to their expectations are treated as enemies and dangerous outsiders. They oppose sexual health innovations, like Plan B or the HPV vaccine, and they censor sex education for youth. They don't want people to have safe lives. They just want them to quit having the kinds of sex they don't approve of.

As with prejudice and hate, nobody's born to be sex negative. You have to be trained to see sex as a bad or dangerous disruption of human life or morality. It isn't natural or normal to fear sex. Sex-negative dogma refuses to face facts. FACT: we were born to have fun in bed. FACT: we all define fun differently.

Sex negativity makes people sick because they live in bodies with brains that know a lot more about their sex life than they themselves emotionally accept. The brain knows people need sex to feel fulfilled. The brain is so sex positive it prepares you for orgasms all day long, whether or not you are too inhibited to have them. The brain automatically exercises the penis every morning and throughout the day with spontaneous erections and provides hungry throbs deep in the vagina when it's time to get off. The brain makes hundreds of other microdecisions each delicious biological step of the way. It is a beautiful biological system.

---

[5] "Domestic Violence." Encyclopedia of the New American Nation. Encyclopedia.com. (October 20, 2018). http://www.encyclopedia.com/history/encyclopedias-almanacs-transcripts-and-maps/domestic-violence.

But if you're sex negative you may never feel that beauty. Here are some of the biggest ways that sex negativity drags people down:

Ignorance of self builds inhibitions

> Most of us are raised to believe that sex doesn't—or at least, shouldn't—matter. It shouldn't even matter that much in marriage. In fact, nice people shouldn't spend too much time thinking about sex. As the social narrative goes, if civilization is the sum of our intellectual achievements, then sex is the shameful burden of our primal roots. It's dirty. It's something you have to do to have children, so put it off as long as possible and then just close your eyes and do it. Preferably with the lights off.
>
> —*Sex and the Self* [6]

It's a strange dogma to apply to one of humanity's greatest and most enduring obsessions. People who buy into the idea that sex isn't important usually end up with miserable sex lives. They never learn what pleases them, they never learn how to please someone else, and they start becoming neurotic. They may not realize how much it tears them down, but once you've internalized the belief there's something nasty about sex, you'll find it increasingly difficult to find relationship happiness. Sexual inhibitions based on myths about sex, myths like "it's bad for you to jerk off" or "too much sex is bad" or believing sex doesn't figure in human health and happiness, are at the heart of a whole lot of personal misery in this world.

Ignorance of others builds self-centered beliefs

People who don't understand their own sexuality have a hell of a time trying to understand other people's sexuality. Every time I read anti-sex propaganda, I begin underlining all the incredibly dumb and antiquated rationales they use to defend their position in my head—almost all of it boils down to "that's why my father, grandma and/or preacher said so I'm sticking to it!" Okay, perhaps if you grew up when they did, that was the best they could learn. Today, however, you could learn facts about sex. But if you automatically reject the new data, the reasons why other people make the sexual choices they do will always baffle and upset you. You fall back on the blind beliefs you had growing up instead of the evidence we have today about how sex and gender work. The more confusing and outrageous the world seems to you as sexual mores change, the more you'll fight an unwinnable war against Father Time because changes in sexual mores are as inevitable as death.

Right way sex is wrong

One of my favorite sayings is that sex is not a one-size-fits-all proposition. Sex is as diverse and personalized as the human who is sexual, but big institutions have warehoused all people into two groups: people who do it right and people who do it wrong.

---

[6] Gloria G. Brame. *The Truth About Sex, A Sex Primer for the 21st Century*, vol 1: Sex and the Self. CCB Publishing, 2011.

For most of western history our religious doctrines, our national laws, our customs, and much of our thinking about sex has simply assumed that missionary position heterosexual intercourse in a monogamous marriage is normal and everything else is a deviation, something that abnormal or sinful people do.

> But medical research and scientific evidence have long since been gathered. They show the only "wrong way" to have sex is to have sex that you or your partner do not enjoy.

— *Sex and the Self* [7]

I've witnessed some dramatic sexological changes in the last thirty years that have opened doors to radical sexual honesty. These days, we have huge cadres of researchers and scientists who are laboring to bring more and more scientific evidence about human sex and gender to the forefront. Nonetheless, those with outdated ideologies still control the debate about sex. Think of all the times one hears so-called experts on matters of love, marriage, and sex say things like,

1. The only right kind of sex is sex between married heterosexuals.
2. Sex and gender diversity is abnormal.
3. Being LGBT is a choice and an agenda.
4. Male sexuality is more vigorous and important than female sexuality.
5. Gender is binary.

"Lies like these are so frequently repeated that they form the backbone of contemporary public opinions about sex." [8] These entrenched myths increase public anxiety about any changes in the sex/gender status quo.

Sex negativity ignores consent

I had an interesting Twitter exchange last week after commenting that I wished the women who accused the president of sexual misconduct got as much mainstream media traction as the woman who dissed Aziz Ansari. One Twitter user quickly tweeted back how former President Clinton slept with Monica Lewinsky, singling out the infamous cigar penetration. I tried to explain that consent is the dividing line between a sex crime and a sexual indiscretion. Lewinksy openly admitted she enjoyed her affair; the women accusing Trump—much like Bill Cosby's accusers and Harvey Weinstein's accusers—allege they were traumatized by their encounters. The guy who was tweeting at me just stuck to the cigar scenario, as if a consensual sex act between adults should be viewed as a crime on the same level as grabbing strangers by the genitals. He could not fathom that **sex between mutually consenting adults is radically different from sexual contact by coercion.**

It's this refusal to acknowledge the moral importance of mutual consent in sexual encounters that crashed Rachel Denhollander's world after she was assaulted by now-convicted sex criminal Larry Nassar. In a recent interview, Denhollander said that when she turned to her church for comfort and support, she was shamed and silenced.

---

[7], [8] Brame, *The Truth About Sex*

Church is one of the least safe places to acknowledge abuse because the way it is counseled is, more often than not, damaging to the victim," said Denhollander, who now works as a lawyer in Kentucky. "There is an abhorrent lack of knowledge for the damage and devastation that sexual assault brings. It is with deep regret that I say the church is one of the worst places to go for help.

—Rachel Dehollander [9]

Not only does sex negativity create sex criminals, it supports sex criminals by blaming victims for getting assaulted in the first place. In their worldview, all disempowered people, whether LGBT, disabled, sex workers, or plain vanilla cis woman either deserved to be abused or are expected to shut up and not disturb the status quo of privileged cis men. The person against whom a sin was committed is treated as the sinner.

Needless to say, people who willfully ignore consent issues are the most likely to harbor sex criminals in their midst—and, even more tragically, are likely to be people who hide the true stories of their own traumas at the hands of relatives or clergy-people for fear of being blamed and shamed the way Ms. Denhollander was. This is the darkest and saddest piece of sex-negative philosophy: it unquestioningly accepts the rights of predators to prey as long as the predators belong to their churches, clubs, and circles of privilege.

Sex negativity stalls human progress

When you are taught there is only one right way to do something, and that you may only do it when you join a club, and the message is repeated to you in all the movies, TV shows, commercials, and sermons you are exposed to, you believe it. You believe it so much that you may believe it even in the face of scientific facts that prove the whole club thing exists to sucker you and that you can actually do that thing anyway you like without negative repercussions. Not only do backlashes against sexual freedom require paradoxical thinking, they reflect how little people know about the flow of sex history. Things change! Things advance! Life is about forward progress!

So, for example, today we know that gay marriage won't destroy straight marriage, women's rights won't oppress men, and that the United States will not fall apart morally if people are allowed to conduct their private sex lives as they wish. If we read sex history, we also know that America was a sexually freer country until Protestant zealots started clamping their dirty hands all over the land of the free in the 19th century, creating anti-sex laws like the Comstock Law of 1875 and the Mann Act in 1910. These acts and other that followed instigated the official witch-hunting of sexual nonconformists.

Here are two factoids from American history which show that our country started out with a clearer, more rational vision of personal freedom on matters of sex:

---

[9] Carol Kuruvilla, "First woman to accuse Nassar says church can be one of the 'worst places' to go for help." Aol.com. February 2nd, 2018. https://www.aol.com/article/news/2018/01/26/first-victim-to-file-complaint-against-larry-nassar-speaks-out/23345068/.

- Washington, Jefferson, and other framers of the United States Constitution viewed marriage and sexuality as matters of religious belief. They didn't want the government to get involved in your sex life.

- Polygamy was legal in the United States until Congress passed the Morrill Anti-Bigamy Act of 1862 as part of a political crusade against Mormonism.

— Sex for GrownUps [10]

Of course, before laws were written to deliberately control people's sex lives, there were other monumental inequities, such as indifference to children's and women's rights. There has never been a society yet that was based on the facts about sex. It's somewhat understandable because we didn't have a lot of scientific facts about sex and gender until the last hundred years, but we have those facts today.

Sex-positive people hold a much brighter future for humanity in our hands. It's time for the world to wake up from the dark slumber of their ignorance and follow our light.

---

[10] Dorree Lynn, Cindy Spitzer. Sex for Grownups. Health Communications, Inc. 2010.

SURVIVING SEXUAL ASSAULT
by Jimanekia Ebor

Sadly, we live in a world where sexual assault survivors are looked at as broken. This is the one of the saddest things I believe you could think about a survivor. Sexual assault survivors are some of the strongest individuals out walking these streets, these individuals who have had their sexual boundaries crossed. I was asked to be a part of this amazing book about sex positivity and would like to use the opportunity to talk about moving forward after having one's sexual boundaries crossed. There are a lot of individuals that do not see and or do not believe that there is anything after sexual assault.

I would love to challenge this, for other sexual assault survivors out there in the world.

Sexual assault can be very complicated, surely. I was not able to recall my sexual assault until many years later. I started to remember the assaults when I first began to work on my spiritual side. Now, I am fully aware that this does not work for everyone. There are many ways to go about finding yourself and healing—I just happened to find myself through meditation. I honestly think sex-positive spaces and meditation saved my life.

Prior to my spiritual work, I knew I was angry and that when I got drunk that I punched people, but I never really knew why. When I started to unpack everything at twenty-five/twenty-six years old, things really started to change for me; I hadn't realized I had blocked so many things out of my memory. As I always say to my clients and survivors that I support, once you start to say it out loud and recall the assault, this is when it gets real and the world begins.

The memories all started to come back to me. I started to remember that when I was around six years old, my cousin touched me for the first time. Sadly, this is story that I share with many other people who experienced sexual assault as adolescents. No, it was not a male older cousin, nor was it even a male. It was a female cousin. Well, a cousin through marriage who was the same age as me. I will not get into extreme details about the things I have remembered, but I do have memory of the assaults from the age of five or six to around eleven or twelve.

In the last memory, I was taking a bath and asked her to come in with me, and she said that it was gross and that we couldn't talk while I was in the bathtub because it was not right, and she did not want to see me naked. This coming from someone who had sexually assaulted me on weekends when she would visit for numerous years. That really threw me for a mind fuck.

When you are young, you often do not realize that things that are happening to you are "bad." Why didn't I think that something was wrong? As I learned more about myself and more about the trauma, I had to remind myself multiple times that I could not blame myself and that I did not ask for this. At the time, it felt good to me, and it became so normalized that I just knew at night we would play games that somehow all led to me being naked. I honestly sometimes try and act like they did not happen, but being an educator and someone who works with sexual assault survivors I now know that pushing everything down does not help anything and or anyone. I am thirty years old and there is still work to be done. I share this because I know this is not just my story. This is the story, sadly, of many adolescents and adults.

I was in college for criminal justice when I was eighteen years old. I had the typical time in college, parting and exploring my sexuality. I was polyamorous before I knew what polyamory was. I was finding and doing things that made me feel good, exploring my sex-positive side. Of course, a lot of people did not understand. Unfortunately, it took me a while to realize that was not my path, a realization that didn't come soon enough to prevent me from getting kicked out of school.

That is when I started to explore what I really wanted to do and who I was, which eventually lead me to think that I wanted to go back to school for psychology. I volunteered as a rape crisis counselor. This was still before I opened Pandora's box and started to explore all the sexual assault that had happened to me. I did not know why at the time, but I have always been pulled to work with those in high traumatic spaces.

That was the most life-changing job ever. I could sit and be that support system for sexual assault survivors. I found what felt good for me; I was finding my place. Following that, I worked with juvenile sex offenders, which was a very tricky job. Throughout the years, I worked in various mental health spaces, primarily with adolescents—I have always been intrigued with working with adolescents. As cheesy as it sounds, they really are our future, and without them we are truly lost. Also, I wish I knew more and had more support at that age. I started to notice that in a lot of my jobs, regardless of whether they were with adolescents or with adults, most of my patients struggled with internal conflict due to sexual assault that had happened when they were younger. I am able to honest with them and continue creating sex-positive spaces that were not readily available to me at that age.

Luckily, I was a big reader as a youth and was always able to read all the things I wanted regarding sexuality and bodies. I was raised by my grandparents, and I would ask them questions as well, but they were not always able to answer the questions as the times and verbiage are always evolving. This left me with unanswered questions about bodies and sexuality; I have always found both to be extremely interesting, as both are always evolving. When moving forward toward a career in mental health, I loved what I did, but I felt like I was missing something: the population that I truly wanted to directly support. It was also very important for me to find something that was ever evolving. While working on my undergraduate degree in psychology, I figured it out: I wanted to be a sex therapist, because I thought that was the only option I had if I wanted to work in sexuality and trauma support. As I was finding my place within this work, I began forcing myself out of all my social norms. I was sure that the things I knew about sexuality were solid, but there was so much more out there.

I continued studying phycology, covering topics like juvenile sex offenders, adolescent mental health, eating disorders, and women with mental health struggles, learning about various levels of care on the way. I still did not feel fully complete. I found an online master's program in marriage and family therapy because, again, I believed that was the only way I could find what I wanted, the only way to reach my end goal. I found every conference I could that covered sexual education, and I went to Sex Geek Summer Camp, put on by Reid Mihalko. Going to all those conferences, I have literally never felt more seen and understood. There is nothing like finding your people and knowing you have truly found what you want to do. Every time I went go back to my job I dreaded it more and more. I finally decided I had to go all-in. I believe that, because I was always able explore things on my own terms, I have always been sex positive. I may not have always had the verbiage to express even what that means, or what that would look like, but it was always in me. I dismissed myself from my master's program because that was not feeding me the way going to conferences was. It was not feeding in the same way that sex-positive spaces were. It was not feeding me in my chosen trainings. Quitting my cushy nine-to-five job was one of the scariest and most fulfilling things. I jumped headfirst into all the sex-positive spaces, exploring my sexuality and becoming a sex educator.

SEX POSITIVITY AND ASEXUALITY
by Shay McCombs

Sex is what makes us human

Well, I don't feel human.
Sexuality and gender are such messy human things,
crucial components of the vivid visceral variety of human physicality.
I've always been an intellectual, my head in the clouds;
I've never been much at home in this body of mine.
Sometimes I wish I were more at home in the physical world,
although I suppose I'm not entirely lacking.
I love the warmth of the sun on my skin,
the smell of rain,
the feeling of dirt between my bare toes.
I melt into cuddle piles with dear friends and family.
I take pride in being strong,
in learning martial arts,
in climbing trees and rock walls.
The most gendered parts of our bodies are the most sexualized.
The curves of my body,
these badges of biological sex spanning from my thighs to my breasts
are simultaneously markers of a womanhood I don't fit
and a sexuality I don't have.
Gender and sexuality are so closely intertwined,
I can't tear them apart.
I want no part in that knot.
I've always related most to the nonhuman characters
the androids, elves, and aliens
because they're a bit distanced.

They're not a part of human courtship or gender norms,
often emphasizing logic over emotion,
they don't get swept up in the confusing messes of romantic subplots.
They're not a part of that knot.
Perhaps that speaks to the profound alienation
of growing up with nobody to look up to.
When everyone around you seems to know the steps to this intricate, complicated dance,
but you never got the memo;
stumbling around, not sure why you're here,
and you don't even like to dance.
I mean, it's not bad, but it's not really your thing.
If this dance is what makes you human,
then you must be something else.
Or perhaps it speaks to the indomitable reach of human empathy,
to humanize the nonhuman.
Because in all those stories of robots and aliens,
the moral is that they're still people
capable and worthy of love.
The point of Data's character arc is to show
that he is a person, even if he's not quite human.
The happy ending for Legolas
is to travel the world with his platonic life partner.
We coo over R2-D2, who isn't even human shaped!
The story of an android is of learning not to discount one's personhood,
that a little distance from all of humanity's colorful messy physical joys
doesn't prevent fulfilling relationships,
meaningful lives,
or personhood.

I was raised in a polyamorous, pagan, sex-positive household. My parents never taught me to hate my body, to feel ashamed of my sexuality, or to think of romance as a battle between sexes. I grew up with hordes of loving godparents, knowing there was someone I could talk to no matter what I was dealing with. I was taught that jealousy is manageable, that healthy relationships take clear communication, that relationships don't have to look like the couples I saw on TV. I was exposed to queer identities and concepts at a very early age, which helped me to explore my own identity. Though I have experienced many of its flaws firsthand, sex positivity has overall shaped my life for the better, and society still needs to hear its message.

For many people, sex is a wonderful, empowering activity. Many people still need to hear that it's not dirty or shameful, that it's okay to want sex outside of a monogamous long-term heterosexual relationship, that their virginity doesn't determine their worth. But when that message turns into an all-encompassing "sex is great!" well, some people feel left out.

Nobody told me it was okay to not like sex. Nobody told me it was even possible to not feel sexual attraction. I spent years feeling like there was something wrong with me, because I waited and waited for the day I would finally understand the appeal, and that day never came.

The monster we're combating is not just sexual shame. Our society is steeped in a complex mix of shame and desire, guilt and temptation. Sex is the forbidden fruit, the dirty little secret. You're supposed to want it, even as you resist the temptation. The virtue comes from the willpower it takes to resist that temptation. If it's not tempting at all, then chastity isn't a virtue, it's a mark of inhumanity.

How many pop singers have I heard compare love to heroin? Am I the only person who thinks that's unhealthy? When poets say they'll die unless their beloved returns their affections, does anyone else wonder why romantic love is the only source of joy in this person's life? What about the way cuddles become romantic once you hit high school, why is physical intimacy suddenly barred from platonic relationships? Our society is convinced that romantic sexual relationships are the ultimate form of connection between adults, that this relationship should fulfill every need, that no other forms of connection could possibly compare—and while I can't speak for everyone, that is untrue, unhealthy, and frankly insulting to most of the people I know!

Any movement that aims to deconstruct society's destructive attitudes toward sex must acknowledge not only the shame but also the obsession. It must not only declare that sex isn't shameful, but also that its appeal is not universal. It must wholly embrace relationships that don't follow the standard romantic template—polyamory, casual sex, queer-platonic relationships, relationship anarchy, kinky relationships—as well as the choice to remain single. It must uplift friendship and teach that sexual and romantic relationships aren't the only ones that matter.

It's not only people on the asexual and aromantic spectrums who are affected by this insistence of the wonders of sex. There are plenty of people with low sex drives, different priorities, or medical issues that get in the way of intercourse; there are shy or private people, or people who simply can't find partners. When most sex-positive spaces are sexual, it makes it hard for those people to feel welcome in the movement. It also excludes children from these political spaces, and youth are already disenfranchised enough. This is especially relevant for communities adjacent to the sex-positivity movement, like the queer community—we need more nonsexual queer spaces!

Of course, it's still important to have unashamedly sexual spaces where interested adults can learn and connect and have fun. Creating spaces that include the less sexual doesn't have to take away from existing sexual spaces, activism isn't a zero-sum game.

Some of these less sexual spaces do exist already. The sex-positive community center in my area hosts classes and support networks with no explicit sexual activities. One of the most effective ways to be more inclusive is to clearly label what level of sexual content to expect, much the same as trigger warnings. I've been to sex-positive events where I had no idea what to expect. Sometimes it was fine, sometimes I felt incredibly uncomfortable because there was more sexual activity going on around me than I was okay with. If the community was more consistent in its content warnings I would feel much safer participating.

There's a delicate balance between exercising the freedom to express one's sexuality and inflicting one's sexuality on the public. I don't think there's an objectively correct balance point; different spaces strike different balances, and it's good to have a variety. But it's important to make it clear from the beginning what sort of balance a given space is going for, both to warn those who might be uncomfortable as well as to set expectations for the rest of the participants.

Activists from more or less my parents' generation worked to counter the wave of sexual conservatism following the AIDS epidemic, when combating sexual shame was desperately needed. To some extent they succeeded, although the movement is certainly not obsolete. While most young people didn't grow up in the kind of alternative communities that I did, open embrace of sexuality is much less controversial than it used to be, even in mainstream culture. The future of sex positivity is a generational conversation. What society needed to hear in the eighties isn't the same as what it needs to hear now, particularly in feminist communities. [11]

How have attitudes toward sex and sexual behaviors changed? Poking around for research on generational differences in sexual behavior yielded some fascinating information (although I'm mostly operating from abstracts since all the studies I found kept the full papers behind paywalls, so if the details contradict me I apologize). A 2015 meta-analysis of studies on sexual behavior between generations found that, while Americans born between 1982 and 1999 (the youngest age group they studied) are the most accepting of nonmarital sex, their numbers of sexual partners are lower than those of every generation since the boomers.[12] In a later 2017 study, these authors found that when they control for age, those born in the 1990s had sex the least often of all living generations, with both a higher percentage of unpartnered individuals and declining sexual frequency among the partnered.[13] A different study comparing three national surveys found that the historic positive trend of adolescent sexual experience reversed among adolescent men, and either stopped or reversed for adolescent women, during the late 1980s and 1990s.[14] While surveys regarding sexual behavior are always questionable, since people tend to answer dishonestly, there's solid evidence that millennials and following generations (from the United States and similar countries) are less sexually active than their predecessors.

Knowing these demographic shifts perhaps paints a different picture for sex positivity. For whatever reason—focusing on one's career, discomfort with one's body, not finding compatible partners—sex isn't as much a part of young people's lives. These generations are more accepting of nonmarital sex, same-sex sexual activity, and teen sex than any previous generation.[15] They don't need to hear

---

[11] Although differences between communities in terms of sexual openness are so drastic that any discussion of society as a whole here is practically absurd. A more accurate statement would be that certain communities have successfully moved away from sexual conservatism and ended up overemphasizing sex, while other communities are still stuck in the fifties, and most places are somewhere in between. Since I'm writing this for a feminist audience, however, I'll focus more on those sorts of communities.

[12] Twenge, Sherman and Wells, *Changes in American Adults' Sexual Behavior and Attitudes, 1972–2012* 2015

[13] Twenge, Sherman and Wells, *Declines in Sexual Frequency among American Adults, 1989–2014* 2017)

[14] Santelli, et al. 2000)

[15] Twenge, Sherman and Wells, *Changes in American Adults' Sexual Behavior*

that sex isn't shameful, at least, not as much as previous generations did. But I do wonder, how many young people need to hear that it's okay not to love sex? How many notice that they're not as sexually active as society seems to expect, how many feel alienated by this cultural fixation, how many worry that something's wrong with them because sex isn't as important to them as it seems to be for everyone else?

The damage is gendered, at least to some extent: where women are more shamed for being sexually active, men are usually shamed for the reverse. There's this intense social pressure on men to demonstrate hypersexuality. It shows up in the way small penises are a cultural laughingstock, how male sexual assault victims aren't taken seriously (because "he must have wanted it"), and in the way male virgins are emasculated and mocked. As a transmasculine person, I'm quite familiar with people invalidating my masculinity when I don't meet hypermasculine gender norms, and I wouldn't wish that on anyone. When it comes to society's attitudes toward sex, I think everyone is harmed by both sides of the coin, but that people perceived as men tend to deal with more of the obsession and people perceived as women tend to deal with more of the shame—though I do think the recent demographic shifts mentioned above have narrowed that gender gap somewhat.

In the end, society's destructive attitudes toward sex cut both ways. Feminist and sex-positive discussions tend to revolve around sexual shame, which is in some ways the more obvious problem and the side which harms women especially. It is for this reason, however, that I chose to focus this writing on the other aspect of sexual norms. Not because shame isn't as worthy a topic—it is an incredibly complex problem, one that changes wildly when it intersects with other identities, and which deserves a more nuanced discussion than I afforded it here—but because I don't hear as much about the obsession, even between activists. People like me, raised by sex-positive families, have hardly been exposed to sex shaming at all. The movement has truly made a lot of progress in combating sex shaming. It's time to turn the problem over and tackle the other side.

Goddess Lilith

contact for prices & services
598-694-2019

CHAPTER 3
PORN AND SEX WORK

Those of us who embrace sex positivity realize that also means embracing consensual sex work and pornography. Contrary to popular opinion, many people are involved with both consensually and joyfully.

A NICE GIRL LIKE ME
by Eva Sless

That look. Oh that look. I've seen it before. On a thousand faces, in a thousand ways. I know it before it's spoken. Eyes dripping with polite condescension. Brows furrowed in fearful concern. That inner moral compass spinning desperately, searching for a direction in which to place me.

The question. The burning question. The question uneasily wrapped in vicarious voyeurism, thinly disguised as curious uncertainty:

"How does a nice girl like you end up in a job like this?"

Or words to that effect.

A nice girl.

A job like this.

Or words to that effect.

A nice girl like me fills the void of human touch lost in the passing of time. Fingers speaking to skin, connecting where connection has been long since forgotten.

A nice girl like me calls to the inside of your loneliness, reaching deep within to draw out that pain and envelop it in warmth. In understanding. In heart.

A nice girl like me makes you feel alive and ignited. Passionate and free.

A nice girl like me holds your secrets and your fears.

Or words to that effect.

A nice girl like me knows you don't mean nice. A nice girl like me reads the code between your lines. A nice girl like me knows the origin of your shame.

Caught up in the bodies of others. Entangling your fears and your shame into my world. Flailing in a pit of self-doubt and clawing desperately at the lives of strangers to pull yourself onto the highest of horses, to look down, to deem unworthy, to judge, point, denigrate, shame. You think yourself a hero. A knight. A crusader who comes both unwanted and unrelenting, wielding your righteousness, brandishing your pity, worn under a mask of care, or help, or rescue.

Or words to that effect.

A nice girl like me doesn't need your white horse. A nice girl like me rides upon her own steed of passion and heart, strong and sure, beautiful and proud, rescuing those who are drowning, gasping, dying in a sea of lonely isolation.

With a word. With a kiss. With a look. With a fire. A nice girl like me takes those battles from you, slays those dragons of solitude, scoops you into her fold and carries you to safety, to comfort, to belong.

Or words to that effect.

A nice girl like me takes the lonely and untouched and gives them a reason, a knowing, an understanding. They are worthy. They are valid. They are human.

A nice girl like me lays beside the body you feel trapped in and sees only skin to be touched and a soul to be caressed. A nice girl like me sees beyond what the world sees. Sees the essence within. A nice girl like me sees you.

Or words to that effect.

The question that you ask is not the question that you mean.

The answer that I give are not the words you want to hear.

What is a nice girl like you doing in a job like this?

I am living. I am loving. I am body, heart, and soul.

I am a secret. I am a whisper. I am a fantasy and a friend.

I am all the world to some, and a passing thought to others.

I am heat. I am warmth. I am fire.

I am compassion and companion, lover and life giver.

I am everything I need to be and everything I want to be.

I am heart. I am whole. I am home.

Or words to that effect.

SEX POSITIVE CAN'T BE WHORE NEGATIVE
by Maggie McNeill

Prior to the early nineteenth century, the sharp lines modern people now draw between prostitutes, mistresses, girlfriends, actresses, dancers, masseuses and other types of non-wives from whom men could obtain some kind of sexual or sensual contact were blurry at best, when they existed at all. Consider that courtesans such as the Madame de Pompadour and Jane Shore were still considered harlots despite the fact that all their liaisons were long-term and their total lifetime count of sex partners was lower than most modern women (who would be extremely offended to be called whores) rack up before graduating from university; also understand that working-class women from Roman times until well into the twentieth century often supplemented their meager earnings by selling sex on the side, and you'll begin to understand why the idea of the prostitute as a specific, "fallen" kind of woman seems so ridiculous to those who know anything about it. The King James Bible uses the world harlot to mean any woman having sex outside of marriage, not just career professionals, and that's not merely an artifact of sloppy translation; up until Victorian times, whether a sexually active woman was married to her partner was what made her "good" or "bad," and her motive for having sex with him was of little concern to anyone but her.

For most of recorded human history, the manifold laws regulating sex work were not intended to preclude pragmatic motivations for sexual behavior, but rather to keep up appearances, guard the purity of bloodlines, and maintain public order. But as industrialization rapidly changed the face of Europe and the young United States, a new idea began to take hold of people's minds: if science could improve man's tools and techniques, why couldn't the same process be applied to mankind itself? The immediate result of turning (pseudo) scientific inquiry upon sex was that taking money for it was no longer considered merely something that "low" or "sinful" women did for a living or extra income; instead, the "prostitute" was defined into existence as a specific type of woman, separate and distinct from other women. And once the idea of prostitution as some uniquely disgraceful activity was invented, and the prostitute was defined as the lowest of the low, it was inevitable that women who would previously have been considered more or less the same as whores would attempt to draw lines between themselves and the new pariah class. Furthermore, once these new ideas inspired western governments to criminalize prostitution and/or its attendant activities, distinguishing oneself from a "common prostitute" became a matter not only of dignity, but of legal necessity.

The first group to successfully shed the whore stigma was actresses, who had since classical times been considered interchangeable with harlots; dancers whose style could be credibly represented as asexual or highbrow (preferably both) followed them, then masseuses and finally, emancipated women who had extramarital sex for nonfinancial reasons. In the past several decades, these groups have multiplied to include burlesque and competition pole dancers, glamour and lingerie models, professional cuddlers, nude maids, waitresses catering to sexual fantasies, and even sugar babies; all of these absolutely insist that they are different from strippers, hookers, and fetish workers in some real (and legally defensible) way. Even people who are directly paid for a hands-on sexual service claim that being certified, spiritual, or whatever makes them distinctly different from other sex workers, and I've actually heard women willing to top strangers at kink parties claim that their lack of a pecuniary motivation makes them not only distinct from, but morally or even psychologically superior to, professional dominatrices.

And I'm here to tell you that if you subscribe to any of this line drawing you are not only full of shit, but complicit in a venerable and wholly odious form of bigotry that has over the past few centuries led to witch hunts, the Red Scare, concentration camps, and conversion therapy for queer people. And if you hold these beliefs and still call yourself sex positive, you're a lying hypocrite. Most people who think of themselves as sex positive would surely denounce the idea that the state has the right to control people's thoughts; they would mock attempts to criminalize certain fantasies, and react with disapproval or even anger to slutshaming, bierasure and policing of others' kinks. Your Kink Is Not My Kink, But Your Kink Is Okay, right? And yet, when the thoughts in question are motivations, and the motivation is money, suddenly all bets are off and many soi-disant sex-positive people suddenly become as prudish as anyone petitioning Congress to ban internet porn. Even more absurdly, some are just fine with sex work as long as it involves no genital contact or only involves contact in front of the camera (which is bizarrely considered to have the magical power to transform a mere trollop into an artiste). Oh, they'll emit high-sounding nonsense about the exchange of money being demeaning (while cruising Tinder or Grindr) or cluck disapprovingly about STIs (while being fluid bonded with four different poly partners embedded in a bigger polycule containing dozens of people). But those are just the excuses they employ when trying to get sex workers kicked out of their local sex-positive community, either officially or by a whisper campaign. In reality, their motivation is just plain old garden-variety bigotry.

But even if you've had these feelings, and even if you've acted on them, that doesn't automatically mean you're a bad person. Morality isn't determined by our feelings, which we can't help; it's determined by the way we act upon our feelings. Nobody is born hating whores; the prejudice is slowly imbibed, drop by poisonous drop, throughout our formative years, from our parents, our peers, religion, the pronouncements of authorities, and, over the past two decades, from the vicious propaganda which anti-sex authoritarians have invested a great deal of time, effort, and money in creating. If you don't actually know any sex workers and I ask you to imagine one, what image pops into your head? Scene: a street corner at night. A woman stands beneath a lamp post; her tired, hardened features are concealed by excessive makeup, and she wears revealing clothes including a short skirt baring her legs, which end in sky-high heels. Maybe she's a teenager. If I ask you why she became a sex worker, what will you say? Drugs. Daddy issues. A "pimp." And so on, and so forth, ad nauseam. It never even crosses your mind that the general public tends to tar kinky people, and women who have sex outside of committed relationships, with the same kind of stigma, slurs, and stereotypes; you may even forget that until Lawrence v Texas in 2003, homosexual acts (referred to as sodomy) were illegal across much of the United States, and gay men were rounded up in the same kind of sweeps that today are reserved for sex workers and our clients.

Were I to condemn you for prejudices you didn't choose to have pounded into your soft, growing brain, I'd be no different from those who claim that sex workers should be criminalized, demonized, stigmatized, or infantilized for our motivations for having sex, or those who condemn queer and kinky people as sick or sinful. But neither am I going to give you a free pass on letting ugliness, bigotry, and hatred disguised as morality, feminism, and concern for children go by unopposed. The queer rights movement didn't gain traction until a sufficient number of straight people began showing support, and the same will be true of the persecution of sex workers. Creating a sex-positive culture requires not only that we respect others' sexual needs, desires, preferences, and choices, but also that we respect their motives for those choices, even if we cannot understand them and would choose differently ourselves. Criminalization of consensual adult sexual behavior has no place in a free society, and it certainly has no place in a sex-positive one. But though it will probably be a while before the evil of prohibition is rooted out from society as a whole, subcultures can evolve much more quickly. Talk to sex workers in real life or online; learn about our lives and work, and resolve to treat us as you would treat any other sexual minority. Condemn antiwhore bigotry and slurs just as vociferously as you would antiqueer ones. Stop drawing artificial lines between yourself and other people, and you'll have made the first step in creating a more inclusive, accepting, sex-positive world for everyone.

PEEPSHOW PEDAGOGY: LESSONS FROM THE LUSTY LADY
by Ron Richardson

In 1987 the term *sex positive* didn't exist. Or, if it did, I'd never heard it, and I don't suppose that should be surprising. In 1987 Ronald Reagan was still in office, AIDS/HIV was God's punishment (in the minds of many) for being gay, and I had grown up in a collection of little shit towns in the elbow formed where Oregon, Washington, and Idaho come together, surrounded by people holding those kind of attitudes.

On the other hand, I also habitually rebelled against common wisdom, and sex was a hobby of mine in the way sports or collecting was a hobby for others. By seventh grade I knew my PE teacher was full of shit when he told the boys in our gender-segregated sex-education lesson that Saran Wrap and rubber bands could be used as a substitute for a condom, in a pinch. I had lost my virginity in a triad and understood that monogamy was not for me, and I knew that the morally relevant consideration for any sex act was the consent of all those involved, not the biological details of what they were doing.

Two days after graduating high school in 1987, this fascination with sex, women, and sex work led me to the big city of Seattle, where I was lucky enough to land a job at a business that was putting the principles of sex positivism into practice—although, again, without having heard the term. The Amusement Center hired me as a cashier, doorman, and janitor. About two years later the name would change to that more well-known moniker, The Lusty Lady.

The Lusty Lady was a peepshow (I'm going to assume you know what a peepshow is, if not please let me refer you to Mr./Ms. Google) like no other in the world. The owner, a man named Bill Cooley, hired a woman named June Cade to be general manager and professionalize the operations of the place. One of Cooley's core philosophies was that there was nothing wrong with sex of any kind, and that the layers of guilt and taboo we had erected around sexuality were damaging individuals and society as a whole. This attitude infused the operations of the place, from top to bottom.

The employment form asked applicants (dancers and support staff alike) how they felt "about men and male sexuality" how they felt about their own sexuality, and what their astrological sign was. Okay, maybe that last question isn't quite so cool, but it was there. All brands of sexuality were accepted at the Lusty Lady. In the 1980s, when the signs outside the business advertised "live, nude, girls," the line up on the stage included women of all ages, sizes, races, shapes, and colors, including one very special dancer, Emerald.

Let me add to the list of terms that didn't exist back in 1987. Back then we'd never heard of cisgender and used words to describe those who were not cis that are considered rude and hurtful today. Emerald was a transgender woman. The management and the staff all loved and supported Emerald fully, the customers were a mixed bag.

More than once I had to deal with some man who had dropped a quarter and started masturbating to the rear view of Emerald only to then be shocked when she turned around and showed what she still had between her legs. Their worked-up outrage was educational to me, as I saw it as a strange, unnecessary display. And I knew Emerald was a very giving, open, wonderful woman who deserved better than their ire.

Emerald went through the entire gender transition process, including more than one surgery, while dancing at the Lady. She would take breaks when she had to, but while she was working she was an endless display of patience for all of her coworkers. The other dancers were insanely curious about what was happening to Emerald's body and Emerald would literally drop whatever she was wearing on her bottom half, sit on the couch in the backstage dressing room, and give illustrated tours on what was happening with her anatomy. She would talk about how the world was treating her differently as she presented more and more female, how she saw the world differently as the hormones affected her perceptions, and the strange experience of finally feeling like her body and identity were coming into alignment.

Her vulnerability, honesty, and candor all blew my eighteen-year-old small-town self away. I had thought I was open minded before, but Emerald was completely beyond my experience. That she was patient with me, and everyone else, gave me the opportunity to see that her humanity was unchanged and independent of any gender identification. She helped me to understand by giving her time and energy to educate me. And she was far from alone in doing so while I worked there.

Another coworker of mine, a fellow janitor, also taught me an incredible amount about race and sexual orientation. Tommy was his name and he was, simply, beautiful. A proud, gay, black man, Tommy talked to me about race in a way few white people ever get to enjoy with black folk. He endured my questions, which ranged from the historical (it was from Tommy that I first heard about Juneteenth) to the sexual ("Tommy," I once asked him, "do you actually orgasm from receiving anal sex?"), and always gave me honest and direct answers. Even if he sometimes had to overcome his shock at this ignorant white boy who had asked him.

It was because Tommy and Emerald were open, that they did this emotional labor (another term that wasn't in wide use then) that I am who I am now. I'm far from perfect, mind you, but I am confident that my transgender kid has always known their gender identity is up to them, that it is none of my business (in the most positive way possible), and that I love them without consideration of it. My friends and family come from all gender, racial, and sexual places and I know enough to not claim to be "color blind." Like the recovering addict, I am still counting my birthdays and know one is never done with bigotry, but what progress I have made lies firmly at the feet of Tommy and Emerald, and I'd like to take this space to publicly thank them, and everyone else like them, who have engaged in that labor to the betterment of others.

I understand that it was labor, and that everyone has a right to tap out from such effort. We can't all always endure the assumptions and slights inherent to such encounters. To all the trans, minority, kinky, poly, and whatever folk out there reading this who are unable or unwilling to do that labor, know that I've got your back. This is not a call for you to change in any way. It is a recognition that my own sex-positive journey could never have bent the way it did without the nudges I got from Emerald, Tommy, and many more like them over the years. It is my thanks to them and to everyone else who engages in that labor, for all that it is often thankless and futile.

It's now 2017 and the lexicon has grown dramatically. I am honored and humbled to have played a small role in that process, to have been a raindrop in the flood of sex positivity and acceptance that has changed the attitudes of our surrounding culture. And the lessons that Tommy and Emerald shared, the labor they undertook, bore fruit. Thank you, endlessly, for all you gave me.

THE BIRTH OF THE BLUE MOVIE CRITIC
by Susie Bright

Excerpted with permission from *The Feminist Porn Book*

I was hired by Jack Heidenry in 1986 to write for *Penthouse Forum*, a pocketbook-size sex journal that porn mogul Bob Guccione published during his heyday.

I had no idea that Jack's plan was rather experimental. All I knew was that I'd never been paid to write professionally before, though I'd worked tirelessly on newspapers and underground magazines since I was a teenager. I got suspended for distributing birth control information in high school. My first sex advice column was written for *On Our Backs*, a then two-year-old underground, anti-establishment magazine dedicated to "entertainment for the adventurous lesbian." I was always the enthusiastic volunteer of the sexual liberation front.

But I'd never watched an X-rated movie. I didn't tell Jack either of my secrets. It was such an amazing opportunity, I wanted him to think I wrote for piles of money all the time and knew everything about erotic theater.

Unlike Guccione's flagship title with its pin-up girl centerfolds, *Forum* was full of sexy words instead of sexy pictures, read by men and women alike. Heidenry contacted me because he admired my writing and editorship of *On Our Backs*. I was shocked he'd even heard of us. Our tiny posse in San Francisco didn't publish our manifesto with men in mind.

Jack asked me to write a monthly column, "The Erotic Screen," to review and report on the latest in erotic cinema. A year later, he added an advice column so I could respond to erotic film questions. It must have been a red-letter day in 1986 for women's lib at the Guccione Empire—Heidenry hired myself, Veronica Vera, and Annie Sprinkle as monthly regulars. I don't know when any leading circulation magazine in New York ever again hired three talented women as contributing editors and then paid them handsomely. I was blissfully out of the loop about how few women worked in these capacities.

I was twenty-eight years old. All those famous hardcore films like *Deep Throat* and *Behind the Green Door* had come out when I was in Catholic grade school wearing saddle shoes and plaid skirts. When I was a kid, I was curious about X-rated movies, of course—but by the time I was a teen, I was a radical, and I considered blue movies, the whole idea of them, to be pathetic. I thought the people who made or watched *those* films must be lonely, at best. They needed to take their clothes off and go have sex with everyone else at the nude beach. My actual life at the time would have made a good porno.

By the time the 1980s arrived, I was creating lesbian erotica every day with a talented band of art radicals at our all-dyke office above a Chinese take-out in the Castro. I worked at a day job in a closet-sized feminist sex toy shop, the original Good Vibrations founded by Joani Blank. It was the only place of its kind. Our great inventory disadvantage was that hardly anyone in the erotic world made anything of interest for women.

My vibrator shop colleagues and I talked about someday publishing a book of erotic short stories by women—it had never been done. I saw only a few customers per day, and in between talking about the miracle of the Magic Wand vibrator, we talked about how no one seemed to believe that women had erotic, aesthetic interests of their own.

At *On Our Backs*, we were inventing everything from scratch. How about mounting a lesbian strip show performed by real dyke whores and strippers who wanted to perform for their own kind? Done! How about making videos of real butches and femmes and punks, people who looked like us, out dykes with real faces, having sex like real women do? Let's do it! It slowly dawned on us that there'd never been an erotic magazine put together by women of any persuasion, straight, bi, or gay—nor had lesbians ever published a periodical, even non-erotic, so blatantly and visually out of the closet. Our names and faces were on the line.

My start at *Forum* was clumsy. I asked Jack, "You know I'm a lesbian feminist, right? I'm not going to change my mind about how I see things." But that wasn't the half of it. I wasn't a professional journalist, despite my political credentials. My first *Forum* review, to my eyes now, reads like a high school book report. Furthermore, I had no contacts in the business, no introductions. I had to buy a ticket like every other dirty old man and march into the Pussycat Theater for a theatrical viewing. I didn't know what a VCR was—none of my friends watched videos at home.

Now I'm glad for my initial deprivation. I ended up seeing rather amazing 35mm films at some of the biggest and most elegant screens in San Francisco and New York. They raised my expectations, in a good way. I was the only woman in the porn theater who wasn't working. I thought at first that the male customers would hassle me as I sat down in a torn velvet seat with my little notepad. But they didn't bother me—they moved away as if I were a detective. I often had the entire aisle to myself.

I also realized that a lot of the men were having sex with each other in the back of the theater, some inspired by, and some indifferent to, the largely heterosexual activity on screen. I remember feeling annoyed when I heard them grunting, and I'd yell, "You're missing a good part!"

I had a friend, now deceased, named Victor Chavez, who worked out of the Local 2 HERE banquet hall. We were both union organizers, a cause close to my heart—but we discussed other things besides unfair contracts! He's the one who opened his briefcase one day and told me that the two books he always carried with him were the Bible, which he set out before us on a table, along with *How to Enlarge Your Penis*, which he told me was the second greatest-selling book in the world, next to Genesis.

Victor had a Betamax video player, and a screen, which he insisted on loaning me so I could be a better critic. He believed in my potential. The screen was enormous, and I could barely fit it in my single room, but I instantly grasped the intimacy of this new viewing experience. I could plug in my Magic Wand and make as much of a fuss as those guys at the Pussycat.

I understood the dual whammy of porn. All those people fucking and breathing hard, it gets to you—at least before you've reviewed a few thousand. It arouses you to distraction. On the other hand, I was a huge movie buff, a film nerd, and I couldn't help but critique the bombs, the gaffes, the weird porn canards—as well as appreciate the directors who were obviously great talents.

You see, erotic filmmakers were the original indie filmmakers. The fact that their films turned you on was no different than a different genre scaring the daylights out of you, or making you cry. Films are great vehicles to elicit strong emotion. When they touch you on multiple levels, simultaneously, we call them "masterpieces."

The hardcore era that began in the late sixties is now be understood as part of the wave of independent films that broke away from the Hollywood studio system. The erotic filmmakers were pioneers in the same league as the spaghetti western directors or the producers of clumsy horror and sci-fi flicks. Sometimes, they were the same people. The permanent ghettoization of blue films was bizarre, and unwarranted by anything but the priggery of political machinations.

When *Forum* hired me, there were a lot of porn fan magazines but no independent reviews or genuine reporting. You would never see an article in a daily newspaper or legitimate magazine about the economics, aesthetics, or workaday world of the adult film industry. (The whole expression, adult as a euphemism for sex came into our vernacular because of legal battles that defined sexuality as a subject forbidden for young people's eyes).

It was truly the twilight zone, only referred to in legal and moral debates about obscenity. No guild reporter actually went out to a movie set or an office, no non-adult journalist knew the numbers. It was untouched territory, and I was the unlikely character who wandered into it with a pencil and pad.

There was one trade newsletter, like a one-sheet version of *Variety*, edited by Jared Rutter, called *Film World Reports*, which was read by producers and directors in the business. It listed the bestselling movies, who was buying what, classic insider bullet news. After all, they were certainly making money and deals, despite the indifference of the rest of the entertainment media. Decoding that sheet was one of my first accomplishments.

Yes, you could buy men's magazines where you'd read breathless interviews with the starlets or read peanut-size reviews that said things like "Steamy! Ceci is SO HOT!" It was advertising barely disguised as editorials. The people who wrote the reviews did not use their own names. It was as closeted a world as a pre-Stonewall gay bar.

The closest thing to erotic cinema criticism was at *Hustler* magazine, who deployed a famous graphic they created called the "peter-meter" to cover the latest releases. With each title, the little penis would rise from the pudgy category to a raging hard-on. "Peter" was always at least at half-mast, until one shocking day, *Hustler* gave a film a complete limp-dick rating. I was riveted by the reviewer, who used his own voice to say how revolted and disgusted he was by this insult to masculinity and good clean, X-rated fun.

Wow. Obviously *Hustler* had not been paid for this review. I decided if they hated this movie, it must be great.

I was right. The film was *Smoker*, by a pair of film students from NYU who'd done art direction for Rinse Dream's *Cafe Flesh*. Their names were Ruben Masters and Michael Constant. I saw *Smoker* the very next day at the Pussycat, and sure enough, it rattled several customers enough to leave the theater. I think it was the moment when David Christopher slipped a filmy blue women's chemise over his chest and started slapping his cock against his belly, masturbating and fiercely monologuing to himself as he spied upon a neighbor next door. He's not announced as trans, or cross-dressed, or any label at all. What he is doing is just his un-explained intimacy, so well-acted and shot you feel like you're in *Hiroshima Mon Amour* a meets seventh-floor walkup in the Bowery.

These filmmakers used a pseudonym, Veronika Rocket. They'd broken so many rules, their genderfuck was so effortless, with such beauty, that I used their film as a benchmark for the rest of my erotic criticism career. I made a pilgrimage to Philadelphia to meet them and visit their original set pieces. Ruben Masters opened the door of her carriage house, looking like Louise Brooks in Pandora's Box and checked me up and down. "Vodka stinger?" she said.

Ruben Masters opened the door of her carriage house, looking like Louise Brooks in *Pandora's Box* and checked me up and down. "Vodka stinger?" she said.

I had so many lucky breaks like that.

Meanwhile, I introduced myself to the baker's dozen of blue film companies in Southern California and New York. I went to the annual trade conference in Vegas, which at the time was a tucked-away ghetto at the Consumer Electronics Convention, far away from all the new TV's and stereos. I hung out in the lady's bathroom at the Sahara Hotel with copies of *On Our Backs* to initiate conversations with the "X" actresses who weren't accustomed to anyone giving a damn about their real stories.

There were lots of men to talk to, of course. Most of the older ones were very conservative. A handful of men ran this business for years, a gin rummy game consortium, and they were as bigoted as Archie Bunker. They had a hard time believing I was there for real, not a joke, not a straight girl on a slumming lark. My *Penthouse* column—and the video library I created at my old sex toy shop— sold so many videos that they had to endure me. They were jaded, and yet naïve about how much their world was changing. They'd say the most incredible things on the record: "Women don't like to see anal sex; that's nasty. Any white actress who lets a black actor fuck her on screen is out of her mind; her career is through. How can a lesbian get pregnant; that's impossible! Don't you have a husband somewhere to look after?"

Some of their sons and daughters were more open, or openly rebelling. Punk rock, queer lib, and feminist sensibilities hit the artistic side of the "adult" industry. It was contagious. It used to be a papa and son business tradition, almost quaint that way. One of the twenty-something heirs to the gin rummy game sat down with me one day and explained how Ruben Sturman, the granddaddy of the peepshow and the adult rain-coater industry, evaded the IRS for so long. How did he manage to never pay taxes? How did he run a business completely outside of the American establishment? Our conversation took place three years before Sturman finally got busted for good. My friend told me in detail how the money was generated, methodically picked up in bags, and moved from place to place.

"Why are you telling me this?" I asked him.

"Because you make lesbian fist-fucking videos," he said.

I didn't realize how daring that act was until he said it. I had no idea that this was the key to mutual confidence—risk.

The lesbian feminist erotic world we'd created at *On Our Backs* was our own little cloister. We were innocent of what was and wasn't outside the law. If we had two lovers crazy about each other who wanted to be videotaped, we didn't tell them what to do. If they put their hands inside each other at the moment of orgasm, to our eyes, it was terribly romantic. To the US Justice Department, it was just about the most obscene act ever. Go figure.

Everything women actually did to get off seemed to be against the blue laws, we found out. Women's orgasms, real orgasms, real female bodily fluids, were a no-no every time we tried to sell our magazine or videos in conservative states. Places like Oklahoma and Florida said that g-spot ejaculations were illegal "water sports," "golden showers," and therefore on their list of community obscenities that violated the Miller Standard. They didn't know anything about female anatomy or physiology—and they didn't care. You can see those same ideas today, in places like Alabama that make possession of vibrators a crime. The old-school porn dudes called them "soft states;" I called them "women-don't-come" states.

On Our Backs, and our video arm, Fatale Video, were rudely introduced to the world of legal obscenity where nothing has anything to do with reality. Strangely, our unintended risk-taking gave us the cred to be allowed into discussions in the hardcore boy's room. They never would have talked to me otherwise.

Video changed everything—in porn first, then in Hollywood. The days of the peep shows and the theaters were numbered; although it's interesting to see the peep show has outlasted the elegant theater. People still like to feed those coins in close quarters—the special claustrophobia of tight circumstances. More importantly, video offered a way in for artists, entrepreneurs, and sex radicals—who, for better or worse, never would've made a movie before. A new small set of geniuses were born, along with a much vaster set of mediocrities. Not different from film, just multiplied like rabbits.

When I first heard from my readers at *Penthouse Forum*, who wrote me by hand, (pre-email!) I realized two things. One, the overwhelming majority of women had never seen an erotic motion picture before, *at all*. Their furtive glances of still photos in men's magazines were mostly female nudes—maybe Burt Reynolds in his famous *Cosmo* spread. But what about men? It wasn't much more sophisticated. Very few men had seen more than a minuscule sampling of erotic films. Ask a random man if he can name five or six full-length erotic movies he's seen. If he is able to make such a list, he's part of an exclusive club.

Watching erotic films, movies that are driven forward by sex scenes, is different than looking at single photos, pictorials, snippets, clips. The medium, the experience of going all the way through an eighty-minute feature, is an entirely different ride than a momentary glimpse, a fast-forward. To prove it, I started throwing living-room movie shows for my friends where I would give away my screener copies and show segments of my favorites. It was like I was offering free rocket tickets to the moon. My neighborhood audience was fascinated—and completely inexperienced.

The living room got a little bigger—I created an educational show-and-tell clips lecture called *How to Read a Dirty Movie*, and another one called *All Girl Action: The History of Lesbian Erotic Cinema*, which I started premiering at independent theaters like The Castro and The Roxie. I hit the festival circuit all over the world, including a daring mission by the British Film Institute to get my movies in, despite iron-clad UK customs rules against them.

One memory stands out: In rural Blacksburg, Virginia, a closeted gay student got ahold of student union funds for "Friday Night Fun!" at Virginia Tech to bring me out there for one of my clips shows. This is a school with a history of devotion to Southern white boys and military service. The students weren't even allowed to watch R-rated films on campus. I didn't find this out until I was moments away from the podium. My young sponsor looked like he'd just detonated a bomb, and his face was covered in sweat. *My Dirty Movie* clips show started, which happens to begin with excerpts of two young handsome army cadets making out on a firing range.

I thought the roof was going to cave in. Blacksburg boys were running for the doors, making vomiting sounds, screaming. The half who stayed in their seats watched a full-spectrum array of sexual and human emotion, delivered by porn's finest auteurs. They got more sex education in one-hundred minutes than they'd had in their entire life.

The stunned president of the Young Republicans, a co-sponsor of "Friday Night Fun," took me out to a fast food dinner afterward. He told me that he found it curious that the scenes of lesbians making love had pleased him, while the scenes of gay men had given him a stomach ache. I was impressed that he was calm enough to observe his own reactions. "I don't disagree with all of what you do," he said, "but I think it's entirely unjust that you receive checks from the government for your homosexuality."

I stared at him with my mouth full of fries. "Oh, it's not that bad," I said, "I only get half as much because I'm bisexual."

The success of the film shows, despite Blacksburg, led me further into the university world. I started a class called *The Politics of Sexual Representation* at UC

Santa Cruz, a rewarding teaching experience. The students were prepared to look at material that was considered ephemeral or taboo and decode it.

In film circles, in the Ivy League, among artists and art historians, this thing called *porn* became a sophisticated interest, with many reporters and scholars following the same leads that had inspired me so long ago. The public developed a sense of normality and better still, *humor* about porn, which had been missing when I began my "Erotic Screen" column.

Much like the topic of gay life, the porn debate seems to exist in two parallel worlds. On one side, it's old hat, a yawn. In the other world, Planet Prude, the legal and public-policy climate is fundamentalist. Politicians and religious leaders employ sex as their bogeyman more vociferously than ever, enlisting liberal as well as conservative support.

The twenty-first-century Gilded Age is one of moralism and slut shaming for the general public—while corruption and Caligula-like license is the rule for the elite. My entree to the golden age of porn looks so utopian now! The seventies and eighties were a heyday for women's progress in journalism, for coming out of the closet, for breaking down once-impermeable barriers in both the media and sex-film trade. I was dubbed the "Pauline Kael of Porn" in 1986 by the *SF Chronicle,* but within a few years there would come to be dozens of reporters and critics covering the erotic film industry and its offerings. It was truly our "Porno Spring!" The art and academic establishment confronted erotic desire; what was once ephemeral drew potent scholarly attention. Among the cognoscenti, blue movies became historic. I was voted into the fourth Estate Hall of Fame of the X-Rated Critics Organization in 2002.

I was lucky to wander in, like Alice with a bottle of something blue and a label that said, "Eat Me." I'm very glad I did. Unlike Alice, I never went back to being small.

HOW TO EDIT LESBIAN PORN
by Sui Yao

When Shanghai native Sui Yao decided to try her hand at editing, she never imagined her first job would be a lesbian porn film. Can a self-identified straight woman cut it with queer sex?

I'm by no means a professional film editor. The first time I tried it was in 2015, cutting a seven-minute short shot with a group of friends for a competition. Against all odds, I won the Best Editing prize. I started asking around for projects, wanting to put my newfound skills to use. In summer 2016, I was handed my first official editing job.

Fan Popo, the "it" queer filmmaker based in Beijing, had asked me to cut his new film: a lesbian porn movie. I had always been vocal about women's sexual liberation, so I was excited by the opportunity, but I spent my first afternoon with the footage in a daze. Watching the material, I felt dizzy. Everything seemed TOO real. I knew I wasn't editing some studio production with lights, filters, and "sexy babes," or the usual woman-on-woman action marketed to straight men, but it still shook me.

The exposed scars on a leg, the omnipresence of hair, the flawed breasts, and the slightly awkward exchange of desire stared at me with stark nakedness. It was, in all honesty, far from what I had imagined. I was in shock. This was the first time I had ever seen other women masturbate or seen two women fuck. I think I was experiencing cunt-phobia.

I was baffled by how difficult it was for me, a woman, to watch and process authentic female bodies in action. My identification as a feminist had no effect on my honest reaction to what I saw. Real human bodies and unpretentious libido are not immediately pleasing to the eyes. We have grown accustomed to a culture in which images of nudity are often affected and fake. In real life, sex is grittier, more hormonal, and more about the everyday. It has nothing to do with being pretty.

The plot of the film was rather abstract, and a lot of the more narrative elements were conveyed through the actor's sexuality and the way they were going at it. I was at no point sure if I was right about anything I was doing.

I had just left my job in advertising and was planning a long summer vacation, so I decided to take the footage with me and work on it along the way. The buzzing of sex toys in the film became the rhythm my heart beat to on that trip, from my Casablanca-bound night flight to a trek through the Sahara, from glittering Paris to my Shanghai homecoming.

I was filled with self-doubt. I didn't really know how lesbians had sex, was I even cutting everything in the right order? The lust these women felt for each other was the through line, and how I juxtaposed scenes of intimacy with scenes of masturbation, for example, would affect the pace and tonality of the whole film. Despite my doubts, I finished the first draft and anxiously handed it over to the director.

When I mentioned the project to friends, many of them smirked and asked me if it was a pleasurable experience. Looking back, I was devastated that I had been so blindsided by preoccupation and hadn't even been able to look at the screen straight. The editing process was provocative, but not in a pleasurable kind of way. Instead, it made me think and reflect.

The role that women play in sex has long been manipulated by misogynist male viewpoints. Ubiquitous misrepresentations in media have warped our perception of what it means to have sex as a woman. A woman's need for enjoyment and self-expression in sex is often times ignored or misinterpreted. Porn that captures real-life sexual experiences between real sex partners has a presence in the West. Chinese women also have real sexual needs, and it is imperative that we can look at our own sexuality without bias and be able to enjoy it on our own terms.

In the interview section of the film, the two main actors expressed the motivation behind their participation. They felt that the lesbian porn they had watched growing up was designed for men. It made them dislike their own bodies and it weakened their sense of identity. To produce a real document of lesbian sex without being misguidance was their hope in being part of the project.

Having watched the playback time and time again, my own discomfort with the material has vanished. I no longer pay attention to unpolished physical details. Instead, I am able to see the women's authentic joy and how they revel in the raw and unaffected pleasure of sex. No feigning perfection, no deliberate seduction. Sex is the most ordinary and extraordinary thing.

HOW PORN (YOGA) CHANGED MY (SEX) LIFE
by Yuri Kotke

I grew up with porn.

When I grew up, the internet was still in its beginning. From a very early age, I learned I could find sexually arousing images on the computer (one of those old desktops with a "turbo" button. As I said, the beginnings of the internet, at least for a country in the developing world.) This kind of story is getting much more common as days go by as pornography, specially internet pornography, becomes more prevalent.

Before that, I looked at magazines such as Playboy or waited until late at night when the more sexually explicit content was allowed to air on TV. Those, apart from some childhood experiments with friends, were the gateway for the world of sexual pleasure for me.

As I got older, well into adolescence and early adulthood, masturbating to porn became a common, nearly daily experience. All that energy had to go SOMEWHERE. And that way, I moved well into my early twenties, going through a relationship and having my first sexual experiences.

Throughout a troubled relationship, I used to go back to porn when my partner didn't want to have sex. It became a source of relief for sexual tension and overall anxiety. But it didn't impact my sex life. Not that I noticed, anyway.

Then, back in 2009, I received an email from sex educator Joseph Kramer, who offered a class on masturbating to porn. He asked, "Have you been masturbating the same way for the past ten years?"

I instinctively answered to myself, "Yes. Wait… Isn't it how it is supposed to be? Can something change in the way I masturbate? With porn?"

I was curious.

This was my first contact with a sex-education class that enticed me, that felt interesting. This wasn't about some mystical way of being or relating sexually, rather, it was about something that was present in my sexual habits. That hooked me. Up to then, all kinds of sex-education classes hadn't attracted my attention, even practical ones, like Tantric sex or other spiritual paths. It didn't feel real to me, someone in their early twenties who was in an isolated location of the world with regards to sexual liberation.

But porn, and masturbating to it, was real. An everyday activity, like washing the dishes.

So I signed up for the class. Without it, I probably wouldn't ever have become a sex educator, a sexological bodyworker, or all that came after.

Pornography, in some big way, defined my life and my choices. For the good.

The first experiments in the class were simple. Masturbate to porn and stop for a few seconds, still touching your body. Take five deep breaths. Then go back to porn.

Just that simple action took me to a whole new level.

The next experiment was masturbating to porn while standing up. While moving my body. I never knew I used to be so still when I used porn. I didn't know I carried those habits back into my sex life with others. I didn't know I was using pornography as a way to remain stuck in an emotional life I didn't see a way out of. I didn't know porn was holding me back from what I could ACTUALLY feel in my body. I had started feeling these sensations, when I was very young, THROUGH porn, so I never saw how it could block me. Pornography had been my gateway to sex. How could it limit me? The beauty of the process was that I was learning how to feel more by using pornography as a catalyst. I never thought that was possible.

Fast-forward to six years later, after I was already a trained sex educator and finishing my master's degree in sex therapy. I saw a new post by the same sex educator, inviting people to his new Porn Yoga project. I signed up right there.

It took one month and over ten practice sessions. They were filmed and I could feel, through the change in my body and in my relationships, how deep this practice was. It altered how I moved my hips. It made me aware of how much energy and pleasure I was generating in my body but wasn't even aware of. It made me feel more confident with my sexual energy. I felt I could wear my sexual self like a second skin now. All that energy I had for so many years but didn't know how to channel, that energy I used porn to downplay, to spend my sexual self and sweep it under the rug, now I was using porn to amplify and direct it.

All of this was done through simple exercises. Placement of attention. Standing up with the knees slightly bent while looking at porn. Moving my attention from the porn to my body and back to the porn. Orgasming while feeling my body and not looking at the porn.

I will share with you a few practices that changed my life.

If pornography has been something you have been using a lot, something you have been ashamed of, or even if you have ignored how it has affected your body and your sexual life, these simple actions can change a lot for you; you will feel the difference.

Here they are:

- Masturbate with the screen at eye level, while standing up, knees bent slightly.
- The Pendulum: During the masturbation session, stop looking at the porn for a few moments. Focus your attention on your body and what if feels. You can keep touching yourself or you can stop. Take five

deep breaths. Return to the porn. Do this two or three times during the session.

- The Mirror: Take a handheld mirror with you for the session. During the session, stop looking at the porn a few times and look at your own face. See yourself in a high state of arousal. Did you know what you looked like when you were this aroused? Drop all judgments and criticisms and enjoy this open space with yourself, aroused and enjoying your pleasure.

- The Loved One: Get a picture of someone you love. It may be a lover, it may be a friend. Anyone of importance in your life. During the session, stop looking at the porn and, in this aroused state, look at the face of the person in the picture. Enjoy your arousal opening yourself to their face. Breathe deeply. Put your attention on their picture. Then return to the porn.

- When close to orgasm, disconnect from the porn and focus on your own body. Orgasm while feeling all your body, with full attention on yourself and your body. Lie down for a few minutes, feeling your body. Savor the feelings in the moment, with gratitude and enjoyment. Let your body integrate this experience and take it with you to your life.

For me, there was a before and after porn in my life. And there was a before and after porn yoga. Try it. Your life will change.

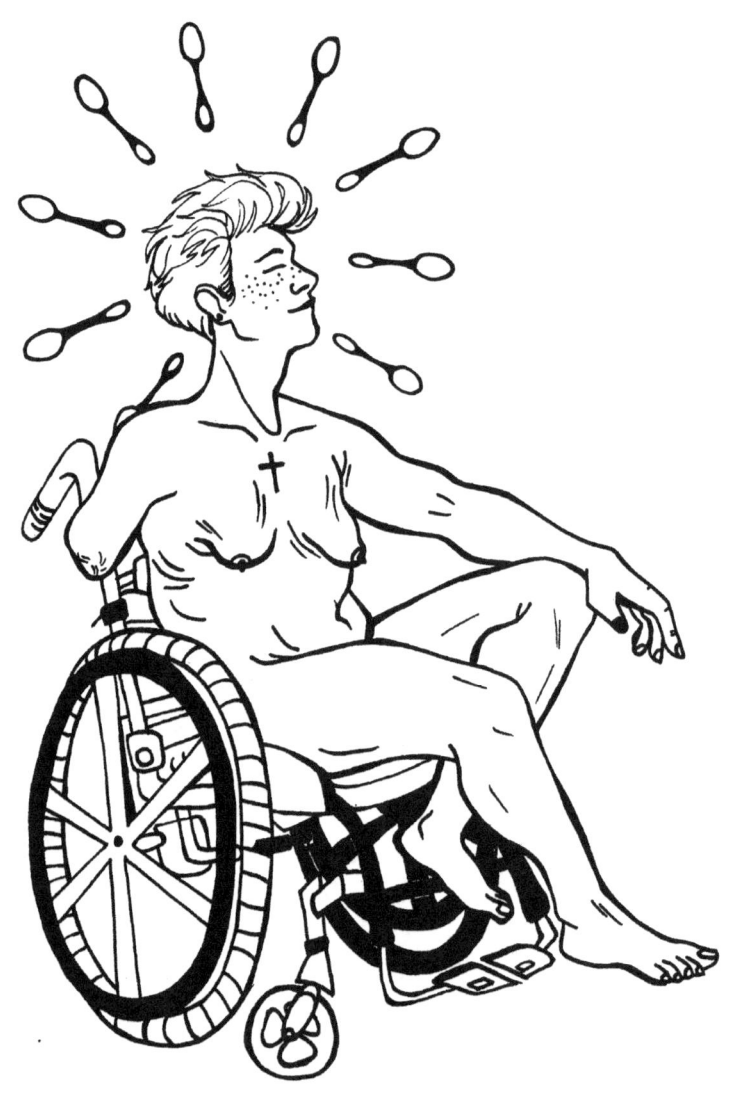

CHAPTER 4
DISABILITY

There's a pervasive attitude that people with disabilities do not have sexual agency. Andrew and Jordan are happy to show you just how wrong that attitude is.

THE REALITY OF WORKING AS A QUEER CRIPPLE AND THE INACCESSIBILITY OF SEX POSITIVITY TO THE DISABLED COMMUNITY
by Andrew Gurza #DisabledPeopleAreHot

I remember finishing my presentation up at the front of a classroom full of young university students. I had just asked them if they had any questions for me about sexuality and disability, and the silence I received back from them was both telling and palpable. I was used to this type of nervousness and uncomfortability, so I waited a beat. After what felt like an eternity, I saw a hand in the front row slowly creep up. I excitedly said, "Yes. What is your question?" The student smiled wryly and said, "Well, can you even have sex? I mean, I just assumed that you were paralyzed and probably couldn't enjoy it, and surely any partner that you're with wouldn't enjoy themselves at all, right?"

I sat there, visibly stunned by the brazen question, full of ableist statements that made my skin crawl. I wanted to scream at her how offensive her question actually was, but then I remembered where I was and that I had to remain professional. I put forward my kindest smile, so full of generosity that I was pretty sure my face was going to crack into a million little pieces, and proceeded to answer her question as best I could. After the presentation was over, I thanked the organizers, grabbed my honorarium and left the classroom. I wheeled out to the accessible bus, and on the way home I broke down in tears over what had happened.

As a self-employed disability awareness consultant who specifically focuses on the intersections of sexuality, queerness, and disability, I am confronted with these attitudes and questions on a regular basis. When I present to rooms full of students, educators, allies, and community members, I invite these types of comments in the hopes of creating a dialog between us and dismantling these viewpoints as we go along. However, even though I ask people to be frank and honest with me, it doesn't mean that some of the things I hear don't hurt me as a disabled man.

Working in the sex-positive industry as a queer disabled person isn't easy, and I want to share with you some of the things that I have encountered while trying to educate people about my experiences as a "Queer Cripple."

Along with the attitudes I outlined in the above experience, bringing disability into the sex-positive community is often difficult because I am frequently asked to present the idea that "sex is for everyone—even disabled people" and that sex and disability is a positive, happy experience. When I first started working for myself, I would take whatever offers I could to present my viewpoints on queerness and disability to an audience, so I would happily comply with their requests. I presented to many groups touting these views. But, to be honest, I have never liked doing it this way; it feels disingenuous and dishonest. By only presenting an overly positive viewpoint of sex and disability, we play into the ideology that the disabled experience is always happy and that, as disabled people, we can overcome anything—even sex! I want to talk about how sometimes sex and disability isn't a happy experience. Sometimes, it sucks, and is full of ableism, rejection, and emotional discomfort. Audiences need to hear this part of the equation when we talk about sex and disability. Instead of thinking that "the disabled person figured out how to have sex. Hooray, all is well" they need to be confronted with the reality of how sex with a disability really feels, and that story often greatly contradicts the sex-positive mantra.

I have also had sex-positive community organizers suggest that the work I am presenting is far too racy and risky. They have asked if I could just "tweak it for the audience." This is troubling to me, because when I hear this it feels as though they want to sanitize the disabled sexual experience for an able-bodied audience to stomach. It feels like they want to wrap sex and disability up in a neat little bow with a happy ending (no pun intended), when it can often be anything but. Asking me to censor the realities of sex and disability is a perfect example of institutional ableism.

Another issue that I encounter working within the sex-positive community as a disabled person is barriers to physical access and accommodation. There have been countless times that I have been invited to sex-positive events where physical accessibility within the space itself hasn't been considered at all. So, picture this: there I am in my wheelchair trying to enter the space, only to find there are no ramps or elevators available, and thus I can't attend. This lack of access is confusing to me, and I often think to myself: "Hang on, didn't you just finish saying that sexuality is for everyone?" Other times, I have been able to enter the space, but there were no attendant care people on hand to assist me, so I couldn't fully participate in the event.

I have applied to conferences that were considered sex positive and have been told they already had other disabled presentations and speakers, so they didn't need my input. This has happened to me a few times now, and each time I am concerned by this. In telling me this, the organizers are usually highlighting that they want a specific type of disabled experience to speak on sexuality, and that is extremely problematic. Sex positivity often only allows for white, straight, cisgender, heteronormative disabled people, and those disabled people who are "able enough" to hold space, while so many other voices and stories are actively stifled and silenced.

I share all of this to say that the sex-positive community has a lot of work to do to become fully accessible. My personal experiences in this field as a Queer Cripple and disabled educator have given me insight into who is really valued here, and I have learned that if you are disabled, queer, a person of color, or anyone who dares to break away from the "sex-positive" narrative, it probably isn't you.

TWISTED BODIES, KINKY MINDS
by Jordan Bouray

Lighting the last of the candles on the dresser, Serena turns back to her lover with one more candle in her hand, a wicked smile on her face, and only a strap-on adorning her body. In the flickering candlelight, Vivian waits in their bed, radiant, her lips trembling, her naked, bound form shivering with anticipation. "You look stunning, my love," Serena whispers. "But you will look even better in blue..."

With that, she tilts the taper, letting the first drops of azure wax fall onto Vivian's waiting body. The droplet of heat on her chest makes her back arch with pleasure, her breasts thrusting into the air as though seeking the source of the sudden sensation, trying to become one with the flame. Another drop, and another, and soon the arching becomes writhing. A stream falls onto the stomach, and the writhing is joined by moaning. More drops, falling from closer to her body, on to more sensitive parts — two here, on the nipples; four here, on the thighs; one there, right on the clit. More drops yet, and soon the writhing turns to bucking, the moaning to pleading. "Take me, Mistress! Please! Take me!"

Satisfied with her art, Serena sets down the candle and blows it out before unhooking the straps that bind Vivian to their bed. Free to receive what she wants — what, by now, she needs — Vivian scrambles atop her lover, locking Serena's wheelchair firmly in place before impaling herself on the dildo in her lap. "Thank you, Mistress! Thank you!" she screams, as her mind shatters with the first of many, many orgasms.

Did you have an image in your mind of Serena and Vivian? An image of how their lustful explorations of each other must appear, what their boudoir looks like, how the candles were set, what shapes the splatters of color on Vivian's body took as they landed? It is very likely you did. We are visual creatures after all, us humans. (Most of us, anyway. Those who have been blind since birth don't tend to be, for obvious reasons.) But if you did, then I have a question for you: Before the last paragraph of that little vignette, did you have any idea that Serena might use a wheelchair?

We live in a world that tells us from the day we are born what kind of people are allowed to enjoy sex. Entire industries are built on the premise that we must possess an incredibly specific, ever-changing, nigh impossible number of physical, mental, and emotional traits before we qualify to join any reindeer games, as it were. I don't know about you, but I haven't ever met those standards. I am too fat (368 lb.), too tall (6' 1"), too ethnic (Asian), and definitely not athletic enough to ever be one of the shining beacons of perfection that our consumerist culture thrives on telling us we are always only one purchase away from being. Oh, and I use a wheelchair. Society at large holds the overwhelming belief that sex isn't something that those of us with physical and mental disabilities are even capable of wanting—let alone seeking out for ourselves.

Disabled. Broken down, the word comes from *dis* meaning "apart from," and *ability* meaning "skill." "Apart from skill." We to whom that term applies are told daily that we are without skill, without skill in work, without skill in hobbies, without skill in athletics. Without skill in bed. Indeed, from the day we can first understand language we are told with ever-increasing intensity that we are incapable in all aspects of life. And it isn't just disabled people who hear this message either. The world is awash in messages of our inferiority, both intentionally communicated and not. We are told, daily, that we are inherently inferior to the traditionally abled, and that we dare not challenge that belief. There is, however, one place I haven't ever heard this attitude: the BDSM scene.

There is an entire subculture built around BDSM, and for those of us with disabilities, that subculture can be liberating. BDSM is built around the practice of asking for what you want, finding out your limitations and those of others, and exploring exactly what those limitations mean. Kink doesn't simply give us a space in which we can comfortably and unapologetically state our needs and wants, it demands it of us, whether disabled or not. Within the BDSM scene, what might limit us elsewhere, what might render us as sexless objects in the eyes of others is simply seen as one limit that can be worked around. One limit amongst many, as those within the scene know well that everyone has limits.

In the vanilla world, there aren't many examples of disabled people seeking pleasure. The thought of a libertine with an other-than-perfect body just seems alien. The idea of pleasure applying to the broken just doesn't register. But in the kink scene, pleasure seeking on the part of disabled people is the norm! I have personally had the immense pleasure of seeing a woman, who was told her entire life that she couldn't ever be attractive to anyone, brought to tears of relief and joy as she was lifted into the sky in a rope suspension rig, wheelchair and all, and fingered to orgasm after orgasm by her friends. I have watched a man, who society at large had written off after he lost both legs in the Second Gulf War come alive as he shocked a willing partner with a violet wand. I have seen a woman born blind bring smiles to the faces of an entire dungeon with her screams of agonized ecstasy. And I myself have had the pleasure of having someone ask me to play with them because they saw me playing with someone else and liked what they saw—not the wheelchair, but my skill with my chosen implement. I can go on and on.

Now I'm not saying that there are no judgmental douchemuffins in the BDSM scene, because of course there are. Any culture large enough to have at least ten people is going to attract at least one asshat, and there are certainly such here. But my experience has shown me that they are not the majority, nor anything remotely approaching it.

Allow me to close with an anecdote, if I may. When I was preparing this essay, I had an entirely different plan for the route I wanted it to take. I intended to take a much more academic approach than I ultimately ended up using, and in pursuit of that end I interviewed several of my friends who are also disabled and active in the BDSM scene.

I thought I had completed all of my interviews when I happened to meet a young woman who was just starting to explore herself and her desires. We met at a munch, her very first munch as it turned out. (For those who do not know, a munch is a gathering of kinky people in a vanilla setting for the purpose of talking over food and getting to know one another.) She was quite gregarious, if somewhat nervous. And understandably so! The thought of approaching people you haven't met, in a group environment, in order to get to know them is scary enough without adding that all you have in common is that you are all kinky!

Nonetheless, she got past her nerves and introduced herself, not just to myself, but to quite a few people at the gathering.

Over the course of the evening, we spoke on all sorts of topics, including what got her interested in kink. "I remember being weirdly fascinated by references to spanking in books," she said. Then she mentioned being worried about being able to safely engage in BDSM because of her disability. Those of us in the conversation with her cocked our heads. I hadn't noticed her disability, and apparently I wasn't alone. That's when she motioned to the left side of her body and pointed out that she was hemipelagic; one side of her body was paralyzed. So, of course, being the nosy former reporter that I am, I asked if I could interview her, and she enthusiastically consented.

It wasn't until I got home that evening that I realized what had struck me the most about the conversation. No one had noticed her disability. No one. Not because they didn't see the disabled person, but because the disability wasn't relevant to the conversation. Visibly disabled people spend our entire lives being judged at first glance, written off because we don't look "right." But not her, not there, not that night. I thought back, and I realized, that I've never been judged for my disabilities in a kinky setting. Not once!

I'm not ashamed to say I broke down in tears.

CHAPTER 5
PLEASURE AND JOY

Sex positivity is about a lot of things including fun and joy and exploration. Here are a few essays that celebrate sexuality in various ways.

OPENNESS, ENERGY, EXPANSIVE ORGASMS, OH MY

by Mac McGregor and Dawn Celeste McGregor

We have always been very sexual people and have become involved with the ideology of sex positivity through people we were fortunate to encounter who helped open our minds to the potential of sex without fear and shame. We had both found the sex-positive community in Seattle before we met, having experimented with BDSM, multiple partners, and other specific types of sex.

We found one another at a sex-positive event, which made it very easy for us each to know where the other stood on sexuality. It took over a year and a half for us to become intimate, but there was never a question on whether we would be compatible.

Oh, and when we did, it was incredible. We were both naturally very open to one another and had quite a lot of experience in the art of pleasing our partners. We discovered that we both got very aroused by the act of pleasing and feeling one another's excitement. We realized that this was one of the things that made sex between us so great. There was no concern about sex being one-sided. And as we discovered that we each equally enjoyed giving the other pleasure, that helped us to be open to our own experiences. We could relax into our own orgasms with the knowledge that our partner was truly enjoying their contribution.

We started to open up to one another more and more, exploring one another's fantasies through cultivating a shame-free mentality, speaking honestly about what turns us on and whether or not we want to try those things with one another, and never judging the other's thoughts. Through this practice we discovered things we had not known about or done before. This type of genuine honesty assisted in melting away anxieties and fears of consequences of self-expression. We could be as creative or as basic as we wanted.

Since we both had worked with energy and its purposeful movement through the body throughout our lives, we decided to play with it intentionally during sex, being open and communicative about our experiences and what we were doing. We had built a foundation of trust and had the desire to move further into a deeper and more spiritual intimacy.

We walk through the process of energetic awareness individually, then, using that energy with a partner, talk about how to use that buildup of energy during orgasm to have a spiritual experience. We all have energy moving through our bodies all the time. We can feel it more intensely when our senses are stimulated. One of the best ways to stimulate one's senses is through sexuality. It's like electricity pulsing through us. Everyone feels it, most just don't know that it's more in their control than they think.

About energy and controlling energy

The process of pouring energy into another person is not something many in western culture learn how to do, and yet it can be used to heal, to connect, to invigorate, to calm, and to stimulate sexually. All living things are energy, and most people unconsciously transfer energy all the time. The trick is to learn to do this with specific intention when you want to. There are many studies on how thought, presence, and touch can change a person's chemical composition, blood pressure, and mental state. So, one can see how this can easily work in sex play. You can literally learn how to change even the tone of sexual play with a shift in your energy, and then send that energy to your partner or partners.

If you don't believe that a thought has energy that can affect you, then think of the grossest, most disgusting thing you can think of. Now try to masturbate thinking of that. Now think of the sexist thing you have ever witnessed and try to masturbate again, which was more rewarding? Thoughts have a great deal of energetic power, especially during sex, when we are opening ourselves in such a vulnerable way. Therefore, learning to be conscious about our thoughts and how to choose our thoughts with intent will help us get the sexual fulfillment that we desire.

What is energy (Chi)?

It is life force energy, or breath—every living thing breathes.

Focus your breath, breathe deeply so that your belly expands on the inhale. To do that you must fully exhale first. Then focus on each exhalation, sending energy from your belly to the palms of your hands. Hold your palms across from one another, facing one another, visualize the energy flowing up as you exhale, then from palm to palm. Do this with your eyes closed for a few minutes and in time you should feel something in your palms. Some people feel heat, some tingling, some feel like there is something coming out of the middle of their palms. Everyone is a bit different in how they feel the energy, and there is no right or wrong way to feel it. Be aware of slight differences at first, if you have never played with energy before.

After this you can begin to create a chi-ball of energy. Focus the energy from your palms creating a ball of energy. You can visualize a ball of water or fire at first, it can also have colors in it. Then you can play with bouncing the ball up and back between your hands.

Moving energy with a partner

First you must decide what your intention is going to be for the interaction. Without focused intent this will rarely get the result you desire. To begin working your energy, you, or you and your partner, can think of yourselves as energetic beings, then visualize yourselves as balls of energy.

Here are some common ways that people visualize energy: fire, water, steam, light, breath, a beam, a tube, heat, electrical current. We change the way we visualize energy according to the result that we want; for instance, if we want our partner to relax and open more, then we visualize water or warmth, like a warm sunlight. If we want our partner to be more raw, passionate and let their wild side out, then we visualize a fire, electrical current, or something more like lightning. Play with these types of ideas and see what works for you.

After deciding on your intention and what way you will visualize the energy, close your eyes and feel it in yourself first. Keep working on this until you really feel it shift things in you. It's a great idea to spend a moment on one's own energy before the sexual encounter, imagining energy permeating your genitalia and erogenous zones—basically lighting your own fire before the encounter. Then you are ready to work on transferring it to an intimate partner.

Whatever you are visualizing—let's use water for an example—focus that to your hands or mouth, cock or vulva, then see the warm soothing water flowing from your contact point into your partner like tube of water flowing from your hands into their body wherever you are touching them. You can even get good enough at this practice to keep someone on the edge of orgasm for a long time and then visualize and control the energy of when they peak. We have learned to make orgasms happen like a wave that keeps washing in over and over and over.

When a couple or triad work on this together, and they all are visualizing the same things with the same agreed-upon focused intent, that is when the most magic can happen. This takes excellent communication and two or three people who have practiced on their own coming together to create synergy. One person may, at times, lose focus in their visualization or their intention. That is normal. Just like in meditation, bring the mind back to the practice and all will continue as planned. Be kind and patient with both yourself and your partner(s) while learning this —energetically, we all have good and better days. Remember that even a very practiced chi master is affected by hydration, fatigue, stress, etc. Other factors that might affect you include whether you feel you are in a safe place to play and/or health issues, but do not give up. The rewards are well worth the practice and patience. Focused, intentional, energetic orgasms and intimacy feed the soul, body, and spirit.

Expanding the self using sexual energy

Once we had been practicing sexual energy play for a while, we started experiencing some very distinct effects within the state of orgasm. When we began to have more extended and/or multiple orgasms, we started to learn that we could also move the energy within our own bodies to achieve a specific purpose. We began to use visualization to turn the energy we were creating into a force of manifestation. This started an entire spiritual/emotional method for us, helping us to heal, transform, and expand beyond our confines.

We will walk you through this process as well.

Expanding energy in the self happens naturally when in the orgasmic state. We can feel the build of that energy, when it all seems to come together into a precipice of intensity and power. The more we release our constraints about how it is supposed to feel, how long it lasts, and how vulnerable we are at that moment, the more fully we can be in that experience.

When coming close to orgasm, pay attention to the movement of the energy in your body. Observe it within this experience as many times as you need to. When you feel familiar with the energetic flow, you can start to try to move it around intentionally, focusing all of it into your genitals by imagining a color or an image that represents what you want your body to feel, such as an opening flower, a fountain, or fireworks. Maybe even imagine diving into your partner, entering them fully—whatever imagery relates to what excites you and is part of your intention. This very well may enhance your orgasm, as well as make it more powerful.

After mastering this you can play with the energy that is within the actual orgasm. If one can be cognizant within the orgasm itself, the energy can be used to heal parts of ourselves, open energy points, and to put energetic intentions into the world. This energy may also induce visions and a feeling of connection with the divine. It is possible to use orgasm and sexual energy to open parts of ourselves that have been blocking us for a very long time.

In conclusion

We have found that being truly open, releasing shame, and eliminating fear of rejection has brought us to a place where we can explore what we desire, creating a foundation of trust and openness. This has ignited a sexual experience that neither of us had ever dreamed of—using sex as a means toward depth, growth, and expansion.

DDF/UB2**: ON BEING SEX POSITIVE IN A SHAME-BASED, INSENSITIVE CULTURE
by Joel Davis

Nothing has the potential to strike despair into the heart of a poz (HIV-Positive) gay man, at least this poz gay man, quite like those all-capitalized letters emblazoned within the text of an online or, for many readers close to my age, print profile. The despair deepens when the word "clean" (as a euphemism for HIV-negative) appears in that profile. Woe has now been paired with hopelessness, its twin separated at birth. The display of dispassion or lack of compassion that persists among some of my peers almost surprises me, but then it doesn't.

I was always a sexually precocious child, and I evolved into a sexually precocious man, impervious to shaming despite what I've already highlighted. Before coming out as a gay man, sex was my secret relief. After coming out, sex was my unabashed adventure. But even the latter does not fully describe what it means to me to be sex positive.

In the absence of nuanced research during the early days of HIV/AIDS, gay men were discouraged from having sex or told to simply "use a condom every time," neither of which were readily achievable behavioral changes I, or many other gay men, could accommodate. For many years, the message of "safe" sex was an all-or-nothing set of rules; there was nothing incremental about it. Other parts of the world, Australia, for example, evolved to an approach that was more flexible and more forgiving. This respectful approached encouraged gay men to engage in safer sex, or what became referred to as *negotiated safety*, a paradigm of behavioral strategies that allowed for individual decisions made across a continuum of possible interactions with individuals, both those who share the same HIV status and those who are of different HIV statuses.

A little later in the epidemic, the female condom was developed and approved but only for use by or with women engaging in vaginal intercourse, not for heterosexual anal sex and certainly not for gay anal sex. Of course, this didn't stop the off-label use. To this day, as far as I know, the female condom is still only approved for heterosexual, vaginal intercourse.

Though certainly evolving, the culture of sex in the United States has always been very puritanical and continues to be mostly so. Such a culture only values sex defined within heterosexual, heteronormative terms. If you aren't heterosexual, if you aren't married, if you have had sex before or outside of marriage, if you have had heterosexual anal sex, or if you had any sort of gay sex, messages about you being acceptable in mainstream American society have been few or nonexistent. When the HIV/AIDS epidemic hit, politicians in position of power wouldn't even mention AIDS by name. The Centers for Disease Control and the National Institutes for Health maintained a very heterosexual, heteronormative bent: gay sex was shamed. And, as stated, even the female condom was wrapped within a tiny, more socially acceptable box for dissemination and use.

Early on, being HIV positive became associated with being dirty, a pariah to be kept at arm's length (especially when contrasted to the use of clean to mean HIV)—a development that has had a lasting impact on me as an HIV-Positive gay man. Over time, gay men, both poz and neg, learned to sero sort, i.e. choose from a pool of partners aligned with a specific HIV status, generally the same status as yours. Risky sexual behaviors like bareback sex, which a good friend of mine would refer to as "natural sex," were shamed, reviled, and considered dangerous and certainly non-conforming—even though individual reasons for engaging in any particular sexual behavior no doubt originate from a very powerful place in each of us. Sharing any sort of bodily fluids was demonized, even though the very first time I heard the term *fluid bonded* was by an HIV-negative gay man referring to the level of intimacy and connectedness he sought with his partner.

Sex is sex is sex is sex is sex, just like "love is love is love is love is love." Sex is powerful, not just about power. Sex reminds us that we are still alive. Sex reminds us that we are still worthy. Sex reminds us that the divine is still possible. Sex reminds us that we are still alive. Yes, that was worth stating twice.

So, what does it mean to be sex positive or, more specifically, what does sex positivity mean for me as an HIV-Positive gay man? What has it meant for me to maintain a sex-positive attitude throughout the many years of navigating the unknown, ignorance, fear, and now, the aging process?

Unlike so many in my generational cohort, I grew up in an environment where I was never shamed about sex. I grew up as a very sexually curious boy in a (fortunately) very sexually permissive home, a positive feature counterbalanced by other painful realities. After coming out, I was extremely fortunate to have had parents who made it crystal clear that they would love any man they believed loved me.

I matured into a sexually curious man unfettered by religious dogma. I came out as a gay man in the sexual heyday of the seventies. I came out in both San Francisco and Los Angeles. I came out in an era of sexual abundance, not sexual scarcity. Being sexual was a celebration. I never stopped feeling that way, even when AIDS hit. But it was different.

I took (and still take) responsibility for keeping my HIV inside my body by choosing modified behaviors and sexual endeavors that keep me engaged and don't subject me to shaming or bullying. I recognize my limitations, specifically my inability to re-contextualize something that, if I did so, would completely sacrifice my cherished memories and tear asunder what I've always considered to be elements that contribute to my quality of life.

I've not been immune to those moments that challenge every ounce of my sense of legitimacy over my place in this universe. In order to maintain my sense of belonging in this world, I've learned how to,not succumb to others' notions of acceptability, not surrender completely to the ignorance of others, and not be surprised by others choosing paranoia over fact.

I don't think my concept of sex positivity has changed over the decades, except that, as I've gotten older, I'm more sexually active in my brain than in my body!

Sex is one of the most life-affirming activities we engage in. In the most profound way, sex reminds us that we are still alive, still impacting our world and humanity. Those two factors were lost in all the early messages gay men received about taking care of ourselves when HIV/AIDS enveloped us, messages promulgated by (perhaps) well-intended professionals and politicians who were deeply uncomfortable with men fucking other men. (Let's be honest: they weren't even comfortable with acknowledging men fucking women in ways other than the standard missionary position.)

Here's why I consider myself to enduringly sex positive:

- I refuse to allow anyone else to transfer his or her shame on to me.
- I refuse to be treated as dirty just because I'm poz.
- I know that it's not my place to pass judgment on the choices of others.
- I see that there are a myriad of avenues to sexual intimacy.
- I recognize that sharing flesh and fluids can be incredibly powerful.
- I recognize the essential nature of human bonding via sex.

I never represent my version of a life as an openly HIV-Positive gay man as anyone else's life but my own. I respect that my experience as a poz gay man may be entirely different than anyone else's.

I only know my truth.

I'M NOT WASHED UP ON THE BEACH YET: SEX, RELATIONSHIPS, AND AGING
by Linda Kirkman, PhD

The saying goes, "You teach what you most need to learn," and I'm sure we study what we are trying to understand. I taught sex and relationships for nearly thirty years before completing a PhD on baby boomers in friends-with-benefits relationships.[16] I study and teach sexuality, sexual health, and relationships because I want to make sense of them. It is only as I move into my sixties after a lifetime of experiences—relationships, reading, studying, and speaking to people—that understanding is coming; an understanding that encompasses only a fraction of the world of human sexuality and relationships. This piece has a focus on Australian baby boomers, referring to my personal experience as well as research evidence on aging and diverse sexualities and relationships.

Human sexuality and relationships are central to everyone yet can be taboo, poorly taught, and not well explained. Sex and relationships form a deep and mysterious undercurrent to human society that people navigate as best they can. Formal structures such as governments and religions have rules that permit or prohibit behaviors and relationships. These structures provide a helpful template to follow, but are harmful in other ways, especially with the patriarchal focus and exclusion—often rejection and punishment—of non-heterosexual, nonmonogamous sexualities and relationships. As people age they can be more confident to challenge these norms and expectations.

Developing an understanding of the diversity of sexuality, sexual identity, and sexual expression, and learning good relationship and communication skills, will help people living in the social world to be happier and healthier in all aspects of their interactions with others. Such interactions include intimate relationships, family, friendships, workplaces, and daily exchanges. While there is a difference between an interaction with our lover and one with the shop assistant, even in nonsexual interactions assessments are being made about our sex and gender, sexuality, relative power, relationship status—things not overtly relevant to the exchange that is happening. Those assessments come with judgments, including value judgments that have the potential to be harmful. Mainstream media influences what is seen as normal and acceptable and portrays very limited approaches to sex, relationships, and gender. As long as sex and sexuality are taboo and poorly understood in the wider world, there will be limited awareness of the diversity that is out there; people who are not considered mainstream will be marginalized or will marginalize themselves. Having a limited understanding of sex, and the bigger picture of gender, sexuality, and relationship diversity, perpetuates a divide. Greater acceptance will build capacity for an attitude of "there is no them; there is only us."

Many of my PhD participants had, like me, grown up in the sexual revolution. Baby boomers started their sexual lives in a time of sexual freedom: after the

---

[16] Kirkman, L. "Doing relationships differently: Rural baby boomers negotiate friends-with-benefits relationships." PhD diss., La Trobe Rural Health School, La Trobe University, Bendigo. Retrieved from http://hdl.handle.net/1959.9/323359.

introduction of the contraceptive pill; with the availability of antibiotics to treat STIs; and before the emergence of HIV/AIDS.[17]

The friends-with-benefits relationships were described as part of their life stories. After a time of youthful freedom, most ended up following the expected social default of marriage, monogamy, and children, and only later in life did they start to think about what it was they really wanted for their relationship style and sexual expression. Those who continued with a more sexually open, nonmonogamous approach found a friends-with-benefits relationship easy to conceptualize and to seek out.

Growing up in the sexual revolution of the 1960s and 1970s led me to lots of sexual encounters and a lack of shame around sexual relationships. It did not necessarily lead to discovering and expressing my own sexual pleasure. The social default was heteronormative, with genital sex and penetration as a focus. Communication skills and consent negotiation were not well modeled or taught, and while pleasure was a goal, broader understanding of the potential pathways to pleasure outside the genital focus was lacking. My understanding of the possibilities of relationships and sexual activity has expanded considerably since those days. The rest of my cohort shows mixed results; some are very progressive.

How are Australian baby boomers doing sexuality and relationships differently today? A key aspect is taking the time to reflect on what it is that they want. Instead of defaulting to the expectation of being part of a cohabiting couple, my participants were consciously choosing intimacy with independence. The friendship was a central part of the relationship, with all the support and shared social activities that friendship represents, with the addition of sexual intimacy. They were also rejecting the relationship elements they did not want. For example, "Goldie" did not want to be the "domestic goddess ... what's for tea, chops and veg again?" This was a clear example of someone who wanted to avoid gendered expectations in her relationship. Living independently allowed her to enjoy the social and sexual aspects of the relationship without being drawn into expectations of domestic labor. Goldie had left home as a teenager and enjoyed autonomy and independence in her relationships as an adult, so it was not difficult for her to make relationship choices that were outside the norm. "Abe" had also left home after finishing school and never stopped living the nonmonogamous, swinging lifestyle—his first girlfriend had another boyfriend so nonmonogamy was normal from the start.

A history of autonomy was not necessary to be socially progressive in later life. "Toby" had been brought up in a religious household where his attraction to other men could not be disclosed safely, and if he chose a life other than heterosexual marriage then the only option was exclusion from his family and the community he grew up with. How he managed to make choices outside his early conditioning is demonstrated by his choice of living with a man in a committed relationship. Both men seek out other partners to satisfy personal interests and desires, following a thought-out and agreed-upon consensual nonmonogamy agreement. Likewise, "Rosemary" and "Jessie" grew up in religious households with narrow,

---

[17] Lewis, M. J. Thorns on the rose: This history of sexually transmitted diseases in Australia in international perspective. Canberra: Australian Government Publishing Service, 1918.

gendered expectations of social and relationship behavior, coupled with sexual abuse from their fathers. Both married young to escape, to husbands who were absorbed in their own activities and not interested in the women's fulfillment or well-being. After her marriage ended, despite her husband's predictions that she would never find what she wanted, Rosemary was lucky to form a relationship with a caring, considerate man who reintroduced her to sexuality from a pleasure perspective and supported the notion that she could take positive control over her relationships. Jessie had two unsuccessful subsequent marriages and thought she would never be in a relationship again, until she met a man at a monthly social dinner she attended. A friendship formed, and only very cautiously did she enter into a new sexual relationship which gave her much joy and led her to conclude, "I'm not washed up on the beach yet." She was careful they maintained separate households as a way to protect her heart and her financial assets. This shows that women in their sixties can change a lifetime's pattern of relationship style, develop and use assertive behaviors to stand up for what they want, and actively seek pleasure and autonomy in relationships.

Everyone has their own story and journey to finding fulfillment and satisfaction. What was striking about all participants in my research was that they enjoyed the sexual aspect of their friends-with-benefits relationship, with some describing it as the best sex of their lives. Participants described benefits of greater self-confidence, better body image, more skillful lovers, and sexual experimentation with things they had not tried before. This included seeking same-sex relationships and exploring same-sex play. Changing social attitudes and expectations about sexual behavior meant that sex in midlife was often more open, experimental, and pleasurable than it had been in the sexual revolution days of the sixties and seventies. This could apply to couple or marriage-type relationships as well as friends-with-benefits relationships, yet the sexual freedom of those times may have paved the way for experimentation with relationships such as friends-with-benefits relationships. People are discovering new approaches to intimate citizenship.[18]

Greater openness and confidence in relationships has not necessarily led to good sexual health understanding and practices for any age group, and baby boomers are no exception. Women aged over forty using the online dating site RSVP know about the importance of safer sex, yet are not as confident as younger women to ask for it.[19] Heterosexual men aged over sixty are much less likely to use condoms with new partners than men aged eighteen to twenty-nine years [20], despite one in five new HIV infections in Australia being diagnosed in men

---

[18] Roseneil, S., Crowhurst, I., Hellesund, T., Santos, A. C., and Stoilova, M. "Remaking intimate citizenship in multicultural Europe: Experiences outside the conventional family," in *Remaking citizenship in multicultural Europe: Women's movements, gender and diversity*, ed. B. Halsaa, S. Roseneil & S. Sümer (Basingstoke: Palgrave Mcmillan.), 41-69.

[19] Bateson, D. J., Weisberg, E., McCaffery, K. J., and Luscombe, G. M. "When online becomes offline: Attitudes to safer-sex practices in older and younger women using an Australian internet dating service." *Sexual Health* 9 no. 2 (2011): 152-159.

[20] Cheng, Y., McGeechan, K., Bateson, D., Ritter, T., Weisberg, E., and Stewart, M. "Age differences in attitudes toward safer-sex practices in heterosexual men using an Australian Internet dating service." *Sexual Health* 15 no. 3 (June 2018).

over fifty[21] and increasing chlamydia and gonorrhea diagnoses in this age group. There is a lack of health policy to support sexual health promotion to older adults [22] and none that promotes relationship skills.

The human need for connection and desire for intimacy persists across the lifespan. Older adults are being thoughtful about their needs and are pursuing diverse relationships that suit their circumstances, with pleasurable outcomes.

---

[21] The Kirby Institute. "HIV, viral hepatitis and sexually transmissible infections in Australia: Annual Surveillance Report 2015." Sydney, Australia. Retrieved from http://www.kirby.unsw.edu.au

[22] "Communicable Disease Surveillance Online Dataset." In Government Department of Health National Notifiable Disease Surveillance System. Canberra: Commonwealth Department of Health. (2017). http://www9.health.gov.au/cda/source/cda-index.cfm

[23] Kirkman, L., Kenny, A., and Fox, C. "Evidence of absence: Midlife and older adult sexual health policy in Australia." Sexuality Research and Social Policy 10 no. 2, (2013): 135-148. doi:10.1007/s13178-013-0109-6

MY FIRST GIRLFRIEND
by Buck Angel

My name is Buck Angel and I am a fifty-five-year-old transsexual man. That means that when I was born the doctor presumed I was a female, because of my vagina. I have lived my whole life with my vagina. During some periods of my life I have enjoyed it and others I have not. This is an earlier experience that I think in some way helped me, as a man, to connect with my vagina later in life.

So, I grew up in the San Fernando valley in the 60s and 70s during a big time for sexual revolution. I remember my dad had a subscription to Playboy magazine and I just couldn't wait for the new one to come every month. The ladies! Wow. They turned me on so much. But wait, I was a girl and I wasn't supposed to be turned on by ladies. I was supposed to be attracted to boys, but I couldn't be attracted to boys because I thought of myself as a boy, as did everyone else on my block.

My parents raised me in many ways as a boy. When my sisters got Barbies for Christmas, I got a GI Joe. I also got to dress like a boy most of the time, my favorites being Levi's and white T-shirts; I loved that look. I remember having crushes on the older girls on my block. I could swear they had crushes on me too. I think they even flirted with me. But nothing ever came from those interactions, except in my brain when masturbated. I had become very interested in masturbation during that time, as I had discovered how to have an orgasm by accident.

Sports was a big deal in my family. My dad was an ex-pro football player, which meant sports were what we did. So, I joined the gymnastics team—this was an after-school activity. One of things you do when you learn gymnastics is climb the rope to the top and back down.

This one day, when I was first learning how to climb the rope, the coach showed us how to grab it by jump up, grabbing with your hands fist over fist, pulling yourself up, and then wrapping your legs around the rope. You then use your arms to pull up and, with your legs wrapped tight around the rope, you slide up. The thing is, your genitals slide up the rope with you.

Well this caused such a sensation that I could not even believe it. As I pulled up harder and harder, and my genitals rubbed harder and harder, I started to have this feeling of joy between my legs. Eventually, I got about halfway up the rope and then it exploded. The feeling exploded between my legs and my legs wrapped tighter against the rope, and I didn't move because I was having an orgasm. I didn't know that at the time, and the other kids below me just be stood there looking up at me screaming, "What are you doing? Why did you stop? Keep going!" I swear I was paralyzed there for minutes, even though it felt like hours.

Eventually I quit gymnastics. I think I was embarrassed because I figured out what was happening to me and climbing the rope was mandatory. I became obsessed with this feeling from masturbation. I missed that rope. So I began looking for other places or things that could give me that same feeling.

One day, while I was in my backyard playing by myself, I found a tree. It was a small tree over near the side of our house, in a part that was secluded but where you could see if anyone was coming. This tree was calling my name. It was skinny and had one branch that came out perfectly like an arm that was ready for me to swing on. So that's what I did. I jumped up and grabbed it with my hands the same way they taught me in gymnastics class.

As I was swinging from the branch, I noticed that I could actually move closer to the tree trunk so I slid over to where the branch comes out of the tree. I then wrapped my legs around the tree and pulled myself up, just like on the rope. As I pulled up my legs were around the tree and my genitals were rubbing and that same exact feeling was happening. I just kept doing it over and over and over. I could not stop. It was as if I was possessed.

I would spend hours with that tree, almost daily when I first discovered it. This tree became my first girlfriend. My lover. My everything. One day my mom asked me, "Why are you spending so much time alone out in the backyard?" I was so freaked out because I didn't want anyone to know what I was doing out there. It was my secret. My girlfriend. My tree. So I told her that I was just playing with our dog, and I liked hanging out back there. Not sure if she believed me or if she even knew what I was doing. She never said anything about it even to this day. I think I should ask her.

Eventually, I guess I got tired of my tree because I don't know when I stopped, but I did. The funniest part to this funny story is this: one day, many years after I had stopped seeing the tree, when my dad and I were in the back cleaning up or maybe installing something electrical (I always got to do cool stuff like that with my dad) he noticed the tree. Not just that it was a tree but that there was this weird rubbed out dent in the body of the tree—the part where my legs and genitals would grind up and down until I reached orgasm. Remember, I had visited that tree for a long time; I must have actually ground a dent in it.

When my dad asked, "What the hell happened to this tree?" I instantly froze up and asked, "What tree?" My dad looked at me funny and pointed, "that tree," and there it was: this huge, big bald spot right on the body of my girlfriend the tree. I just looked, shrugged my shoulders and said "I don't know" But somehow I don't think he believed me.

A SIZE QUEEN SOLUTION
by IM Jae

As a woman who enjoys men of an above average sized genital endowment, trying to find a romantic partner is always interesting. Yes, I am what is referred to as a "size queen," and I am adamant about it in my love life. Somehow, I have almost always connected with men who have a penis of at least six and a half inches or larger, going all the way up to eleven inches. (There were two who were around five inches.) Through my various field studies (dating relationships and lovers), I discovered that I am most compatible with well-endowed men and will only achieve stimulation of some of my best internal spots from longer penises. (Thicker is also great!)

So, what's a single, size-minded girl to do in this age of online dating? I'll spare you the assorted horror stories, as well as the hundreds of fascinating dick pics, and suffice it to say that I created dating profiles with my seven-inches-and-above penis requirement. One of my online friends told me about a dating site focused specifically on well-hung men and the people who are into them. I joined that one and found a few similar sites. Unfortunately, neither these or more traditional dating sites really produced any good potential dates for me. Plenty of interesting conversations and pic trades, but that was about all.

As I've been involved in a variety of social activities for years, I was very aware of all kinds of special interest real-life meet up groups. I had also heard rumors of mythical private parties where women got together and had well-hung men parading around in front of them. The idea of an in-person group for my particular interest inspired me to start yet another internet search: The Quest for the Elusive, Secret, Size Queen Party!

I was not able to find anything to substantiate the rumors. I also failed to find any current groups or events, other than an occasional gay men's bar having a size queen party that had nothing to do with big penises. Just a catchy name, I guess. And oh, so many queen-size mattress and sheet-set advertisements. Too bad there wasn't a man bearing a king-sized penis to go along with one of the mattress and sheet-sets!

But a woman on a quest for a mighty cock does not give up! So in September of 2016, I organized a meet up for women who love big cocks and men who have them. Our first meet up was on September 22, 2016. We had seventeen people attend! There were ten women and seven men with a particular "seven or better" attribute. We met after work that evening at a classy but relaxed sports bar/restaurant. I was anticipating that maybe only ten people would show up, but much like a "grower" penis, our table kept getting longer and longer as more people showed up. Everyone seemed a bit nervous, but I knew a few of the women, and we were able to work together in guiding introductions and keeping the conversation going. Most of the men were running late, and we'd give them a round of applause as they joined us. Watching them arrive was like seeing a sixteen-year-old's surprised, shy expression of joy when they've been invited to senior prom. So adorable and uplifting seeing men almost blush as they were publicly appreciated for their bodies. We had lots of great conversations on a wide assortment of topics, with cock size and related issues featuring prominently. I know a few people traded contact info and even went out a little after the event, which was nice to hear. Overall everyone seemed to have a lot of fun and they were excited about the prospect of trying the meet up again.

The group was a nice mix. We had two sets of couples with varying degrees of openness in their relationships as well as a man in an open relationship attending on his own. There was a lesbian who attended, as she and her partner were seeking a guy to be their occasional lover. Overall it was mainly single people looking for someone to date or a friend for sexual fun. The group was also racially diverse, among both women and men. Age range was a few in their mid-twenties, most in their thirties and forties, a few in their fifties, and one couple in their early sixties.

Group attendance has varied over the last year and a half, but we are generally meeting once a month. The group continues to be diverse in all the aforementioned areas, except we rarely have any married people attending, other than at the first few events.

The big question everyone has is how I determine if the guys actually qualify. I verify that the men have a penis that is at least seven inches in length by requiring them to provide a photo with the following criteria:

- Make sure both the base and head of your cock are showing in the photo.

- Keep the measuring device pressed firmly against the side (or top) of your penis for better accuracy. You may use a ruler, tape measure, or US dollar bill as a measuring device. Keep in mind that a dollar bill is only a little over six inches long, so you need to be well past the end of it.

- Make sure both ends of the measuring device show.

- Include a note in the photo that has both the date and "For IMJ" or your username.

I have found this system works well for weeding out men who don't qualify. Of course, there are always some who try to angle the ruler a lot to make up some distance, and most of them forget to include the note the first time, so I make them take the photo again. Once I explain that the note helps to ensure that men aren't stealing pics off the web, they are usually more eager to retake their photo. It also helps that I am an artist with a great eye for measuring! I can generally give a size estimate in person that is accurate within a quarter to a half inch. When it comes to photos, I have a private system I use for assessing the measurements. Usually the guys who complain about my system tend to also be guys who don't actually qualify. One of my favorite photo verifications was from someone about eight inches long who drew a heart on the note around the date and "For IMJ," which was so sweet. He totally got extra points for that. On a side note, I consider the use of penis pumps and other cock "enhancers" to be a disqualification. You need to have all-natural man meat for this group.

I encounter a lot of expectations that the Size Queen group is going to be a very seedy and sordid event. To dispel some of the myths, let me tell you more about our get-togethers. In spite of always advertising that we are meeting in a public restaurant, men still ask me if the guys get verified in person at the event. No. I'm sorry, but we aren't whipping out cocks at a restaurant. That kind of sausage is not on the menu! On a positive note, the men who actually qualify for the event almost never ask that. Very rarely have women asked me that either. Now we might (totally will!) get out our phones and share pics, (both men and women will do this), but we work very hard to not flash the wait staff our sexy pics. There have definitely been times when the wait staff has overheard some damn juicy conversations, even though we try to keep it discreet when we see them approaching.

A lot of the men let me know ahead of time that they are not eager to hang out with the other guys who might be attending. They are just focused on meeting women. However, once we all get to talking, they end up finding that here are other men who understand both the blessings and challenges of being well endowed. The women are usually a little nervous as well, but they are happy to know I've done my best to verify the size on guys and they can focus on seeing if they have any chemistry or compatible interests. About half way through the event you can start to see the body language of everyone really relax. There's a lot of laughter, but people also bring up thought-provoking topics. We share stories of our various size-related experiences and also tips for finding new brands of condoms, sexual techniques, success/failure with dating sites, etc. There ends up being a lot of networking and friendships that people never expected.

For a group focused on cock, it is a perhaps surprisingly thoughtful and friendly gathering. The regular attendees (including one of my best friends and right-hand woman) and I do our best to keep things upbeat and make sure everyone gets to talk. No one is sitting in the corner alone. Instead, we do introductions every time someone new shows up. The men are usually happy to be around women who value both their cock size and them as a person, and they aren't worried that women will reject them for being too large. The women aren't concerned the men will be too small, and no one is judging them negatively for expressing their interest in well-hung men. As a group, we make a ton of sexual innuendos and sexy jokes, but everyone is thoughtful about making sure they are not touching anyone without permission or belittling anyone.

Since we have started to develop a somewhat regular group of attendees, we are looking forward to having our first private party. It won't be a sex-positive party, but we'll definitely allow (encourage!) male nudity. The ladies and I are still trying to convince the guys that games like "penis ring toss" will be great fun! Some of the fellows are game, but others just look at us like we're out of our minds. Whether we play any silly games or not, I look forward to seeing what the next adventure is for our very special Size Queen meetup group!

LEARN A NEW ORGASM: HOW TO UPGRADE YOUR MASTURBATION TECHNIQUE
by Betty Dodson

Many women, and a few men, experience long-term difficulty incorporating their current method of masturbation into partnersex. Some have carried their childhood masturbation pattern over into adulthood, and it's now the only way they can get off. Some are lying face down on their tummies stimulating their genitals with one or both hands pressed between legs that are tightly squeezed together—not conducive to sharing orgasms with another person. Others are humping folded blankets, wooden floors, riding the arm of an overstuffed chair, or pressing against hard counter tops. As kids, the idea was to come fast to avoid getting caught. If we were lying face down Mom, siblings, or the baby sitter couldn't see what our naughty little hands were doing.

All of the above are examples of Pressure and Tension Orgasms (more on these later). While these orgasms are probably the most prevalent kind for a majority of people, they are limited in terms of bodily sensations—a quick blip on the pleasure scale. The other problem is that they rarely translate into sharing orgasms with a partner, but the solution to this problem is simple! It's time to upgrade your masturbation technique.

First let me emphasize, there are a gazillion ways to get off, and there's no such thing as having a "wrong" kind of orgasm. After years of observing my own orgasms, plus hearing from all the women I've known personally and have worked with professionally, I've observed four basic categories: Pressure, Tension, Relaxation, and the combination that I call a Rock and Roll Orgasm. This last combines elements of the first three; while breathing fully during a buildup, we are squeezing and releasing our muscles rhythmically with direct or indirect clitoral contact. Total Relaxation Orgasms, or what I've also termed "Sleeping Beauty," are most rare. To remain totally relaxed while breathing deeply, someone else must do genital stimulation in a manner that is nearly perfect. Ha! If you find that person capture them quick!

While no two orgasms from self-stimulation are precisely the same, most women use some form of direct or indirect clitoral stimulation, with or without penetration. The body responds with movement, or no movement, along with varied breathing patterns from holding the breath to panting. Some women remain utterly silent while others make a variety of sounds. The mind can be paying attention to what the body is feeling, focused on sexual thoughts, or conjuring up a sex fantasy—just as long as it's not planning a dinner menu or running the laundry list.

Pressure Orgasms: (No hands.) In one workshop, a woman said she pressed her clitoris against overstuffed furniture. Another pressed against the hard nose on her teddy bear. Some little girls squeeze their legs together to get those good feelings. Others say wearing tight jeans got them off, and more than a few were very fond of their bicycle seats. As a preteen, I was crazy about riding horses before I got interested in boys. Some women who grew up with a strong prohibition about touching themselves directly made a transition to stronger orgasms by letting water run on their clitoris from a bathtub faucet. I began rocking on a pillow pulled up tight between my legs until the "tickle" went away. At some point I just naturally segued over to my fingers and assumed everyone did the same. Not true.

Tension Orgasms: Direct genital rubbing combined with muscle tension gets most of us through puberty, into young adulthood, and for some, through the rest of their lives. Tension Orgasms rely on leg and buttock muscles being squeezed tight with the rest of the body held fairly rigid. While holding the breath, a fast motion is used on the clitoris or penis until orgasm explodes in a quick burst. These fast tension climaxes are silent and many of us grew up masturbating this way to avoid getting caught by our parents or siblings. These quick tension orgasms often carry over into many men ejaculating prematurely during partnersex.

A few women have orgasms with muscle tension only, without any direct genital contact. One woman climaxed by hanging from the top of a door to create tension in her entire body while squeezing her vaginal muscles tight. Another woman had orgasms from climbing a rope in gym class. In contrast to coming fast, a friend of mine developed tension orgasms without any clitoral contact into an art form. Now in her early fifties, she is in great shape with the isometric exercise she gets from straining against various forms of erotic bondage and keeping her body rigid during elaborate scenes of suspension.

Most people claim to be too busy to spend any quality time enjoying sex, so it will come as no surprise when I say Tension Orgasms are the most common for the largest number of people. While there is no such thing as having a "wrong" kind of orgasm, some are definitely better than others. When a person spends more time building up sexual arousal by breathing, moving, and allowing the body to express a little joy with sounds of pleasure, it creates a more joyful and satisfying experience with orgasm. Fast sex is like fast food—it takes the edge off hunger, but it's not all that nourishing.

Relaxation Orgasms: These are difficult to achieve alone because it's nearly impossible to be totally relaxed while doing some form of genital self-stimulation. My relaxed orgasms first happened in my teens with manual sex from a boyfriend's delicate touch. During long sessions of kissing and genital fondling, I was the classic Sleeping Beauty. To avoid exhibiting "animal-like" behavior, I kept releasing the buildup of sexual tension by consciously relaxing my muscles. This took concentration, but I felt my reputation was at stake. At one point, when I could hold back no longer, the orgasm would come and get me. As long as I did nothing to make this happen, and he didn't put his penis inside my vagina, I was still considered a virgin.

The best way to experience Relaxation Orgasms is with a partner. A few teachers of eastern sex practices have their students take turns giving and receiving manual genital sex with explicit verbal guidance telling one another exactly how to vary the stimulation. They are taught to slow down, relax the pelvic floor muscles, breathe deeply, and allow their sexual energy to build gradually. Rajneesh, a Tantra teacher from India, called this a "valley orgasm," sinking down into the sensation instead of building up as in a "peak orgasm" (which is what I call a Tension Orgasm). Rajneesh believed that sex in the future would involve more fun, joy, friendship, and play than the serious affair it is now does. I totally support this image.

Combination Orgasms: These are my favorite, so I am a bit biased here. This style of orgasm uses tension and relaxation, as well as some form of direct clitoral stimulation with either fingers or a vibrator, along with vaginal penetration. The Combination Orgasm is what I teach in my masturbation workshops. Once I realized I could jump-start sexual arousal for women who had never had an orgasm by using an electric vibrator, I began teaching them how to harness all that power for pleasure. Even women who were already orgasmic with their hands could take their orgasms to the next level by masturbating much longer than the usual few minutes. The key to enjoying any electric vibrator is to manage the intensity of the vibrations. I recommend the Mystic Wand, which has five speeds that allow the user to control the intensity. The idea is to build up slowly, not to slam a strong vibe directly onto a cold clit—eek!

After getting in touch with the pubococcygeus (PC) muscles by practicing Kegel exercises, begin slow penetration with a dildo while squeezing and releasing the pelvic floor muscle, then add clitoral stimulation with a vibrator while rocking your hips forward (inhale and flex the PC muscles) and back (exhale and release the PC muscles). Your muscles will be engaged in a way similar to those of an athlete in motion. The combination of these five elements—clitoral stimulation, vaginal penetration, PC muscle contractions, pelvic thrusting, and breathing out loud—makes the Combination Orgasm the one that translates most easily to partnersex. During intercourse the woman, or her partner, simply adds her preferred kind of clitoral contact. In my opinion, the best approach is to have the woman control her clitoral stimulation, the same as a man does with the angle and speed of vaginal thrusting. Sharing mutual orgasms combines the best of both her and his worlds, creating more harmony between the sexes.

CHAPTER 6
GENDER

Sex Positivity includes a consciousness about trans and gender fluid inclusivity. This can mean not only being supportive and accepting, but also willing to explore your own gender identity.

MEANINGFUL SUPPORT: HOW TO BE A BETTER ALLY TO TRANS PEOPLE

by Sara Blaze

I think I've always found the unusual to be fascinating, particularly with respect to the human condition. As a teenager, I devoured books about individuals with multiple personalities. I couldn't fathom what it would be like to be trapped in a body with parts of a shattered identity fighting for dominance. I imagined what it would feel like to wake up in situations I didn't put myself in or deal with the aftermath of actions I didn't voluntarily take. The ingenuity of the coping strategies developed to manage this condition fascinated me.

That fascination with the human condition endured, but unfortunately fascination doesn't always create true empathy or the capacity to interact skillfully with those different from oneself. I selected the topic of transgenderism as the topic for my Psychology 101 paper and dove into the research. I scoured the internet for, and marveled over, before-and-after pictures of individuals who had had a sex change. I learned about body modifications commonly undertaken. I learned about common methods used by health practitioners to correct this mental health condition. I didn't know anyone who identified as transgender, but with all the research I did, I felt like I had a pretty good handle on the topic.

Now, a decade later, I realize I had only scratched the surface of what it means to be transgender. Writing the paragraph above was painful, as it was intentionally written to reflect my former use of language and the conclusions I drew at the time. I understood the "what." I had a grasp on the surgical options, the physical changes hormones create in the body, what criteria doctors use for diagnostic purposes, and all kinds of statistics about suicide, personality traits, success rates, and long-term outcomes. What I failed to appreciate is that real people are affected and that none of what I learned was useful in actually understanding how transgender people struggle, both internally and in navigating their day-to-day life. Now I see that, in the end, my focus on the medical minutia of transition, and my failure to pull away from the idea that transness is a choice or a mental health condition, were symptomatic of our culture's oppressive attitudes towards trans people.

I am a white, middle-class, cisgender female. As such, I am not an authority on trans issues nor do I purport to be. Rather, I am an ally and a person who has been in relationships with transfolks. From my vantage point, I have witnessed harm done to transfolks by individuals who have a lack of knowledge and understanding. But I also have to continually address my own internal struggles on what it means to be a good ally and a good partner.

This is my primer on how to be an ally.

Don't allow hate to cloud your humanity

The adage, "if you don't have anything nice to say, don't say anything at all" has never been more relevant. At our core we are all the same, all human. All human life must be provided the same respect and the same dignity, and it is this belief that is behind the statement that "trans rights are human rights." It isn't okay to hate someone because you're afraid, you don't understand, or because you can't relate.

There is a lot of outspoken and rancid opposition to the mere existence of trans people. Parents disowning children. Governments restricting benefits, opportunities, and community. Hate groups opposing adequate medical attention, education, and equality in human rights.

I can appreciate that looking at trans issues can be uncomfortable. It has challenged, and continues to challenge, my own unconscious bias, and I've had my own missteps along the way. If you are uncomfortable, I challenge you to consider how uncomfortable it must be to feel unable to exist without fear of violence, discrimination, or expulsion. This is often the lived experience of trans folks.

Learning to leave space for each person to simply exist on their own terms is a really good place to start. Even if you never knowingly interact with a transgender person, you can vastly improve their existence by simply practicing acceptance of all people.

Understand that gender has nothing to do with genitals

First, let's deconstruct the concept of gender. The fundamental misconception is that the term gender means one of two classifications—male or female. In short, your sex refers to your classification as male or female and is assigned to you at birth, based on the appearance of external anatomy. Gender, on the other hand, is a collection of socially constructed ideas about what behaviors, actions, and roles a particular sex (male or female) performs. When a person is cisgender, it means that their sex and their gender are congruent. When a person is transgender, it means that their sex and their gender are NOT congruent.

This concept is challenging, and that's okay. But if you endeavor to always keep people's humanity at the forefront of your mind, it is not insurmountable. Consider some thought experiments commonly used to challenge the idea that gender is determined by genitals. What if your husband lost his penis due to some horrific work accident? Would he still be a man? What if your wife had an extremely high risk for breast cancer and opted to have a double mastectomy? Would she still be a woman? I'd be shocked if you'd conclude that the loss of sex characteristics strips an individual of their gender. Why then, are we so concerned about the genitals of trans people?

If you can accept that the loss of a sex characteristic does not strip a person of their gender, it is not a huge leap to contemplate that a woman can have a penis and still be a woman and a man can have a vagina and still be a man. The sex characteristics of their physical bodies are irrelevant, it is the essence and personality that define an individual.

This can be particularly challenging for cisgender men, given that society can be very homophobic. When my cisgender male partner and I started a relationship with a transgender woman, he struggled with how people's perception of him would change because he was involved with a woman who has a penis. He identifies as straight and engaging in sexual relations with her did not change that. He was attracted to her femininity, as he would be attracted to anyone. The rest is just semantics and creativity. All sex organs bring pleasure, why do we care so much what form they take?

Using correct pronouns and chosen names is crucial

Pronouns and names are generally not something cisgender people consider changeable. Because of this, it can be difficult to suspend your belief system and let in new information.

I recall the first time I came across someone who used gender-neutral pronouns (in this case, they/them). It was my first exposure to such pronouns, and at the time I actually thought it was onerous and unnecessary, but I was determined to do right by this individual. I worked hard at incorporating their pronouns into my language, even though it felt awkward and uncomfortable at first. It gets easier and when you start to recognize that making the effort is akin to affirming their humanity, it becomes worthwhile.

Even if you don't personally know anyone who is transgender or nonbinary, consider looking at your use of language. When greeting people you don't know, consider gender-neutral language instead of gendered language like *ladies, guys, mister,* or *ma'am*. In my experience, this is where the majority of misgendering happens, and it happens because it is done unconsciously, not with malicious intent. Using terms like *folks, people,* or *friends* ensures that you avoid inadvertently misgendering someone.

Beyond that, there are a number of other ways to support the use of chosen pronouns and names. Normalizing the sharing of pronouns is one good example, like including preferred pronouns in signature blocks or online bios. Using an individual's preferred pronouns and name, even when that individual is not present is another, as is correcting (but not shaming) other people when they get it wrong. Apologizing when you get it wrong, correcting yourself and moving on is particularly important, as is supporting your loved one when navigating unfamiliar territory, keeping in mind their unique needs and circumstances. For me, this last can look like stating my boyfriend's gender in my opening sentence to a stranger. "Have you met my boyfriend?" or "I will have a beer and so will he" or "he and I were just at the zoo." Sometimes, support is having hard conversations with individuals who have inadvertently caused hurt, while at others it is simply being a shoulder to cry on when things go horribly sideways.

Shake the belief that activities, items, or behaviors are gendered

We are conditioned to categorize everything into convenient, tidy boxes. We do this as parents without any real thought. Girls play with Barbies, boys play with trucks; girls can be emotional, boys must be stoic—and society persecutes children who do not fit into those norms.

Playing with dolls will not make a boy trans any more than it will make him gay. Neither does his desire to wear a dress, apply nail polish, or reject playing team sports. If a child is trans or gay, it is already within them. By forcing gender norms on a child, you are not pushing them in the right direction, you are actively subverting a part of them that already exists. These biases start at home and intensify as children enter the school system. To be an effective ally, it's imperative that these stereotypes are examined and ultimately rejected.

Educate yourself

Gender issues are nuanced in a way I never imagined when I was researching the topic years ago. When you have friends or loved ones that are transgender, it's important to delve deeper into these nuances, to have a deeper understanding of their worldview and how you can support their individual journey. Much of it is simply adjusting your view on certain concepts to allow for a different perspective. For example, in the past, I've said, "when you were a girl" to refer to my boyfriend's life before he started his transition. He explained to me that his experience didn't match my understanding. His experience is that he was never a girl. Even though he was assigned female at birth, he has always been a boy. His truth and his lived experience trumps my ignorance, as it should.

Another example of this happened at a conference I attended with an activist friend of mine. She tweeted how disturbed she was to hear the term "socialized male" being used repeatedly at this sex-positive conference. I had understood this term to express that a trans woman would have a different experience/upbringing than a cisgender woman and I couldn't understand why she was upset with the use of this term. I sought her out and asked her to share her thoughts with me. She explained that the term has, in recent years, been co-opted by TERFs (Trans Exclusionary Radical Feminists) as evidence that trans women are not real women.

Your learning will be ongoing, be open to it.

Speak up. educate others. do the heavy lifting whenever you can

Transgender people have to continually defend their existence. They face endless invasive questions about everything ranging from their transition to their genitals, and it can be exhausting. As an ally, take on the role of educator whenever you are presented with the opportunity. This doesn't always mean answering every question that another cis person asks though, pointing out that some questions (particularly ones that involve medical details or genitals) are inappropriate is often the most helpful course of action an ally can take.

While unfortunate, it is ultimately true that people can hear truths better from someone that they feel resembles them. Being cisgender, my voice and privilege often carries more weight than the voices of transfolks. Using this privilege to educate others and to be the first line of defense against hate and uninformed opposition.

Recently, I had a conversation with a man who was wrestling with whether or not he should come out of the closet as gay because, over the years, he's found himself very attracted to trans women. We chatted at length about what defines a woman and what defines sexuality. Before this conversation, these concepts were virtually foreign to him. Armed with new knowledge, this man will be better equipped to communicate with trans women without having to be educated in the process.

Don't do the trans résumé

One day, my girlfriend and I were out at the beach for the day with a group of people, some of whom were unfamiliar to us. When they picked up on the fact that my girlfriend is trans, they started sharing stories about all the people that they knew were trans. Another time, my boyfriend and I were out for dinner with a group of people. He and I exchanged social media information with a couple so we could keep in touch. All of a sudden, after looking at my partner's profile, this woman started talking about trans issues because she noticed from his profile that he was trans.

I see and recognize that this is a way that people try to show that they are cool with trans people, but it's gross. The best way to show trans people solidarity is to continue to treat them exactly the same as you did before you knew they were trans. Being trans changes nothing. If it changes something for you, you need to look at the source of that within you and not project it onto other people.

Learn to sit with discomfort

For my girlfriend, being trans was an overt and very visible part of her identity. For my boyfriend, being trans is a feature of his identity but not the defining feature. Sometimes, I find his desire to be private hard to deal with. When I examine the source of my discomfort, I find it is my desire to be seen and/or be supported. By this, I mean that I want people to know that I'm an ally or I want to co-opt his experience as a method of educating others, but I can see that these desires are rooted in my ego, while his desire for privacy is rooted in his need for safety. As his safety is paramount, I sit with my discomfort.

Discomfort can also be experienced when, as an ally, I have to call in a fellow ally, whether it be for a hurtful use of language or hurtful actions. On occasion, I've taken on this role at the request of my partner. When called in, it is our natural inclination to want to apologize for these missteps, but sometimes an apology is unwanted or unwelcome. It can be uncomfortable to not apologize, as apologizing tends to assuage feelings of guilt. Recognize that often the best way to support those you love is to respect their needs.

Revel in uniqueness

On most levels, my relationship with my transgender boyfriend is exactly the same as my relationship with my cisgender boyfriend, and the differences between the two stem from nothing other than their individual personality traits.

That being said, if you find yourself in an intimate relationship with a trans person, delve deep. Never assume that what works for one trans person will work for all trans folks. Each person has a unique relationship with their own body and their own journey. Being an ally and a partner means celebrating and honoring the things that make them unique. It includes learning and using language that empowers your partner. It's about supporting them to be the best they can be, whatever that may look like. It's assuring your partner that they are valued and cherished. And if that sounds remarkably familiar to how you would treat any partner, you're right. All people deserve love and affection. Trans folks are no different.

Gender is an intensely personal thing and our language and knowledge is ever expanding. Some who read this may vehemently disagree with me, my understanding, and the way I navigate these issues. In a year from now, it's also very possible that I'll cringe at some of my language choices. As our understanding deepens, our approach changes. And that always has been and always will be good and right.

POWER, PLEASURE, AND JUSTICE: TOWARD A TRANS-INCLUSIVE AND ANTIOPPRESSIVE SEX POSITIVITY

by Tai Fenix Kulystin

Every time I sit down to write this piece and think about the particular way I experience sexuality in my trans body, the ways that my combination of identities, presentations, and experiences make up and influence my own sex positivity, I can't help but think of power. I think about power a lot, both personally and professionally. In my work, I help people step into their own personal power in a variety of ways, including getting more in touch with their body and desires, as well as bringing attention to the ways societal power dynamics live in their body and influence their relationships. In my personal life, I love playing with power by intentionally and consensually playing with who is in charge for the pleasure and satisfaction of all involved.

If we can play with power, we can see that power is socially constructed. Gender is also socially constructed. As are notions of sexuality, race, ability, neurodivergence, class, money, nationality, language, and really just about everything made up by society. For something to be socially constructed does not mean it is not real nor that it does not have an impact on our bodies and our lives. Quite the opposite, actually. What it does mean is that these things are created through cultural agreement. This means it is shaped by us and that it has changed throughout history. This also means we get to shape how it changes in the future.

Gender and sexuality are not the same thing, though they inform each other, just like all identities and ways of being inform each other. They, like all identities, have to do with the body. Eventually, everything comes back to the body in this reality. We may be able to categorize ourselves in a myriad of different ways, into identities or parts or souls or so many other things, but there is one truth we can always come back to: reality is here, right now, and our body is what keeps us in the here and now.

Our identities are ways of talking about our bodies. We use them to describe cultural influences on our bodies, to describe the trauma of oppression and how we are or aren't influenced by it. Privilege is another way of saying we are not affected by a specific type of cultural trauma. I cannot think of gender or sexuality, or any of the many ways we divide humanity, without thinking of power. Especially social power. Gender, sex, and sexuality in contemporary

United States society is directly influenced and impacted by supremacy and colonization, which utilizes social power as a way to keep us disconnected. Sex positivity is one of many ways that we can work to create a world that instead centers sovereignty, love, and justice.

Before I get too much further, it is important to mention my identities so you understand where I am coming from in writing this. I include these to be transparent about the ways this society rewards or punishes me for existing, the particular privileges and oppressions that influence my experience, and the ways I hold power or am systematically disempowered. I'm a genderqueer trans person. I was assigned female at birth (AFAB), which is important to mention because I am not trans feminine so I do not internalize transmisogyny and therefore my experience as an AFAB genderqueer person is different and more privileged than one who is assigned male (AMAB). I have transitioned both socially and medically, but I am not going to focus on that because medical transition is not a requirement for being trans. I am also white, middle-class, fat, neuroqueer, able-bodied, a sex worker, and a witch. Sexually speaking, I am a polyamorous kinky queer switch, though sometimes I use the term queersexual to emphasize that I am emphatically and exclusively attracted to other queer people.

I have dedicated my life to sexual and relational healing through sovereignty, self-understanding, and embodiment. As much as possible, I strive for my work to be antioppressive, sex positive, and trauma-knowledgeable. I am a pleasure activist, meaning I organize my world around pleasure, I believe we all deserve pleasure, and my activism comes from a source of pleasure. I work as a somatic sex educator and therapeutic trauma coach and have degrees in psychology and gender studies. My teachers have been many, including folks dead and alive (encountered both in-person and through written works), and I have had students of my own. I offer private therapeutic coaching sessions, tarot and astrology readings, pleasure-focused bodywork, ritual design services, and workshops on a variety of topics.

So, now you have some knowledge of where I am coming from, both personally and professionally. I can't speak to all types of oppression, that is not my place, nor would I want to. I can speak from my own experiences of external and internalized oppression. I can also speak from the ways that unconscious participation in and benefiting from white supremacy has impacted my body and experiences, as well as from the ways my transitioning to being now mostly misgendered as a man means I am newly benefiting from patriarchy. All these words are trying to explain, as best I can, using the language of this time and place, the ways that my body, my experiences, and my worldview are limited and controlled by the culture I grew up in. It would not be important in the same way to categorize myself in a culture that is built on sovereignty, justice, interdependence, connection, and the celebration of difference. However, this is not that culture.

I would love to be creating a light and fun piece that illustrates how phenomenal it is to live in a trans body (which it is… though it is also often terrible because of transphobia). I would love to tell you how amazing it is to have sex with trans people, which I have had the pleasure of experiencing from both sides and multiple angles. Sex with a trans person means questioning everything that you know about how bodies work and how bodies are "supposed to" interact with one another. Sex with a trans person also means dropping all pretense of what you think you know about bodies and sexuality and being with the reality of what is here and now. Hopefully all sex is that way to some degree, but often our ideas about sexuality and bodies get in the way of our current experiences.

Regardless of the surgeries we have had or not had or the which hormones are dominant within our bodies, trans people have trans bodies and our bodies destroy the idea of any sort of default. This is part of why we are so feared and hated. This society does not want any of us to be aware of our bodies or the power we can embody within them. This society is afraid of our claiming any sort of power for ourselves or self-declaration of identity. Those of us with nonnormative bodies disrupt the idea of normalcy, which includes trans people, but really includes anyone who does not fit into the cultural "default" We call attention to the fact that we are not simply cogs in a capitalist machine but unique individuals with desires, hopes, dreams, and personal power. Trans bodies disrupt the current gender paradigm simply by existing (and we have always existed).

Sexual and gender oppression both have roots in patriarchal white supremacy, which is itself antierotic, and this supremacy is what sex-positive culture is really opposed to and trying to help us heal from. This isn't always the focus or awareness of sex positivity, but it needs to be. Patriarchy (aka male supremacy) and white supremacy both benefit from keeping us separate, disconnected, and unaware of our own power.

My experience of sex positivity is that it often (though not always) comes along with awareness of the multitude of ways gender and sexuality are expressed and lived through the human experience. Still, though, sex positivity is overwhelmingly cisnormative and heteronormative, unless it is explicitly coming from a queer- and/or trans-inclusive perspective. Pansexual sex-positive spaces often end up still defaulting into heterocisnormative power structures, usually not out of intention, but out of a lack of awareness or ability to center queer and trans voices and experiences.

Dr. Cornell West said, "Justice is what love looks like in public, just like tenderness is what love feels like in private." Justice and tenderness need to be at the center of our social movements and work against oppression, therefore they need to be at the center of sex positivity. I think sex positivity is often approached (mostly by cis hetero people) as a fun social club where everyone feels positively about sexuality, rather than as a necessary social movement working to change the sex negative attitudes and beliefs in society. Too often sex positivity is taken to mean that someone is interested in or open to sex, and often includes pressure to "prove" sex positivity through being sexual with anyone (usually cis man) who shows an interest in you. This is a perpetuation of patriarchy twisted to fit sex-positive culture and needs to be rooted out of the movement.

My sex positivity is focused on promoting body agency, autonomy, and personal sovereignty for everyone, within sexual encounters and beyond. This inherently includes being able to have any kind of consensual sexual experiences that we want to have, or to not have sexual experiences at all. This requires as awareness of the systems of power that are in place to keep us divided and disconnected from our own power and from each other. This also inherently includes declaring and embracing your own gender, whether it be cis or trans, intersex, agender or hypergender, binary or nonbinary, or any combination thereof. It also means accepting the identities of others as real, true, and right for them, and knowing that sexuality and gender can be changeable throughout a lifetime or can be fixed and that neither experience is superior to the other.

Ultimately, if our sex positivity isn't intended to dismantle patriarchal white supremacy, what is the point? Our sex positivity needs to be antioppressive, anticolonial, and aware of the ways our lives are shaped by our identities and our identities are shaped by each other. We need to center the lives, voices, and experiences of the people who are impacted the most by discrimination and oppression, especially queer trans femmes of color. We need to side with the oppressed and powerless, rather than being "neutral." To paraphrase Desmond Tutu, no one is truly neutral in the face of injustice; those who are silent side with the oppressor. I am not the first to say this, and I will not be the last. It is vitally important to my own liberation and experience within sex positivity as a trans person to work toward justice for all who are oppressed. We all need to be in this together.

So, ultimately what do I want you to know about gender and sex positivity? I want you to know that gender is real. My gender is real. Your gender is real. All genders are real. Gender roles are social constructs to be dismantled, and all that gender is, in the end, is one part of who we are. It is not the same as our bodies, our personalities or character traits, our interests, our mannerisms, but it is related to all these things in some ways and also not at all. My body does not determine my gender, nor does your body determine yours. All gender and sexual identities are real, including agender and asexual identities. All people deserve love, justice, and tenderness. All bodies are good bodies.

If you are trans or intersex and you are reading this, I want you to know that your gender (or lack thereof) is real. You are amazing and your existence is important. You matter. You deserve to be here. You deserve love, support, kindness, and to be cared for exactly the way you need. You deserve to be seen. I am glad you exist.

If you are cis and you are reading this, I want you to know that it is your responsibility to learn what you can about the lives of trans and intersex folks and leverage your privilege to help make our lives better. This goes for any ways you (and I) are privileged, any ways we are not affected by specific cultural and intergenerational trauma. We need to be aware of the power that we hold in these arenas and work to share that power so we all may heal together from the ways our bodies are affected by these cultural traumas.

To all of us, we deserve love and pleasure. Pleasure is necessary for us all, including sexual pleasure for those of us who want it, but also pleasure in the broadest sense of the word. We are social animals, and we all need and deserve love, belonging, and pleasure. Remember what Dr. West said, and work toward love for everyone. Fiercely demand justice and stand up for what is right in the name of pleasure and love. Be also fiercely tender, kind, and loving to all you are around. This is how we change the world and create a new paradigm that is better than the one that is currently dying.

TWO SPIRITS
by Beau Black

One day, while with a few friends, the topic of self-discovery and gender identity came up. One of my friends expressed that they had been feeling as if they did not identify with the gender assigned to them at birth. They mentioned feeling as if they were Two Spirit. At this time, I was not fully aware of what this term meant, but there was something that resonated with me. After much discussion with my friends, I came home and did some internet searching and something clicked. I had found a piece of myself, a part of my identity that was inexplicable before. I have always been Two Spirit, but it took someone else using the term for it to fall into place. The term Two Spirit is used among many native tribes to describe one who not entirely masculine nor feminine, but somewhere in between or along the gender spectrum. Prior to colonization, Two-Spirit people were celebrated, honored, and revered for their uniqueness. These individuals were often healers and balance keepers among the tribes. My family is Chippewa (Ojibwe/Ojibway) but I did not grow up immersed in my tribal culture.

I am a masculine of center, queer, butch, Leather Daddy, boi, and a switch. My appearance and energy are masculine, with feminine undertones. I float along the gender spectrum, neither one extreme or the other, but somewhere in between; I love the juxtaposition of the two. I embrace all the aspects of myself by wearing sexy bras while simultaneously packing. There was a time in my life when I wore feminine clothing, such as skirts and dresses, but I hated being cold, so I stopped. I have a fascination with makeup and wore it regularly in my early to mid-twenties. On a random day in 2004, I decided that I no longer wanted to wear it daily, but will still wear eyeliner to achieve a certain aesthetic. I prefer to wear men's clothing and cologne and have used the men's restroom on several occasions. Let's be honest! A bathroom is a bathroom, and we should all get over it already. Everyone has to pee at some point.

Gender-neutral pronouns can be difficult to navigate in professional lives if you don't follow the binary norms. I am actively working to educate both my client and coworkers about gender variant folx and the use of proper pronouns. Speaking with them about inclusive language and providing encouragement to ask, rather than assuming a person's pronouns, has been a positive experience.

I am a member of BDSM/kink, Leather, and sex-positive communities in Seattle, Washington. I am fortunate to live in a very diverse and affirming city. Being Two Spirit in my sexual life has been the easiest portion of my life journey. While I am always open to connections with people who vary in gender presentation and orientation, my current partners have femme, queer, bisexual, and cisgender-women identities. Along with my Two-Spirit identity, I also recognize that I am demisexual. Navigating the expectations of sex can be difficult for people who don't understand those two things. Mutual attraction, chemistry, and connection matter to me the most.

My romantic and sexual energy is quite intense, depending on my mood and my partner. I have been very fortunate to have sexual partners who honor my masculinity and femininity, and everything in between. I have had several positive comments from partners about my dual identity. Most of them find is hot as hell or "Sexy AF." To be honest, I do feel incredibly sexy and confident in my body when I am with people who understand my identity. That I crave both the soft and the hard, the giving and receiving of mutual pleasure. I enjoy rough and dirty sex with a mix of tenderness here and there. I am constantly evolving sexually. I used to be painfully shy! Now I am growing and learning to channel my inner sadist, or Dark Prince as I like to call it, in both sex and play. My leather community has helped me to embrace my authenticity, uniqueness, and multifaceted self.

Discovering my Two-Spirit self has helped greatly to boost my confidence. I am able to float between top and bottom, dominant and submissive. I feel fluid in many areas of my life. It allows me to experience life from many vantage points. Embracing who I am has made my life more rich and profound and I hope to encourage and enrich others by living out loud. Even though we live in an evolving world, there is still so much education needed. We all need to learn and grow to create a world where people can be accepted for who they are. It is our responsibility to honor each other and create space where love and acceptance can thrive. It is not our place to judge one another. My hope is that one day soon we can learn to honor and accept the gorgeous and vast diversity the world has to offer. There is so much joy and beauty in the world. Too many people are missing out by simply being afraid of what is different or being too ignorant to step outside of their comfort zone and see the bigger picture. I am a Two Spirit, dirty, kinky, sex-positive human and I wouldn't have it any other way.

EDUCATION

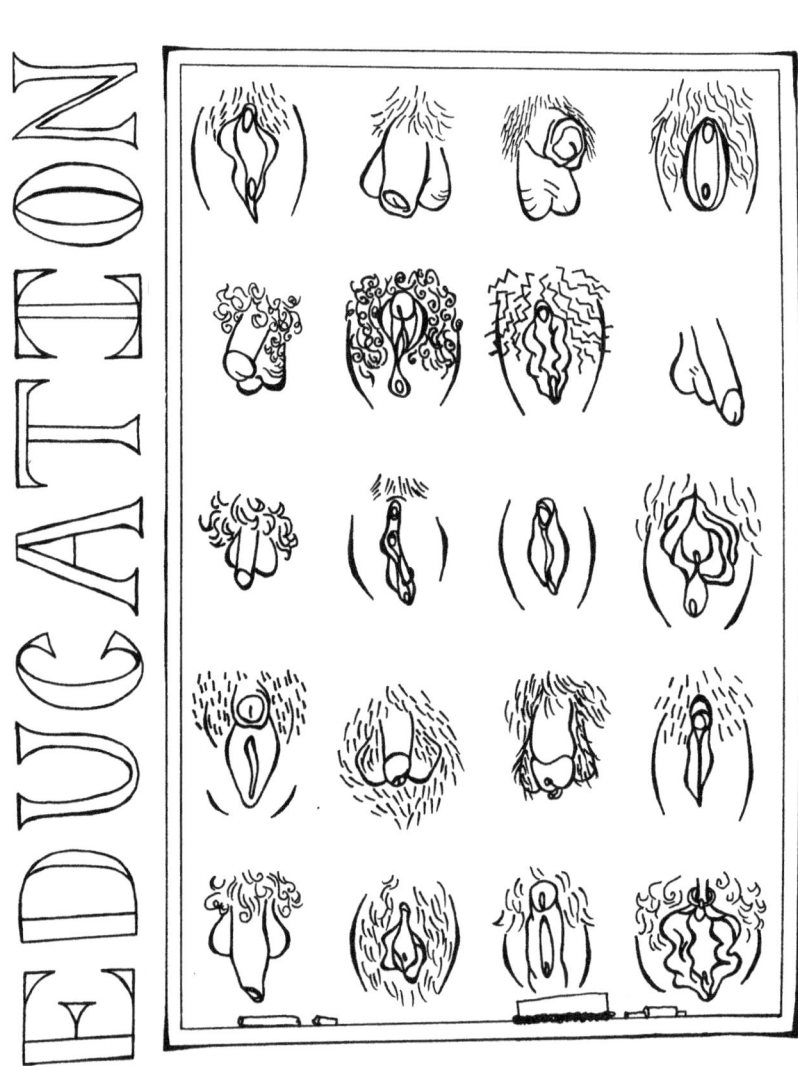

CHAPTER 7
EDUCATION

There are many avenues to sex-positive education, from one-one-one coaching to creating workshops to academia.

SEX-POSITIVE EDUCATION
Interview by Jeremy Shub with Deej Juventin and Uma Ayelet Furman

Good to see you, where are you?

Deej -- Brisbane, Uma and I are both live and work in Brisbane.

So, who are you, what is sex positive to you? Why is this important?

Uma -- Okay. When people ask what I do for a living, I would usually say that I'm a Sex Educator and a Tantra Teacher. I see that as something a little bit different to sex education. I have always been in this world, it's always been my world, I would say the sexuality world, I've been involved in lots of different aspects of it, and I've been doing tantric work and sex education work and sexological bodywork full time for about a decade now. Before that I did that just as my hobby, just as my vocation, something that I was interested in.

Let's start with, what's sex positivity to you, and why is that important maybe.

Uma -- Sex positivity for me has a lot to do with inclusivity, acceptance and awareness, so I guess the first piece is being aware of whatever is out there in terms of sexual expression, in terms of sexual orientation, in terms of gender presentation. Having that awareness, which is part of our education as humans is something I try and pass on to other people, and to learn for myself. And you might not want to be all things but acceptance, tolerance and acceptance is a big part of sex positivity. So awareness, acceptance and inclusion.

I'm really passionate about the idea that we can all live together. We don't need to separate ourselves because of different gender presentations or different orientations or because we are into different kinks. I think everybody has a lot to teach everybody else, and in a perfect world you'll do really exciting things with people who think exactly like you and you'll do really exciting things with people with who you have not much in common. You teach each other, about your world. That would be a perfect sex positive world, in my eyes, where everybody is happy and accepting and understanding and everything is, my kink is no better than your kink and, my sexual orientation, whatever that is, is what it is now, and it might change later and it's not better or worse than yours.

And we try in our little humble way to create this type of energy, this type of environment where we teach and how we teach. And we try and pass on this concept that we do have a lot to teach each other and that we can practice with people who we don't, we are not necessarily attracted to and there's lots of positivity there and there's lots of things to learn.

Thank you. Maybe jump over to Deej and do you want to try a similar version of who you are?

Deej --What came up as Uma was speaking is that, I think in some ways it's about survival on a global level. We've spent hundreds of years practicing our cognitive capacities, and maybe thousands of years denigrating the body and what it experiences, and so we've become really powerful as a species, we've got these really powerful cognitive narrative capacity, but we've sort of lost our wisdom because we haven't been paying any attention to the body and eroticism, and to the living charge of life. I really think we are suffering the consequences of it. Things like global warming and the tension that we have in our bodies; The body has its experiences and the mind has attitude about it, so we are putting a lot of our effort i into the tension that goes on between the body and the mind.

And on a personal level the survival piece: I grew up same-sex attracted in a very homophobic time, before the generations of gay people came out and so the message I grew up with was that because of my desire, my sexual attraction, the three options were to be murdered, to be incarcerated or to be exiled. So that massive shame, that same-sex attracted people grew up with at that time, was either go with that flow and kill yourself or get to that wonderful opportunity when you realize maybe it's not me that's wrong it's the social construct and to be able to turn all that on its head and pull it all apart and come back to actually maybe sex is a useful thing, maybe sex is a positive thing. Maybe even my attraction is something to be proud of. And that was a generation thing and I was really in that time of growing up, so it very much was survival to me because I wouldn't have, I personally wouldn't have survived if I hadn't been able to turn that shame into positive.

So two questions. Do you regard yourself as sex positive and could you tell a personal story, either something in the bedroom or something in the outside world where your experience about sex positivity or sex negativity stood out.

Uma -- I would regard myself as sex positive, but I think being sex positive is a constant process. Rather than saying I am or I'm not - because if it involves education, and knowing about other people's experiences, because I don't know everything. And I wouldn't like to be in a place where I think I know everything. So I think the process of education is continuous and the process of acceptance and inclusion is continuous. And, I regard myself as very fortunate and privileged in a sense because I grew up in my micro cosmos, that was quite positive sexually, I didn't grow up with shame. I didn't grow up being told sex was bad, or that I shouldn't be proud of it or of having fun with it, but I grew up in a place that's relatively conservative, and as I've gone through life I've always realized that I was kind of the odd one out. I was the one who was making the most noise in an apartment building and the neighbours would be waiting downstairs in the morning and trying to shame me for it, for being open and positive. I was the one who had polyamorous relationship at quite a young age and then again, the people in the neighbourhood saw three people or four people living together, and would get really concerned and come and lecture us and tell us how it's a bad thing.

But what I noticed as well is that, if you have a sense of pride inside, that positivity, internal positivity that says, I'm not doing anything wrong, it carries out, so people might come and tell you off. In my culture, I grew up in Israel, which is very much a culture where everybody interferes or everybody is involved in everybody else's life and nobody holds anything back when they think they have something to tell you. Being internally positive has helped me translate it out and just say no, there isn't anything wrong with this, and people had to, in a sense, accept it. And so that's always been my journey around that: if I feel positive internally, it will translate, it will manifest to how I present it externally. It's not an easy thing, it's not pleasant when you go outside your house and neighbours are gathered and they are all screaming at you, but then, it's that choice of well how you negotiate, and do you take that on, or do we choose to educate and turn it around.

That's easier said than done, and in some cultures, a lot more dangerous to speak back, than others. And that's why I talk about my privilege because there was no physical danger, I wasn't under any threat of being, or any physical threat or even mental. So, that was useful, and what I strive to do is use that to support others who might have not had such as positive experience around that. I think that's our place, as one who feels quite privileged in not having a lot of sexual shame and trauma, in her past, I feel it's one of my roles to support people that have, to support them in being there and saying hey, we can change that.

Yeah. Wonderful. Thank you. It makes me want to circle back to sexological bodywork in a moment but first I'll ask Deej for some comment.

Deej --Uma's and my friendship, our relationship, is based on our sex passivity. We met when Uma was 20, I might have been nearly 30, and in an extended sort of community of wild people living in Sydney who were doing all sorts of things, there were lots of sex workers and all sorts of different people, but Uma and I were the most sex positive amongst them. I think that's partly why I liked her, because she just loved having sex and I loved having sex, and everybody had different interests and I think she and I amongst the family, were the most into sex, and then we went onto create a whole career out of it. So that worked. Is that enough? That's all that's coming up.

Yeah. So maybe share about Sexological body work, assuming that I have no idea what you are talking about, because anyone reading this book will have no idea what you are talking about. So if you can say a little bit about what your work is and if you can loop it around sex positivity that's good. Otherwise, just have a bit of a rave about sexological bodywork and the impact of that on either Australia or globally. Any connection to Joseph Kramer you want to mention or any other people who've inspired you around that.

Deej --That question that you've got there about who are you in the world of sex positivity. We are educators who teach somatically, so we teach about the body through the body and that's what we've had success in. We've developed quite a simple and effective methodology that allows us to, rather than talk about things, and think about things, to get people doing things through their body in a relatively safe way and we've set the stages of what it takes to create safety in a group that allows people to bring their awareness into their body and experiment and explore with each other.

Sexological Body work is an aspect of somatic, or body-based sex education. So it's the hands-on component, but it's also using breath and touch and movement and sound and placement of awareness, so using our body's tools to experiment with doing things in different ways so that we can create more sensation through the body, more connection with ourselves and more connection with each other.

We never really know what to say about it because it changes every single time we do it, but mostly it's teaching people about their bodies through their bodies and finding ways to create really safe ways to do that. It is also for the material to be research based. So it's using science and using information that, like neuroscience is delivering in terms of learning theory, like we know 95% of what is known about the brain and nervous system, and we've learned in the last two decades and that's just given us a lot of information about how the body learns. The body learns that first it needs to be safe. Then we need to engage our curiosity and perhaps with guidance, use our curiosity to try new things out, and through trying those new things out we have new experiences. But the newness is only laid down in the body through practice over time, so Sexological bodywork is also of intentional practice. So Yoga of Sex. And Joseph Kramer has gone and created a course called Yoga of Sex. So it's that intentional practice piece that through creating environments where we can both experiment and, where we can experiment over time to create new experiences and access more pleasure. And so Joseph Kramer has been heavily influential in our work, and Chester Maynard has been heavily influential. Uma and I have done a lot of work with Kenneth Ray Stubbs as well, and I think he's really affected our capacity to be present and to attend on multiple levels. I think that's something that somatic sex educators do as well; we pay attention, and we create learning situations so it's not just about active listening, we are actively attending to our students, so that we can support them in working out what it is that they want, rather than putting on them what we think might be useful for them. It's a very co-created way of working, and it's not about a teacher being the source of information, it's about actually the interaction with each other being the source of the information that might be useful for learning.

Uma -- Sexological bodywork is more of an educational modality rather than a therapy or healing modality. And it's that collaborative effort between practitioner and client or practitioner and student around finding a way to educate the body, finding ways to learn more and sometimes finding ways to overcoming particular blockages, issues, concerns, but not in a treatment type way: the client doesn't just lie there and receive a healing or a massage, and the client doesn't only sit there with you and talk about what's going on. It's that combination of, let's feel into what's going on and let's see what practices will support whatever it is that's happening for you.

Whether it is that you are saying, "wow, my body feels really good, I want to learn how to make it feel even better", or maybe it's, "oh, my body's feeling a little bit, and I have a concern around an aspect of my sexuality, I want to find out how I can overcome this particular concern". And we are very clear about not having any particular system or dogma that says well you must do A, B and C and then D will happen. Because we are very aware that we are very complex creatures, especially when it comes to our sexuality, and there are so many different elements that make one's sexuality, different amounts of shame, and different aspects of what brings us pleasure and our fantasy world and so on. In our eyes it really needs to be a collaborative process because the practitioner can't know in advance what's going to work for each client, and the client doesn't know either, we have to try different things, we teach the clients what we call little micro skills, and we see what works. So it's different then when we think of yoga, traditional Hatha Yoga or a series of practices that you do in a very structured way, that gets you a particular result. Our yoga is very different because we have what we call, the building blocks: we teach our clients a lot of practices around how they can use their breath, but not in a particular way. We can we can do this, and we can do this and we can do that. We talk about movement as a way of creating the play between tension and relaxation, the opening of the pelvis, but again everybody's body is built differently so how they would move and how we would teach that movement would be different.

We look at touch and sensation, and of course we all have different degrees of numbness and awake-ness; in our skin, in our nervous system, and that has to be tailored. So it's a collaborative effort that is about client and practitioner working together in session, giving enough tools for the clients to then go home and practice those tools and develop them. And then the client comes back to the practitioner and says okay, this has been working, that not so much, let's see what we can develop. Let's see what we can add or adjust to this, and that's the process. And it can be a short process, or it can be a really long-term process. It really depends on the clients, their learning objectives. Their intentions.

Great descriptions you two! You shared something in your work which is scientific, research medial almost, and then you also mentioned Kenneth Ray Stubbs, who I know is interested in Shamanism, and Joseph Kramer, who has Taoist background, and you are also talking about yoga, so there seems to be an esoteric Eastern sacred sexuality mixed in with some of your Western evidenced base.

Deej --We try to ground the sacred in the body, so in our professional trainings we ask the students to put the word 'energy' aside, for the duration of the training to see what other language that they could use to describe that experience that is happening, because our body base, our somatic language is quite primitive and there's very little shared language about what we are experiencing in our bodies. So just as a learning exercise, but that's sort of how it started, but what we realized over time I think is that we were really interested in this bit of grounding, in whatever the experience is in the physical organism, that's the sort of the part of the education field that we occupy. So we are really informed by other traditions, we are really informed by Tantra, we are informed by Taoism, we are informed by Shamanism. We do subtle energy work as professional development, more or less for ourselves. But we look at, how that might actually work in the physical body, and what language we can use to describe that in the physical body and so really what can we do, what can we do and what does it feel like, in tangible terms? By tangible I mean striving to try to come up with shared language, when shared language doesn't really exist for what we are talking about.

So that stuff that's coming out in neuroscience about the nervous system really geeks us out. We love it. We love learning about what physically happens in the brain and the nervous system, when we do different things and learning, how the brain and the nervous system shape themselves and how they grow, just the endless information that's coming out around that.

How we regulate each other, how we co-create each other-co-creation came as a sort of educational concept, but the stuff with Stephen Porges Polyvagal Theory and mirror neurons and interpersonal neurobiology and all this sort of stuff, has shown that actually co-creation is a truth: we co-create each other's brains and nervous systems and interactions with each other and the world around us and we regulate each other. And that regulation isn't random. We can intentionally do things to regulate. Those are the pieces we are interested in, how we can intentionally work with that then and it's new science, so maybe it's not going to be true in five years time, but it's true at the moment. How can we use it to learn and to grow and support and to connect and to regulate each other?

If you are talking about mirror neurons that you two stand as these sex positive people, if I can use that word, what circles past you would you see having effect, what feedback do you get or testimonials, or how do you see the reach of your own work? Not personal but the work you do.

Deej -- I think one of our primary motivations to do professional trainings is that we can ripple out and we can connect with and affect more people by training other people to do what we do. Or do similar things but by training people to feel confident to go out and work as practitioners.

Uma -- And we also, in our professional training, we have a real intention of creating a very inclusive and sex positive space in the training itself and educating the practitioners about different gender presentations, sexual orientations, and lifestyle choices. We would love to do a lot more of that, but that is a whole training, or it could be a whole training in and of itself, but as part of our program, this is very much included in our program and we live what we preach. We don't divide the room into man and woman and tell the boys to work with the girls and all of that, we really intend for everybody to work with everybody, knowing that there will be something to learn, even from the people that you really don't want to be with. And we do that, and we create spaces, from workshop spaces that happen in festivals, all the way up to our professional training, where this is our structure, this is what we do. We are the people who do that.

Deej -- Everyone works with everyone, so it's the intention to bracket attraction or dis-attraction, for this time. How can we interact with each other and what can we learn from each other outside concepts of attraction? I think the gender pieces do have major ripples. People come to our professional trainings to learn somatic sex educator skills, but they also learn quite a lot about inclusivity. When we have the conversation we do 101 of what is sex and what is gender, which interestingly in Australia, isn't a big conversation. In California it's a basic conversation, but in Australia, people who have been working in the area of sex and sexuality come to our professional trainings and it's very often the first time they've heard this about, what is sex and is it binary or is it beyond binary, and what is gender and is that binary or beyond binary?

I don't think we deliver it in a way the activists necessarily are happy with, but we deliver it in a way where the people who maybe experience themselves as binary are open to it, open to these concepts and open to these ideas, and very often they have epiphanies. Wow, I've just realized that my whole concept of my own gender is different to what I thought it was, or my own concept of my own sexuality is different from what I thought it was. And I think that's not preaching to people, it's not telling people what they have to think, it's just creating a space where people can feel, have some information and feel into things. At the same time we take care of the activists through language, by not using the words man and woman and being really particular. We teach through the body so we are teaching about genitals, we talk about genital configurations, and the incredible variety in genital configurations, rather than just talking about penis type structures or just talking about vulva type structures. So that inclusivity of the incredible variety we have in our bodies, is a great starting point, I think.

I think one of the things I'm proud of is getting this going in the UK. Uma and I went, in combination with Katie Sara and set this up in the UK and now we've handed it over to them. They've got really fertile foundations there and they've responded incredibly well and people are doing a lot of stuff, a lot of amazing stuff in the UK, so when you said ripple, it's that concept for us, by teaching in a lot of places, we can hopefully create more sex positivity I guess. We can create a more accepting world.

Yeah, that was my question about the international scene, and where you travel, and what do you notice and what effect is your work having on people in other countries.

Uma -- It's really interesting to look at different cultures and their attitudes to sexuality. Sometimes on the surface it looks the same but then when you teach people, you get to see underneath the surface and you see those, sometimes subtle, sometimes not very subtle, differences and the wounding that comes with each culture, and the same, and the different aspects of shame that come with each culture. The challenge is for someone who's not part of the culture, coming to teach people, and that is always a challenge. Because coming into a new culture you don't really know what the differences are, until you are right in there, and it takes a while to absorb that, so there are advantages, because people see an example of another culture, because you are bringing your qualities in and they can see that, oh we can do this differently. But then there are challenges because you have certain expectations of your students which might or might not come to fruition.

Deej -- You come from a place of great ignorance when you teach internationally, but it works because, they've invited you so they are sort open to that you are going to fuck things up and get things wrong, but I think there's also that bit when you are outside a culture, particularly shame, because shame is the illusive one isn't it, I mean shame hides in every way it possibly can. I think when you come from outside, I think you get a bit more perspective. Maybe it's easier to see some of the ways that people are hiding, or people are holding back, or people use shame to limit their experience in the world.

I'd like to hear if you have a particular story to share about a different culture, and also I want to circle back to shame as well, because I think that's really critical how you guys work with that, But you are both laughing so I'm guessing there's some experiences that you've had where you were surprised by being in another country.

Deej --What do you want to say Uma?

Uma -- I've done quite a bit of work in Singapore and Deej and I have gone and taught in seminars there and workshops, and what we notice is there are simple things that you couldn't teach. It was very, very hard to teach Singaporeans how to upregulate their breath, meaning when you teach people about breath you teach them how they relax their bodies through breath, and how they can excite their body through breath, but Singaporeans are so far up on that excitement scale, they are so stressed out with life, that if you ask them to excite themselves a little bit more they are just about to explode and have a panic attack. So, we had to drop this whole part of our teaching because it wasn't useful for people. It was taking them to this place that's beyond excitement because they are already so excited. It was taking them into anxiety. So that was really amusing to see and think oh, okay, I can't do that. Also, the idea of collaboration was really foreign to them, because their education system is very particular in places like that; teacher says, student does. Student doesn't question teacher. Student is not allowed to question teacher, it's rude to question teacher, and we want out students to question us. But again, impossible to do in a culture where that is considered highly impolite.

Also it was really difficult to get people to connect with each other because staring into another's eyes is considered very rude. And very challenging. So simple practices of let's sit here and just look into each other's eyes for five minutes, which would not be challenging to most people here, is challenging there.

That was impossible over there. So we realized that, the cultural way of communication, the cultural shame was very different in what we have here. They are simple things but you have to adjust what you are doing and they can be quite challenging because you have particular learning objectives to get through, which might or might not resonate with that particular culture.

And also, we ran a sexuality conference, with some local people, and it was in a big shopping centre that had conference rooms. So we were in one conference room and there was a handbag sale in the next conference room. We had 80 people who came to our conference, they had a line going around the block. Waiting to get into the handbag sale. Two signs side by side. [laughter]

Deej -- It would be interesting to see if they did the same experiment in Australia, what would happen.

Yeah, handbags versus sex. And where there places you've encountered where you would say they are more sex positive, or where would hot spots be in the world of sex positivity? Or countries.

Deej --I don't know, I guess California, but I think Australia is doing well in a sort of low-key way, because Australia's got that, no worries concept, where it might not be very obvious. But I think things are really moving here, I think there's an incredible momentum on interest in sex, and the body, and talking about and learning about it. Like a big shift from when I started working in this field. People are prepared and willing and wanting to talk about sex.

UK people don't really want to talk about sex. The interesting thing about the UK which surprised us when we got there, working with people who were working with sex, is there was an assumption there that if you work with sex, you work with trauma. Like a complete assumption. They'd used this expression just assuming we agreed, and we were like, no actually, we got through got through quite a large portion of our career without having to work with trauma at all. I mean we do now but there's a real assumption there that sex equals trauma or if you work with sex, you work with trauma. Whereas in Australia, it's quite easy to separate those out. A lot of people who aren't living with trauma- sex therapists and different people-come to Sexological bodywork..

So tell me about shame? And how you work with shame and the relationship between shame and your philosophy, and the relationship between shame and sex negativity and sex positivity. Let's talk about shame and how there can be a transition from shame to a celebration and a thriving of sexuality or worthiness.

Deej --Yeah. Mine might be skewed by my personal experience, professional I think it's an important part where really attending comes in, as practitioners really being fully present and fully interested and curious in the full range of human experience. So Uma and I use the term 'horizontalization' of experiences. So pleasure isn't more interesting than pain, numbness isn't more interesting than pleasure. Whatever shows up, whatever the person is experiencing is equally of interest to us, we are equally curious about it because shame comes out of the mind's attitude about what the body is experiencing and what the body is doing, so if we can show up with equal curiosity an interest for whatever's been experienced there, I think that can be pretty powerful, because that's not how people live in the world very often. I think all sorts of healthy practitioners do that, and they do that very effectively and that's one reason it's useful to have sessions with various healthy practitioners because it's a place where people can, even if it is talk, and feel and be who they are and for that to be accepted, and I think that sort of Carl Rogers thing of empathy, congruence and unconditional positive regard is enormously powerful in terms of working through shame. He was extraordinary with being able to just knock it out in those three expressions. But just really showing up, really connecting, really accepting.

And we talk about interpersonal neurobiology, so we get that piece of science, that as we sit with each other we are regulating each other. So therefore as practitioners, we need to be really present, really grounded, really aware of how we are in our bodies. So that we can be regulating our client's bodies, by which I mean so that they can, their bodies feel safe, rather than just their minds but their bodies start to feel safe, start to arrive start to feel present in the room, and then it becomes possible to talk about and explore these really hidden parts of our experience. Do you want to go Uma?

Uma -- Personally, as a practitioner, I wait for shame to show up in the room, and then most people who come to me would not say oh I'm experiencing shame. Shame is often very much hidden, and it manifests in different ways. So I'm experiencing, sometimes sex negativity, towards others, and sometimes there's sex negativity towards self. And when it is present it will eventually show up, so I don't necessarily bring it up as okay let's sit now and talk about your shame. Because that feels too analytical for me. But then when shame shows up in the room while we are doing something, so here we are doing some kind of a breath and touch practice, and the client comes out of the moment, the moment is interrupted, and they are experiencing it as some kind of shame. And then we can look at it with curiosity, what Deej was talking about and notice it, allow it, and then learn how to come back to the moment.

Joseph talks about shame as being an interruption of the present moment. So if shame is an interruption, what we need to teach is how to come back into the moment. So here's my shame, and I'm noticing it, I'm allowing it, I'm curious about it, I'm not in it, I'm just acknowledging it and here is my tool to bring myself back to the present moment, to what is actually happening in my physical organism. So I can recognize it in my life and I know that oh okay, that's a piece that's not actually, doesn't necessarily need to be part of who I am.

As a practitioner I intend to teach my clients that they have a choice around their shame, that they don't have to be in their shame, all the time or, really, at all. They have the tools to learn to, I don't know if it's learning to let go or learning to come back to the moment.

Deej -- We got the expression 'resilient edge of resistance' from Chester Maynard, which is about intending to work at a place where there's just enough of what's showing up, but not so much that people get overwhelmed, and learning happens when we can be experiencing what we are experiencing, just enough of the edginess, that we still at least know where presence is, we still at least know where ground is and as Uma says, we can navigate our way back to ground. So that's what we are teaching people to do, to experience what they are experiencing, and know what is just enough and also come back to presence to rest and to nurture and to integrate and to reflect and all those things, because I think culturally, we've been taught to actually hang out. To not do something, or hang out past the edge, is a habit for a lot of people. It's just too scary so we just won't go there, because every time we do go there, we go way past our useful edge and get overwhelmed, so it's teaching a different process that allows people to experience just enough if without being overwhelmed.

It makes me wonder, talking about these practices that you do, what do you notice about the graduates of the training or what do you notice about completion with clients?

Deej -- Graduates, we've just finished an intensive, and it's interesting because it's such a structure that we created, we are clearly there. They say it's life changing and we are like, mmm, what about it was life changing? I don't know if I know the answer to, what about it was life changing. That it was safe, that it was connected, that people were in their bodies, that people were accepted. In some ways I hope that that's not enough because if that's enough people are really suffering out in the world a bit, but maybe it is, maybe it is just that bit of really showing up, being present and being accepted, that changes things.

Uma -- I see people's ability to feel grows, but at the same time, feeling their physical body and but also feeling emotions. Those pieces grow whether you are doing one of one work or group work or a practitioner training. But at the same time, their ability to regulate themselves grows. So people gain a capacity and choice around regulating their emotions, around feeling more in their body or feeling less in their body, that piece of choice and regulation really solidifies in a person's body. So it's emotional choice, its physical choice around how we want to be in our bodies. And the ability to actually be in one's body and be with one's sexuality is therefore peeling off the layers of shame.

Deej -- A lot of it is curiosity and confidence. Curiosity to try other things or to experiment and confidence that it's okay to be feeling what you are feeling. And I think maybe that is an antidote to shame. Confidence to feel what you are feeling, and curiosity to have a go at different things.

Yeah. That's great to hear. Uma, what happens when you peel off the shame, in that analogy, what's left underneath?

Uma -- Freedom.

Freedom, right. Yeah. Is that a natural state, as like babies say, is that what it would look like or is there an adult mature version of the freedom? Are they similar things?

Deej -- Freedom to place your awareness when you want your awareness to be. One thing Joseph says is, "freedom is the placement of awareness, the choice and the placement of awareness", and when shame is not there you've got a lot more freedom to put your awareness where you want it to be.

Uma -- But when people get to that place, they often talk about that place as being familiar. So I think it is very it's not unlike that child-like state, if we were fortunate enough to have a good childhood, good enough parenting and no trauma, it's very much like coming home to that state, only we are in an adult body. So we have that freedom and lack of judgement in a body and mind that has experience and agency. That's even better. So we know not to put our hand in the fire and we can actually get up and walk. Almost everybody that gets there, talks about a coming home. And that place is familiar. And they can often relate to their last memory of that, at a young age.

Deej -- As educators of adults we are intentionally trying to get them back to their toddler mindset in a way, like that place where they can just be curious and experimental and not evaluative, and not comparative, and not stuck in their perfectionism, so that they can get back to being clunky and having a go and seeing what it's like.

Which is subtly radical.

Deej -- It's subtly radical yeah!

Real guerilla culture changing gesture to say that people can have that experience. So much of culture seems to be oppressive, repressive, controlling about feelings experience and interactions, and there's so much loneliness and isolation and fear and drug addiction and suicide and violence. I think your suggestion that we can have that freedom is really radical. I think you two are radicals.

Uma -- Ooh I like that.

Deej -- I think we are, but we don't experience ourselves as that. I think we are so radical that we don't experience ourselves as radical, because it's simple I think, it's about this, what we are talking about, for us it feels simple. Pay attention, notice, discuss, be with, connect, but yeah it produces quite radical change in people.

I think you really focus on the safety, and when people feel safe, one to one or in a group, then there's a possibility of expansion and the exploration, without a reprimand or without being told how to be or how not to be. So you guys weave some magic to make that safety is my guess.

Uma -- We take a lot of time and care to create that safety in lots of different ways. And so whoever we facilitate for, we plan it very carefully as one of the biggest pieces, safety and education, and that's has really proven to be a really great system for us and for others. So if that means I have to create safety somatically, that it's not enough for me to say to people you are safe, it's not enough for me to sit them around in a circle and talk about their fear, I actually need to make them feel safe rather than telling them that they are safe; and how do we do that. So there's lots of different ways that we can do that and that time spent, you might spend a bit part of your allocated time creating that safety and not as big a part for the learning and certainly not a big part of us just blabbering on and on and on, but once you are safe, you don't actually need a lot of prompting to have a learning experience, you don't need a bit piece, you just need the freedom to lean whatever it is that you needed to learn, at that time. But we take a lot of care. It's not magic, it's actually a lot of hard work. Yeah. To create that.

Deej -- And one of the main things we try to get across to the people we teach, you know, plan, put lots of effort into it and focus on safety and connection and grounding first. Get people into their bodies, and get people feeling safe with each other before doing anything.

Yeah. I'm curious if you have a message for someone reading this book, if you could sum up or condense, distill your wisdom and your own learnings or your messages, what would you like to end this interview with?

Deej -- I think it's just something about – there's just so much potential and possibility in what we can feel and how we can support each other and be in our bodies and living vibrantly and erotically. We don't have to do massive things to do that, I think it's actually quite simple things, like paying attention and accepting what's there, can make a massive difference.

And in some ways, finding ways to do it together. Isolation doesn't help, trying to do the culture of the individual, doesn't particularly support all this, it's where do you go to meet healthy practitioners or go to meet out or go to groups or go to discussions, connect with other people, there's lots of people doing amazing things around.

MY SEX-POSITIVE JOURNEY
by Nekole Shapiro

I first heard the term *sex positive* in 2008. When I heard it, my ears perked up and something inside me felt like it was righting itself in that perfectly uncomfortable way. I knew I needed to do more investigating. What I did not know was that I would eventually become a sex-positive birth and sex educator.

At first, I just took the phrase at face value. *Sex is positive—of course sex is positive!* And, while that idea may sound simple, purposefully living in alignment with it as a belief quickly proved challenging. I came to see clearly how alarmingly sex negative our society is.

Not only does this make it difficult to live a sex-positive life, it also means we have to face off with our own enculturation and the unconscious patterning that comes with it. Beyond all that, when we understand that sex positivity is ultimately an extension of self-acceptance, we come to see how we have been hurt by sex negativity. To live sex positive is to address and counter all of this. It's just not as simple as enjoying sex.

The more I investigated, the more confused I became, because nearly everyone who talked to me about sex positivity was almost religiously polyamorous, kinky, and queer. Did you have to be poly, kinky, and queer to be sex positive? Couldn't vanilla, hetero, monogamous folks be sex positive too? My research taught me that this was due to the sex-positive movement being a result of work done primarily by members of the LGBTQAIU and kink communities.

Members of these communities—no longer willing to feel shame about who they are—have done the hard work of disavowing sex-negative norms that oppress them. They have communed, learned from one another, and spoken out often in the face of serious danger. To be sex positive is not only to believe that sex is positive, it also means joining a sociopolitical lineage of sexual reclamation spearheaded by those who have been oppressed for far too long by sex-negative societies. With this knowledge, it became clear that not only did I need to personally tend my sex positivity, I also needed to support and create public forums designed to increase sex positivity in my community.

All of this deepened my belief in the second-wave feminist assertion, "The personal is political." My personal work is incomplete if I am not also working to impact the political environment in which I live. Likewise, to focus purely on the external is to create unsustainable change. It was clear that I needed to regularly tend to both internal and external aspects of sex positivity.

I first focused my sex-positive work on birth. A local sex educator wanted me to take a class she was teaching called Clitoral Revelations. As she explained the contents of her workshop, I realized that I had birthed my first baby through an incredible network of tissue I DIDN'T EVEN KNOW I HAD! *How on earth could I have grown up in a massage school, done yoga since I was a child, attended an Ivy League women's college where I was PRE-MED, and somehow not known about the clitoral complex? How!?* The answer is simple: society is sex negative. Sex negativity keeps us from being fully educated about all things sexual and, because we're uneducated, we are more susceptible to abuse.

I became ravenous. I could not stop looking up materials on the anatomy of the pelvis and the clitoral complex. With each new bit of information, I remembered my first birth and could feel how my being shut off from my pelvic floor and clitoral complex kept me from fully embracing my birthing process. This awareness facilitated a powerful reclamation that allowed my second birth to occur at home and in water, which facilitated it being a fully ecstatic experience. I literally sang operatic arias as she slipped through my birth canal! I do not believe I could have realized this experience without having been introduced to sex positivity prior to her birth.

As I did this work for myself, I began to feel like I had discovered a secret that needed to be shared with others. *What would birthing outcomes be like if everyone could embody their pelvic floor and clitoral complex?* It became clear to me that it was time for me to step back from the world of academia and focus instead on following in my mother's footsteps. I needed to teach others how to embody birth as I had. It wasn't just that I had the information. It was that I knew how to use the information I had acquired to both free myself and leave room for my tissues to release to birth.

This is knowledge that has been passed down to me from countless teachers and cultures. My mother, desperately needing to recover from the impact of horrific abuse, has spent her life learning and sharing what she has learned. I lived at her feet, learning not only the tools, but also how to teach them every step of the way. At that point it felt as though the curriculum poured out of me, and Embodied Birth was born. I designed 100 hours of material that's meant to help anyone bring sex positivity to a birthing room. I've now been working with families and birth workers for close to a decade.

I also focus a lot of attention on raising my children to be sex positive. Again, I didn't think this would be terribly difficult since I grew up in a massage school in Hawaii. I really thought I was fairly sex positive already. Then my toddler grabbed my husband's penis. *WHA!?? OMG! WHAT DO WE DO!??* We didn't want to shame her, but *how should we talk to her about it?* Eventually, once we processed our own distress around what had happened, we were able to see clearly it was simply an issue of consent. We explained to her that Daddy was not comfortable with her grabbing his penis and then agreed to remind her of that boundary if she ever tried again.

Obviously, moments like these happened way more often than I had anticipated. I have since found near-daily opportunities to teach my children sex positivity. We discuss consent often, I teach them to love their bodies, model healthy relationships, discuss methods of communication, give anatomy lessons, discuss power dynamics, and so much more. I will say, it's incredibly rewarding to have conversations like the one we had the other day: "Kids, when you guys play like that it's really hard for me to tell if you actually want the game to stop or if you are just saying, 'No' as part of the game."

"Don't worry, Mom. We have a word we say when we really want it to stop."

As I worked with adults to bring about sex-positive birthing experiences, I kept running into more challenges than I had expected. I really thought I'd teach people the material, give them practices, and boom…they'd be on their way. But in reality, I would teach the material and their eyes would sort of glaze over. I'd give my clients exercises to work on at home and they wouldn't do them. What was going on?!

When I brought this struggle up to Allena Gabosch, she chuckled at my naiveté and said, "That's because of sexual shame." *What? Shame?! What are you talking about?* After explaining what she meant, I queried, "Boy, I wonder what birth outcomes would be like if there was no sexual shame!" Her response was clean and quick, "I don't know, but let's find out."

We started a monthly meeting with parents to brainstorm how to raise kids without sexual shame. This continued for five years. After numerous dynamic discussions, and a few sessions out of state, we eventually evolved that meeting into the community Facebook page Raising Kids Without Sexual Shame. We then spent a good year thinking about what we should do with all that we had learned from those community discussions. It was fairly clear that much of what was getting in the way of adults being able to talk to their children about sex in a positive way was that they just needed more time to talk about sex themselves. Most adults are so confused and distressed about sex that talking to children about it just seems impossible. We created a multilevel workshop series for adults on sex, intimacy, and relationships that is designed to foster community dialog in a sexual shame-free setting.

Doing all this work made it quite clear that not much was going to change if we didn't address trauma. So many people have experienced what can seem like an insurmountable amount of oppression and abuse around birth and sexuality. Sexual oppression and abuse in a sex-negative society has created a social climate in which isolation is rampant. Trying to remain functional, people lock their stories and the complicated emotions associated with them behind tightly-packed control patterns. We need dependable mechanisms to release this distress if we are ever going to create sustainable change for ourselves and our society.

Perpetuating sex positivity in our lives, and in society at large, demands that we heal our own trauma. Who knew that my recovery from PTSD following the September 11 terrorist attack would become highly applicable to the work I was doing around sexuality and birth? I certainly did not.

While I was creating Embodied Birth I attended a peer counseling course taught by a friend. I saw how I could adapt the curriculum, merging the peer support and embodiment work I had used to recover from my own PTSD to focus specifically on birth and sex. You can learn more about Holistic Peer Counseling by reading the textbook or by taking one of our correspondence courses online. For years now, we have fostered an online community that supports people through the emotional roller-coaster that comes with bringing increased consciousness to the topics of birth, sex, and anything else that comes up along the way.

And that's the short version of my sex-positive journey. That you are reading this suggests you are also on this journey. Expect it to be challenging and rewarding and know that many of us are here with you. When each of us decides to focus on bringing sex positivity to our lives and to the world around us, we make a huge step toward counteracting centuries of sex-negative influence. Good luck on your journey. May you too come to say what I say often: *life is never dull.*

TO LOVE FREE OF CHAINS
by Lasara Firefox

We start where we are now, the present moment. Two kids, both in stages of early adulthood. Their sexual orientations are nebulous for the most part, except that being open is a point of early negotiation. Consent plays a central role in conversations that make room for honest and transparent fumbling and snuggling without fears of being found in lies, without fears of breaking hearts.

Moving back in time, there are snapshots of how we raised our children with vocabularies that include words like nonmonogamy, polyamory, choice, and consent. It's been a long road. One that begins before I was even on it, so I give thanks to the trailblazers who went before.

In our younger years, with babes in arms and littles knee-high to a grasshopper, people asked, "But what do you tell the children?" We said, "Anything they want to know." People asked, "Aren't you afraid…?" of this thing or that thing, some specter that we didn't let into our home. We said, "No. We aren't afraid. And more importantly, we're unwilling to lie to our children—" even by omission. That which we don't tell resounds as strongly as what we choose to share. The way of our loving does not hide in darkness. It stands in the light.

Even the best times weren't always easy. Conflict wasn't hidden any more than devotion was because all of these are what build true relationship. Family. The extended family of loved ones tied together by both love and learning. We never said it was easy, love and commitment to family don't always mean staying together. The separation of the nuclear model—in as much as that model existed at all—was a challenge, but we kept loving. Because love is big enough to hold it all: pain, dissolution, transformation, reconfiguration. We came out of the divorce with new commitments in place. We've been true to them.

This redefinition of family is also part of open loving.

Having offered honesty to our children in their formative years, they now offer it back, asking questions, telling stories of clarity, confusion, and questioning: "My current flame is not sure about poly. But now he's interested. Can he borrow some books?" "My crush wants to be in an open relationship but doesn't know how to have the conversation with her boyfriend. I told her I'll help."

My older one leaves for college. "Mama, I'm lonely for cuddles. I miss having friends around who I sleep with." "It's ok, kiddo," I say. "This too shall pass."

Two weeks later; "So, that loneliness thing? It's over! I'm dating two boys and my other lover has moved here. And I just met a new guy! Now I'm overwhelmed. Can we talk about how to prioritize?"

As parents, we are not invested in our children identifying as open. We feel pleased and even proud that they choose to come to us with questions ask for support talk out relationship complexities. My heart blossoms seeing my older child organize her ways of loving, creating her own languages structures, adventures, indulging in experiments with more joy, less fear. More acceptance, less shame. This is perhaps the thing we can offer: handing our values down to our next generations, this integrated ease of knowing there are all kinds of ways to love.

Our children curl deftly into their own identities knowing that "open" may be an orientation like any other, that in our house, "queer" includes this arena of identity too. We have built this. Our children have fewer irrelevant threads tying them to outdated relationship expectations and they have more tools with which they may build the loving world closest to their own true expression.

In the most engaged cases, learning to love is not a one-way street. These young ones who I am humbled to have in my life continue the process of teaching and learning with me. We have always done this dance; they offer as much as they take in. Success is our proof. Our heart-lead experiments of trusting our children in their curiosity, trusting ourselves in our integrity, trusting one another in a foundational commitment to love, family, community, relationship in all its complexity.

The future we envisioned has arrived in the bodies and minds and spirits of these beings who came from us. Now we are honored by the gift of glimpses of the unfolding, which has already arrived: pansexuality; gender-rejectionism, and nonbinary expression; and loving in whatever ways feel right to the whole.

FIVE THINGS I LEARNED FROM TWELVE YEARS OF SEX-POSITIVE PODCASTING
by Cunning Minx

An accidental educator

This may sound odd, but I never set out to be a sex-positive or polyamorous educator. I simply happened to have some free time in the spring of 2005, when my poly then-boyfriend told me about RSS and podcasting. Since I had lost a prior long-term monogamous relationship to a lack of self-awareness and communication about needs (including sexual ones) and I had also been struggling with my first polyamorous relationship for the previous few years, I figured *why not podcast about polyamory?*

After all, our little polycule had already made a host of classic poly newbie blunders, and those might make good fodder for an internet radio show. Perhaps I could warn a few dozen people not to make the same mistakes I had, and I would move on to another project within a few months.

That turned out not to be the case. By the second episode of *Polyamory Weekly*, I already had a listener comment from AggieSez, who went on to literally write the book on solo poly a few years ago. I was shocked to see that hundreds of people had downloaded and listened to the first few episodes, even with the awful audio quality of those first few shows. The release of iTunes 4.9 in 2005, with its podcatching services, brought another boost to listenership numbers. I quickly learned that there was a dearth of online information about polyamory, and there was little that was as interactive as a podcast.

Imposter syndrome

Listeners began to write in and ask for advice, but there was a problem: I felt supremely unqualified to give any advice to anyone. I was still busy fucking up my own poly relationship; who on earth was I to give relationship advice to anyone else? I awkwardly skirted the issue by adopting a technique of listing questions listeners could ask themselves in order to decide what to do next, all the while claiming that "I don't give advice." Hello, imposter syndrome! I mean, I to this day have no training, education, or degree related to sex or counseling. I'm just a woman with a microphone.

But as the emails continued to pour in, I came to understand that there were poly-identified nonmonogamous folks all around the world, and many were isolated, alone, marginalized, and feeling that they were weird, wrong, weak, sinful, or worse for their proclivities. After the first year or two of podcasting, I realized that there was an opportunity here. People needed a safe space to hear and talk about what poly relationships are really like.

So I set out to shift the focus from telling stories of my own poly foibles to hosting a community resource. I wanted the podcast to be a place where anyone anywhere could come and feel safe, part of a like-minded community, and free to ask whatever questions or share any stories they liked. Being no sex or relationship expert, my goal was to be like the host of a great party and make sure that everyone felt welcome, got introduced around, were engaged in some great conversations, and went home fulfilled and happy.

I'm pretty damn proud to say that the podcast has accomplished that. The credit for that goes to the listeners, who called and wrote in with their questions, corrections, and suggestions for improvement.

Five things I learned

So, without further ado, these are the things that the awesome listener community taught me about how to be a great sex-positive educator:

1. Many voices are more powerful than one.

Being a sex-positive educator isn't about me. It's about being a resource for everyone. Sure, I have a personal poly journey that I can share, but what about those who don't hear their stories reflected in mine? To be fully inclusive means pushing outside my comfort zone and bringing on guests that have experiences far beyond my own, like those who self-identify as transgender, asexual, or disabled. We bring on people of color, millennials, septuagenarians, and sex workers. We even give monogamists a voice! Some are experts in their own right; others were simply friends and connections willing to share their stories. For the podcast to be a safe haven for everyone, everyone should be represented.

2. It's okay to be wrong.

If you've ever published anything on the internet, you're probably aware that there is a host of people out there eager to correct your mistakes the instant you make them. I've been called out a few times, and my attitude is generally one of gratitude that people took the time to do so. I mean, they could have just stopped listening; it's easy enough to do. Taking the time to write in with a correction means they care enough about me and the show that they want it to be better. Any sex-positive blogger or podcaster will tell you that feedback is a treasure; don't waste it!

Philosophically, I hate to miss the opportunity to learn from others. It's not like I know everything just because I have a name, a blog, and a podcast. In fact, one of the reasons the podcast became more inclusive is because listeners wrote in and asked for the spotlight to shine on their subculture for a bit. In fact, one of the best characteristics of a good sex educator is curiosity: we should all be willing and eager to explore unknown worlds in our own backyards and convey our findings to the public as accurately as possible.

I'll never forget one of the first truth bombs a listener laid on me after an episode discussing the male view in porn. My impression had been that men created and watched porn while women, I dunno, read romance novels? This erroneous belief was dashed by a single reader email, "Fanfic," she wrote in, "check it out. You're a Buffy fan, right?" And so I discovered that people (mostly women) had been writing fantasy erotica (mostly male-on-male) about popular TV and movie characters for AGES!

3. There is nothing unique about polyamory.

That may sound odd from someone who has been spending every minute of her nights and weekends speaking, writing, and teaching about polyamory for the last twelve years, but it's true. Absolutely nothing I teach is unique to poly; everything is applicable to creating and nurturing healthy communication in relationships of any kind. In fact, our very first listener survey revealed that over 50% of our listenership self-identifies as monogamous! Self-awareness, courageous communication, shit-owning, compassion, and vulnerability are handy tools for addressing a wide range of relationship and sexual challenges.

4. There is no substitute for a live community.

As a podcaster, it's easy to hide behind the microphone and limit interactions to email or social media messages. But, as I always advise on the show, there is no substitute for engaging with your real, flesh-and-blood poly community to help you through the tough bits. We all need to spend time in meet space with like-minded folks to share our stories and renew our spirits.

It has been a privilege and an honor to go to events all over the world and meet poly folks at everything from BDSM conventions to science fiction events to poly conferences. In fact, one of the most rewarding aspects of being a sex-positive podcaster is having the opportunity to sit down with poly people and hear their stories one-on-one. Just as we say that it's hard to be successfully poly in isolation, it's hard to be a good podcaster without spending time with and in your community.

5. Vulnerability is powerful.

When I taught podcasting classes, I taught that an important element of podcasting is finding your voice. And by that, I didn't mean the literal sound of one's voice; I meant the presence and persona you as the podcast host put forth into the world.

Podcasters are often asked how much of their personal life they share on their shows, and the answers may vary, depending on the topic. But everyone agrees that to be effective, you must share at least a little of yourself. You must be willing to be vulnerable. Yes, the voice on the internet is a persona, but that persona is and should be the real you. While it's okay to keep some things private, I strongly believe that the more of your authentic self you can share, the better your show will be for your listeners—and the more it will give back to you. And no, I don't mean just those best and happiest moments that we share in snapshots on social media. I mean the vulnerable moments as well: those moments when we are wrong, discouraged, or heartbroken.

I have shared much of my personal life with listeners, from a heartbreaking breakup to my transition to solo poly to coming out to my family to leaving my job. After my first poly relationship imploded, I had to wait three months to talk about it on the podcast, because I couldn't even consider what I'd lost without bursting into tears on the spot. I tried telling that story over and over on mic—but I kept ending up weeping bitterly. When I finally mustered the courage to speak about the breakup on mic, "vulnerable" didn't begin to describe how I felt. But I shared what I could, including the pursuant loneliness and self-doubts, questioning if I was still "really poly"—or was I just dating around like a regular single gal?

Vulnerability is hard, in both our relationships and in our work, but I wholeheartedly believe that the more we can embrace it, the more powerful we become—both as people and as sex-positive activists. Sharing the real you is powerful.

When people ask me about starting a podcast, I usually advise against it—unless you want to never have free time on nights and weekends ever again, I say! But the truth is that I've gained far more from my accidental part-time career as a sex-positive educator than I ever knew was possible. Not only have I learned more about sex, relationships, tolerance, compassion, and the world that I ever thought possible, I've also been able to meet some amazing people along the way. It's true that podcasting is a more intimate medium than just writing or even teaching; I feel connected to everyone who has ever written in to the show or said hello at a conference. In the end, I'm simultaneously humbled by and proud of what we have created together.

So, to future sex-positive educators and podcasters, I'll change my usual advice and say yes, do it. Do the thing. Podcast your passion. It will take you to amazing places and change you for the better.

SEX-POSITIVE PARENTING
by Taryn de Vere

Remember in Sleeping Beauty when the three fairies bestow their gifts on the newborn princess? Imagine if the fairies had the choice of gifting repression, shame, and guilt or self-love, knowledge, and delight. Which would you prefer they gave your child?

Without knowing it, many parents pass on the same lessons that they received; by doing this, many parents pass on sexual shame, guilt, repression, and self-loathing.

Sex-positive parenting is motivated by a desire to raise children to see their bodies and sexuality as a normal and healthy part of the human experience. I think most parents would want their children to feel self-love, take joy from their own bodies and, later in life, perhaps joy in other people's bodies as well. Sex is a normal part of the human experience. We all have the capacity to give ourselves and others pleasure, yet these are subjects that are rarely discussed between parents and their children, and this silence creates a sense of taboo and shame around the subject of sex.

As a sex-positive parent I try to be honest, open, and upfront with my children about sexual subjects. I have to be careful in how I talk to my children at times, not because I wish to deny them knowledge, but because we live in a world that would be alarmed by a five-year-old talking about masturbation. I have to fight against a world that is designed to socialize my children into feeling shame for their biology.

Consent comes first

Teaching children about consent is the first lesson in sex-positive parenting; it begins with babies who can understand *no*. We teach consent by showing children how to understand and respect other people's boundaries while also being aware of their own. If your goal is to teach your child that only they have control of their bodies, you will have to respect their *no* as well—consent cuts both ways. If every parent was doing this work I believe we would have an almost sexual-violence-free world.

As children grow older the consent learning deepens in subtlety. We teach them to look at the body language of the people around them: do they look comfortable? Do they look happy? What are the power dynamics at play? Could this person be uncomfortable to tell you they are uncomfortable? The interactions in question will be in the context of children playing, not sexual activities of course, but they still form the basis of a good understanding of consent, empathy, and awareness of the many ways a person can say no. This learning and skill set is invaluable for keeping your child safe. It gives them language and awareness around what society deems appropriate and inappropriate and also makes it much less likely that they will perpetrate sexual coercion or violence themselves.

Teach by example

I believe most of parenting is role modeling, as children learn by watching what we do, not by what we say. So, in order to parent in a sex-positive way, we need to first become sex positive ourselves. This growth and learning is a lifelong project, but as we learn, so do our children. For most of us, we are learning with our children, learning as we go along. It's better to try, mess up, and apologize than it is to not try at all.

Use the right language

Knowledge is power and teaching children about their own bodies is vital to the process of creating a self-aware, self-loving person. How can we love ourselves if there are parts of our bodies that we aren't allowed to even know the right name for? Calling all body parts by their correct names from the start helps to destigmatize genitals and sex. Doing so without conveying your own discomfort would be even better, but it is preferable to use the right words, realize you've conveyed some shame, and apologize to your child than it is to never try—so keep trying. We're all humans learning, and our kids are thankfully very forgiving of us.

Tackle difficult conversations with courage

Being a sex-positive parent requires courage. It means having lots of potentially difficult conversations with your children. Age appropriate discussion can and should be had with children about sex, body autonomy, sexuality, abuse, power, patriarchy, sexual health, contraception, masturbation, objectification of women and girls, consent, abortion, media portrayals sex and self-love, porn, critical thinking, and self-awareness. Some parents are afraid to broach these subjects for fear of saying the wrong thing. There are numerous studies to show that children who have talked with their parents about sexual matters tend to become sexually active later than those who don't, and they also are more likely to use condoms and birth control than those whose parents haven't talked to them. Talking to our kids about sex and related subjects makes them safer.

Teach critical thinking

An oft overlooked, but in my view essential, component of sex-positive parenting is the teaching of critical thinking skills. Once a child is taught to analyze the world around them, they are capable of seeing through the harmful messages of shame and stigma that much of the media encourages. I like to ask lots of questions to build their critical thinking skills. "What do you notice about the bodies of all the women on this TV show?" "Why do you think they are all the one body type?" "What messages do you think this show is trying to teach you about women?" etc. Kids are remarkably astute, and once they have the language they can see right through the media and advertisers attempts to give them negative messages about their own and other people's bodies.

Celebrate all kinds of bodies

A final tool I offer is to acknowledge and celebrate the various types of the human form in front of your children, declaring each one beautiful. We're bombarded with images of the "ideal" way to look and so few people's physical appearance match that image. The more you can do to reinforce the beauty that can be found in the variety of human appearance the better.

As a parent, my goal for my kids is that they will be full of self-love and free of sexual shame or repression. If they choose it for themselves, I wish for them wonderful, consensual, fulfilling sex lives. Imagine a world where everyone felt comfortable in their bodies, where they're at ease with their sexuality and sexual selves, where the word vulva is met with the same reaction as the word knee. Luckily for us, we don't need magical fairy godmothers to bestow that on us, we can create that world though sex-positive parenting.

EXTENDING KNOWLEDGE AND SOLVING PROBLEMS: THE CREATION OF THE JOURNAL OF POSITIVE SEXUALITY

by D J Williams, Idaho State University and the Center for Positive Sexuality (Los Angeles)
Emily E. Prior, Center for Positive Sexuality (Los Angeles)

Introduction

There is little doubt that, despite the ubiquity of sex, American society remains generally sex negative. Compared to other western democracies, the United States has lagged behind in protecting the rights of LGBT persons; acknowledging the legitimacy of safe, freely chosen sex work; recognizing and accepting diverse consensual sexual practices and alternative relationship styles; and addressing occurrences of sexual violence in a humane fashion. A sex-negative culture, of course, allows myths about sexuality and sexual behavior to develop and proliferate, while impeding progress toward effective solutions.

The Journal of Positive Sexuality (JPS) emerged as a creative response to a pressing social need. Like many sexuality experts, we recognized years ago that while scholarship on human sexuality was advancing quite quickly, the practical application of such knowledge, at least in the United States, remained stagnant. We realized that a longstanding, pervasive general culture of sex negativity has much to do with the stagnancy of practical progress. While the topic of human sexuality has received considerable attention from multiple disciplines and has led to important new knowledge that could improve policy development and direct practice in the helping professions, much of US policy and professional practice remains rooted in sex-negative myths. This is not to say that sex positivity is abundant in academia; it is not. Much of academia remains reluctant, at best, in welcoming creative scholarship on sexuality. However, based on recent multidisciplinary scholarship, sex positivity, or a positive sexuality approach, is capable of helping to resolve diverse sociosexual issues and problems.

Addressing a need

In assessing the state of knowledge and its application in the field of human sexuality, we realized several key issues that seem to prevent sociosexual progress:

Academics study sexuality from different disciplines and methodological approaches, thus there is a need for more integration and cross-disciplinary understanding;

>a. Most scholarly resources (academic journals) are inaccessible to policymakers and helping professionals;

>b. Much academic and professional discourse on sexuality focuses exclusively on risk, while ignoring sexual pleasure, well-being, and sexual empowerment; and

>c. Many journals, especially in the humanities and social and behavioral sciences, publish longer articles, which nonacademics do not have time to read.

We were also familiar with innovative publication strategies designed to address similar issues in other disciplines. For example, the American Sociological Association publishes a peer-reviewed journal, Contexts, which features well-written, nontechnical articles that are appealing to a nonacademic audience. The *Journal of Gambling Issues* (JGI) is a respected online publication that offers high quality, peer-reviewed research articles to both academics and professionals who focus on gaming and gambling behaviors. We also liked the online, peer-reviewed *Brief Addiction Science Information Source* (BASIS) journals, published by the Cambridge Health Alliance. *BASIS* papers include large, original, quantitative studies summarized succinctly in only two or three pages. *Contexts, JGI,* and *BASIS* are each peer-reviewed, while the latter two are fully available via the internet without monetary charge to authors or readers. In the field of human sexuality, we have greatly appreciated the *Electronic Journal of Human Sexuality* (EJHS), which published full-length research articles. However, although *EJHS* articles remain accessible online, it discontinued publication in early 2015. Given the above issues that prevent the production and application of knowledge in the field of human sexuality, while also following the lead of innovative peer-reviewed publications noted, we created the *JPS* in February 2015.

JPS Aim, scope, and purpose

JPS is an online peer-reviewed academic journal that focuses on all aspects of positive sexuality as described by Williams, Thomas, Prior, and Walters in the first issue of the journal. Specifically, positive sexuality acknowledges the importance of sexual diversity; the multitude of sexual identities, orientations, and practices; the need for open and safe communication and education concerning all aspects of sexuality; empowerment of sexual minorities; and collaboration to help resolve sexual problems within society. Positive sexuality is consistent with the World Health Organization definition of sexual health.

The journal is multidisciplinary and is designed to be accessible and beneficial to a diverse worldwide readership, including academics, policymakers, clinicians, educators, and students. It invites original submissions from diverse epistemological and methodological approaches on any topic that explicitly pertains to positive sexuality. A full range of qualitative and quantitative methods is acceptable.

The primary purpose of *JPS* is to share current empirical, theoretical, and practical research about positive sexuality and its implications across academic disciplines and to various practitioners, students, and interested people. Occasionally, *JPS* publishes full-length articles; however, shorter articles that are reader-friendly (not too technical) are the preferred way that this purpose is accomplished. *JPS* currently publishes three issues a year.

Early success

By 2016, the second year of publication, over 12,000 file downloads (articles being downloaded/viewed) have been recorded. Not only are articles being downloaded in the United States, *JPS* has been accessed by readers from over 100 countries have accessed *JPS*, including Germany, European Union, Spain, Canada, Australia, the Czech Republic, Romania, Ukraine, the Russian Federation, and Turkey. Although some of these countries match or surpass the United States in sex-positive scholarship, others are "behind the curve." We seem to be reaching a large worldwide audience. We have learned that several professors are utilizing the journal in their classrooms, encouraging students to read these easily consumable articles as a part of their regular coursework. As *JPS* became established, the Center for Positive Sexuality (as publisher) reached out to the National Coalition for Sexual Freedom (NCSF) and the Community-Academic Consortium for Research on Alternative Sexualities (CARAS) in an effort to increase collaboration and support between the three organizations. Subsequently, *JPS* is the official publication of CPS, NCSF, and CARAS. We appreciate the efforts and support of these and other organizations that facilitate positive sexuality research, education, and practice in various forms.

Conclusion: Into the future

We are pleased with the development and early success of *JPS*. We appreciate the work and support offered by our outstanding editorial board, members of our collaborative organizations, and the many individuals who read and promote *JPS*. Because sex negativity remains so entrenched in western society, we hope that the number of readers, contributors, and supporters continues to increase well into the future. We need to reach far more policymakers, educators, and helping professionals. By making sex-positive knowledge more accessible and understandable, perhaps our society can move forward in effectively resolving a variety of serious sociosexual problems.

Further reading:

Williams, D J, Christensen, M. C., and Capous-Desyllas, M.. "Social work practice and sexuality: Applying a positive sexuality model to enhance diversity and resolve problems" *Families in Society 97*, no. 4 (January 2016) 287-294.

Williams, D J, Prior, E. E., and Wegner, J.. "Resolving social problems associated with sexuality: Can a "sex-positive" approach help?" *Social Work 58*, no. 3 (July 2013) 273-276.

Williams, D J, Thomas, J. N., Prior, E. E., and Walters, W. Introducing a multidisciplinary framework of positive sexuality," *Journal of Positive Sexuality 1*, (February 2015) 6-11.

Williams, D J, Thomas, J. N., and Prior, E. E. "Moving full-speed ahead in the wrong direction? A critical examination of U.S. sex-offender policy from a positive sexuality model," *Critical Criminology 23*, no. 3 (February 2015) 277-294.

Authors' note:

We would like to thank the editors for their support of *JPS* and for the opportunity to contribute to Sex Positive Now.

CHAPTER 8
RELATIONSHIPS

Sex Positivity is about celebrating all relationship structures from monogamy to polyamory and in between.

TEN TIPS FOR FULFILLING RELATIONSHIPS (OF ALL TYPES!)

by Eri Kardos

Relationships, as you probably already know, are complicated. Have you ever stopped and thought, "Hey, there must be a way to feel super connected to my loved one(s) all the time?" As a coach who helps people feel more connected, I work with people around the globe to help them navigate their relationships and explore new ways of creating meaningful intimacy. People come to me because they are tired of trying to fit the mold of "find your Disney prince/princess and ride off into the sunset for happily ever after." They want to experience REAL love in real life!

The book you are holding is filled with amazing information about sex-positive culture. You may already be deeply involved in this culture, or perhaps you picked this up to learn more about it. Either way, learning tools that have been developed within this community can help with you navigate any type of relationship. Whether you are single, partnered, monogamous, polyamorous, confused, or curious, there is so much to explore and learn. One of the greatest tools I have found for building intimacy and opening space for vulnerability is *intentional connection*.

Here are ten tips (many of which stem from the sex-positive communities of kink and polyamory) that will help you build intentional connection and create fulfilling relationships, no matter what structure you choose.

1. Know yourself

Most of my clients feel this first step is cheesy, until they DO it and then bask in the connection and joy that it creates in their relationships! Before you engage in any relationship, take some time to reflect on what you want from the experience, both as an individual and as a relationship partner. Where are you in your personal growth journey? What is your intention for this connection(s)? What needs, desires, and boundaries do you have? What demons might pop out of your closet when life gets intense? What do you need for self-care along the way so that you do not lose connection with yourself? Ultimately, you are the only one responsible for your own pleasure, safety, and growth.

Takeaway

This is YOUR love story and you get to write the script—so what do you want to create?

2. Communicate clearly

Once you've taken inventory of the desires and boundaries of your heart, mind, body, and soul, it is time to share them with your partner(s). If you are not feeling confident in your ability to voice them, try journaling and sharing via email or in a letter. Discuss the hopes and desires of all parties involved to reduce surprises and set you up for fulfillment. What are each of your hopes and fears for this relationship? Walk through hypothetical situations and allow yourselves to talk about the scary topics—it may prevent harmful events in the future. Ask yourselves, for example, what if an unbelievable career opportunity arises in a different state? Or, how will you handle finances in this relationship? Or, how might you handle romantic feelings for another person? Take inventory of your relationship. Are there any unresolved issues you haven't brought up with your partner(s)? Is something bothering you that you that has not been addressed yet? The idea that your partner can read your mind might sound sexy, but this is highly unlikely and can set you up for unmet expectations.

Takeaway

In the end it is sexier and easier to navigate the complexities of deep connection and love when everyone communicates clearly and is on exactly the same page.

3. Let go of assumptions and expectations

Even as you're contemplating your desires and intentions for a relationship, having specific expectations can lead to feeling unfulfilled. Instead, consider thinking of your relationship as a journey that you're traveling together—you may have a destination in mind, but you may also miss something delightful along the way if you rigidly stick to a predetermined path. Similarly, if you make assumptions about your partner, you may be missing wonderful things they can offer you that you never even considered.

Takeaway

Know where you want to go with your partner(s) and allow yourself to be surprised by the path you take on your way there.

4. Set boundaries and make agreements.

Before you head off on a grand new relationship adventure, take some time to talk about language use. How will you describe your relationship and boundaries to others? Do these labels mean the same thing to you both, or are there nuances you might need to clarify before you go? There is power in language—use it carefully. What agreements and boundaries might you need for this relationship? Sexual boundaries? Emotional boundaries? Spiritual boundaries? Think through your individual needs and consider making requests of one another. Deciding on a plan ahead of time and staying open to the idea of renegotiation allows for more comfort and ease in the dynamic. I strongly suggest creating a relationship agreement, with the understanding that it will change as you, your partner(s), and your relationship evolve. For more detailed information on how to create one, please check out my book, *Relationship Agreements: A Simple and Effective Guide for Strengthening Communication, Reducing Conflict, and Increasing Intimacy to Design Your Ideal Relationship*.

Takeaway

Creating your own relationship agreement will guide you through tough times and the good times and help you to experience your relationship like you never imagined.

5. Explore dealing with jealousy.

Jealousy can be successfully navigated with a few learned skills. Kathy Labriola, author of *The Jealousy Workbook*, likens jealousy to a smoke alarm. It can be a helpful tool for alerting you to potential danger, informing you that it's time to check whether your relationship is actually on fire or whether it is just a false alarm. With practice, you can calibrate this tool so it doesn't go off every time you metaphorically burn a slice of toast, but does sound the alarm when there is an actual fire. Sadly, most of us don't use it as a tool. We assume that when the alarm goes off there is always danger, whereas underlying fears of abandonment or being replaced are usually at play. When your partner has time and space to listen to your emotions, reactions, and fears, be sure to share them. Action is not always needed—just being heard often quiets the frightened inner voices of jealousy.

Takeaway

Jealousy can be a good thing—especially if you use it as a tool!

6. Care for yourself

One of the best ways you can take care of a relationship is by taking care of yourself. Life is often filled with intense experiences and highs and lows—how will you process them? Journaling, drawing, meditating, dancing, and doing yoga may all be helpful, and talking with others who are in similar situations may help as well. Make sure to create space and support for yourself so you can process and refresh.

Takeaway

If you don't take care of yourself, you won't be able to take care of your relationship—especially when it needs your presence and support.

7. Care for your partner

Once you have taken care of yourself, turn your attention to your partner(s). Do they need anything specific to feel secure and fulfilled in the relationship, whether it's words, a massage, or something else? Check in with them regularly about their desires and energy levels. Consider learning about Gary Chapman's *5 Love Languages* so that you can care for them in a way that will resonate with them.

Creating a secret signal for telling your partner(s) that you love them can be a fun idea for strengthening your bond. Maybe a squeeze on the back of the neck, drawing a heart on the lower back, or using a sign that can be seen across the room. This can come in handy when you are in really loud or silent places and can't express your love verbally. Be bold and break the mold—create fun rituals and experiences together that are off the beaten path!

Takeaway

If you want to experience a connected partnership, get creative in the ways you express that connection to each other, like creating your own secret codes.

8. Use your calendar

We've already noted that relationships are complicated, and this can extend to scheduling too. Use your calendar and spend time intentionally making space for everyone involved. Remember that relationships are rarely just a matter of bodily sensations—they usually involve the hearts of people who deserve time, compassion, and respect. I suggest setting up a regular date night and determining ahead of time who will be the "Date Night Driver," alternating who is in charge of planning the adventure. This way you get to have the experiences you both want, including having time blocked off but unplanned for those who like spontaneity but have a hard time aligning time with their partner's schedule.

Takeaway

Scheduling time can actually lead to more spontaneity in your relationship—you'd be surprised!

9. Educate yourself

If you want to create a relationship that continues to grow over time and become more sexy, more passionate, and more connected, then it is imperative that you continue to learn more about ways of relating! With so many wonderful resources out there on more traditional and alternative relationship styles, kink/BDSM, open relationships, safer sex, conflict resolution, and jealousy, you can easily find information from a variety of sources and in a way that appeals to your specific learning style.

To learn more about sex and relationships, you could schedule time with a professional coach; check out your local dungeon or sex store for classes; pick up books that address relationships (A short list of books to get you started includes *Opening Up* by Tristan Taormino, *More Than Two* by Eve Rickert and Franklin Veaux, and *The Ethical Slut* by Dossie Easton and Janet Hardy); reach out to the different sex-positive communities via FetLife and other social networking sites; or check out the plethora of online resources including podcasts, websites, videos, and forums.

Whether you are monogamous (or –ish), single, or in an open relationship, make time to brush up on safer-sex education before you connect with more than one sexual partner or switch to a new monogamous partner. Get tested for STIs (Sexually Transmitted Infections), understand your results, and share them honestly with your partners. If having "the talk" is difficult for you, search online for Reid Mihalko's "Safer-Sex Elevator Speech" (it's even in video form) and practice until it becomes easy. Learn how different STIs are transmitted, think about what impact they might have on your life, and decide on your comfort level with sexual risk. STIs are often accompanied by social shaming, and it is time that we respond with compassion and educated questions instead of fear and shunning.

Takeaway

Your relationship can only be as much as you know, and there are so many ways to explore methods of connecting beyond what we see on TV or in the movies.

10. Stimulate your "in love" brain parts

Want to fall in love all over again? Researchers have found that when people in relationship do something that is new, exciting, and challenging for all parties involved, it stimulates the same areas of the brain that are activated when we are falling in love. Your dopamine levels rise and those rose-colored glasses appear again, even if you've been together for ages. So shake things up and embrace experiences that are new, exciting, and challenging for you! Luckily, the sex-positive world is all about curiosity and exploration. Welcome to the community!

Takeaway

Whatever relationship structure and feelings toward sex and sexuality you choose, you're welcome in the sex-positive community. The tools developed within this culture can lead you to keep growing and keep falling in love with your partner, your relationship, and yourself!

SWITCHING SPEEDS
by Kevin Patterson

So, a friend of mine asked me about my nonmonogamy.

Really, he's more of an acquaintance. A friend of a friend. A bro-y cisgender, heterosexual, black guy. Just like me. While helping our friend-in-common move apartments, he decided to ask me about the juicy details of my polyamorous life.

Do you know that part in *Harry Potter and the Order of the Phoenix* where Dumbledore's Army is meeting for the first time? In an effort to elect Harry as leader, the other students start rattling off his achievements from the previous four books as proof that he's the right person for the job. But for Harry, this isn't an awesome highlight reel. It's his life. He doesn't look at it as an exciting retrospective on an action-packed journey. He sees it, accurately, as a list of all the times when he had to make hard and fast decisions or face the most dire of consequences.

That's the kind of space I found myself in. This acquaintance, through the storytelling of our mutual friend and from brief glimpses on social media, knows about my nonmonogamy as a series of risqué stories. Granted, I can definitely relay a few not-safe-for-work tales about wild nights and adult activities that would be unacceptable within a strictly monogamous relationship, but that's not the lens through which I view my own life.

So, instead I turned on the analogy machine and told him my polyamory was like baseball. Pausing to let him conjure images of bases collected and dingers knocked out the park, I moved over to talking about pitching. A pitcher at any level of organized baseball knows that you can't just hurl the ball the same way at every batter. You can't even pitch the same way to the same batter if the game's circumstances have changed during or in between at-bats. Multiple situations require multiple strategies.

As it comes to polyamory, a different approach is necessary with every partner you're involved with. In many cases, switching between different authentic aspects of your personality multiple times in short-shift is absolutely necessary. You may need to be the calming presence for a partner who is anxious about changes at their job. You may need to be a cheerleader for a partner who is undertaking a brand-new project. You may need to be a provider of racy banter for a partner who is eagerly anticipating a hot date with you or someone else. And just to shake it up, you may spend your lunch switching chat windows on your smartphone so you can be all of those people over the course of your hour-long break.

Not only do you have to remember who to be, polyamory also requires remembering who your partners are. Meaning, you have to stay on top of which partner prefers to drive versus which partner prefers to relax in the passenger seat. One of your partners loves chocolate. One of them is allergic to the corn syrup that's often found in chocolate. Should I remember to open doors and walk on the outside of the sidewalk? Or should I remember that chivalry is an outdated concept that infantilizes women?

At the same time, it's not just who you are for your partners' sakes but who they are for yours. I can say unequivocally that every person I date engages me in a different way, which makes perfect sense when you don't view people as interchangeable warm bodies in wild sex fantasies. Even more important than that is the fact that each partner draws from me a unique but authentic aspect of my being, like a multicolored pen. All ten colors are in the barrel, but each partner presses down a different lever.

One person in my life might encourage my ambitious side. All of a sudden, the projects that I'm a part of might see more attention. Another love might bolster the activist within me. She might invite me to protests or social justice initiatives that I might have been otherwise unaware of. Dating an educator might find me delivering my usual long-winded diatribes, but instead of being on a couch at a party amongst my closest friends, I'd be presenting them as a workshop at an academic conference. All of these are things that I had the capacity or interest in doing, but maybe need the proper push to follow through with.

Along with all of this switching speeds, you also have to give yourself room to hit the brakes. As multifaceted as polyamory may require you to be, you still need to be able to opt out and find time for self-care or introspection when you need to. That may mean going fishing or meditating or getting some exercise, but whatever it is you owe it to your partners and to yourself to be able to focus on what you need to maintain your personal wellness. At the same time, your partners owe it to you to give you adequate space for that maintenance.

But nobody wants to hear about all that. Certainly not the acquaintance that was asking the questions. He didn't think I'd start talking about how often I juggle emotional labor. Bringing up how my partners stir underdeveloped or underutilized aspects of my personality pretty much ended the conversation.

There's nothing sexy about emotional literacy or calendar management or taking time to process your feelings before having deep discussions with people you love. But all of that stuff that would also benefit monogamy, that stuff that nonmonogamy absolutely thrives on? It's booooorrrrrinng! Sometimes it's sometimes boring to live that stuff out, and it's definitely boring to listen to. Therein lies the problem: the representation problem.

No monogamous person with an interest wants to hear that a polyamorous relationship can be as uneventful or as tedious as their own. They want lurid accounts of threesomes, foursomes, and moresomes. That's why our media appearances, created by monocentric sources, are often so slanted toward that end. Even critics of polyamory focus their barbs on the ideas of sexual health and fidelity. It's all anyone on the outside thinks about.

So, we have to ask ourselves why are we looking to cater to their perspective in the first place? Why would we allow ourselves to be the freakshow in a monogamous human circus? Cunning Minx of the *Polyamory Weekly* podcast ends every episode with the catchphrase: "Remember...it's not all about the sex." But that podcast is an informational resource for those who are practicing or interested in polyamory. It's not entertainment fodder for people whose only real questions are "Who's sleeping with who and how?"

So, how do we alter that representation? We use our own voices to tell our own stories. We give the boring relationship stuff as much exposure as the sexy stuff. We make sure to remember our audience. That new poly-interested person who's trying to find their own way needs to hear about navigating shared Google calendars more than they need to hear about a play party. They can then use their new Google Calendar skills to organize their own play parties—which they subsequently refuse to talk about with their own monogamous acquaintances.

CLAIMING YOUR POWER WITH NO
by Kris Lovestone

"Can you take out the garbage?" my mother asked. Although phrased as a question, it was really a demand in disguise. I didn't actually have the option to say *no*, and I knew it. I grew up with this being the norm. Everywhere around me, whether at home and at school, we children were taught that we had to do what we were told, not make waves, take care of other people's feelings, and always be nice.

We were literally trained to be docile and conform. We were squeezed and shoved into a culture of inauthenticity where we couldn't show our true authentic desires, couldn't stand up for ourselves, and most definitely could not say no. This fostered an understanding, a belief inside me, that I literally did not have the freedom or permission to be who I really was inside, even though I lived "in the land of the free." I had to be what was expected of me and fit the cultural norms regardless of my true authentic uniqueness.

As an adult, I carried this erroneous belief pattern with me as I dove into relationships and sexuality. I would say yes to everything asked of me because I didn't know that I could say no. I had never known anyone who did it. I was polite. I wanted to never give anyone any reason not to like me, and my relationships were destined for failure from the start because my partners could never really know who I was inside.

Not knowing how to say no prevents us from defining and demonstrating who we are. Saying no is the means by which we carve out a distinct and unique self by demonstrating what we will and will not accept, what is and is not okay to do with us, and what our limits and preferences are.

Giving yourself permission to say no is a radical act, a gift that you give to yourself—a gift that no one else has authority to grant you. Learning to wield the power of no is nothing less than a revolutionary act in a person's life, in which they take the power to mold their life into their own hands.

In the face of oppression, abuse, and marginalization, seizing the power to say no can be a life-changing event. Learning to say no in this way is standing up for yourself against exploitation, and the more you exercise your capacity to say no the more you train yourself to be able to do it. Like a muscle that you exercise to develop, your "no muscle" gets stronger the more you use it.

Only when a person has the ability to say no, and have their no received and honored, is there a possibility for them to settle into the freedom to be their authentic sexual self. Only when a person can say no powerfully can others trust that their yes is actually meaningful—for when a person cannot say no their yes is meaningless.

These days many people subscribe to the belief that saying yes to everything is a spiritual practice, but I call bullshit. Saying yes to everything just empowers the dominant cultural norm of conformity at the expense of your life's uniqueness and your true authentic desires. Only by learning to say no can you truly come to know who you are and what you truly want. Only then can you have a chance to build the life of your dreams. Saying no is the gateway to knowing yourself and being true to yourself. Once you can say no, people know who you really are and can have a relationship with a real person, rather than a cultural clone that is still charging the matrix.

I strongly believe the successful path forward for our world requires harmony in relationships, and that comes from relationships of equals rather than ones of dominance and oppression. Learning to wield the power of no levels the playing field by taking your own power out of other people's hands. It offers inspiration to other people because you become a role model of authenticity, transparency, integrity, and courage.

Only when we all can say no powerfully is a sex-positive world possible, a world where we can be free to be the sexual beings that we actually are in an atmosphere of consensual sexuality.

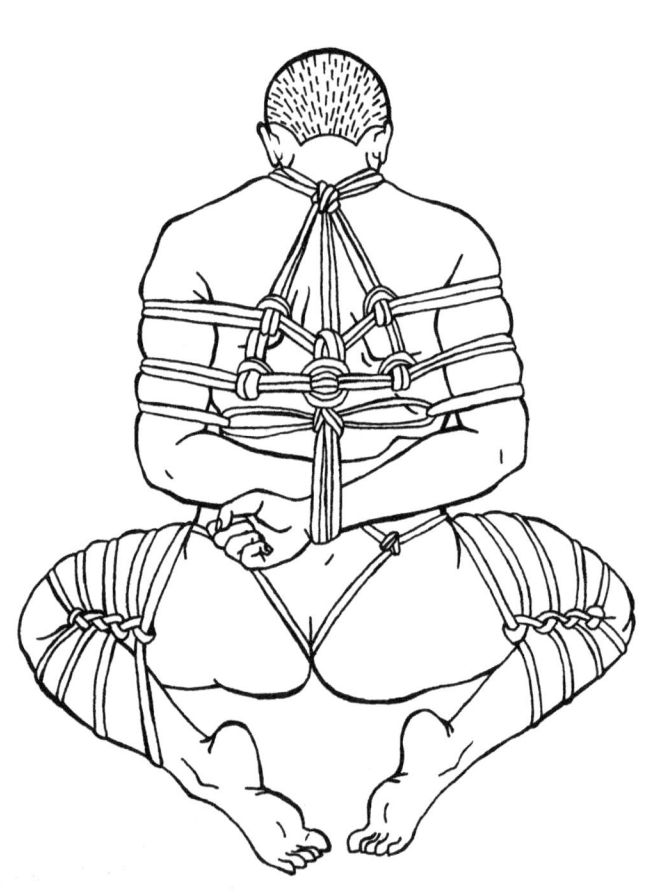

CHAPTER 9
KINK

Many people conflate BDSM and Kink with things like the 50 Shades of Grey. In reality consensual BDSM is life affirming and sex positive.

SPINNING THE WHEEL OF DESTINY
by Patricia and Mark

For us, sex positivity has been a way of transcending preconceptions, received wisdom, and shame. We have grown, both individually and as a couple, because our sex-positive approach has enabled us to explore and has opened us up to new possibilities. Sometimes this practice of conscious sexual exploration and adventuring has required us to see ourselves in new and different ways and to be open to unrecognized sources of pleasure. This is especially true in the realm of kink and BDSM, which were considered marginal and even pathological when we were growing up.

In recent years, kink has become more mainstream as both fashion and as an acceptable form of sexual expression. This is due in part to the internet, which has provided easy access to information that was unimaginable just a few decades ago—but kink can still seem strange and a little scary to those who are unfamiliar with it.

Even before we met, we both had a deep curiosity about sex and had visited BDSM clubs, though as outsiders with very little knowledge. Sometimes, the experiences were erotic; sometimes they were not. Sometimes people in the scene displayed an enthusiasm that came across as a kind of zeal, an effort to convert that was a little unnerving; though our reactions probably had more to do with our anxieties and preconceptions than with the reality of what was taking place.

Our background is in Tantra, and one aspect of that tradition can involve the conscious and intentional violation of taboos, including sexual taboos. We've sought to apply that aspect of Tantra to our own lives. At the same time, Tantra (especially in its westernized form) involves spiritualized sex and maintaining an attitude of worship for one's partner.

In 2005, we decided to attend Dark Odyssey, a pansexual event that includes play parties and an array of classes and workshops. We agreed treat our attendance as a Tantric experiment, with the specific intention of expanding our sexual horizons and growing as individuals.

Nevertheless, we were extremely nervous about going. For our own peace of mind, and against the recommendation of the event organizers, we reserved a hotel room off-site, in case things got too intense or overwhelming. We stayed in our hotel room for reasons of physical, rather than emotional, comfort. The experiment worked. The event opened us to new and unexpected understandings of ourselves and sexuality in general. On opening night, we attended a mixer that featured a carnival-type wheel known as The Wheel of Destiny. Instead of prizes, each pie slice on the wheel referenced a kinky activity—from fellating a strap-on wearing clown to fire play. Participants were invited to spend three minutes experiencing whatever destiny the wheel prescribed. It was an offer that we couldn't refuse. Nevertheless, we approached the wheel with considerable trepidation. Here are our stories:

Patricia's story

I thought, "What the heck, I can do anything for three minutes" and nervously took my place in line. Everyone was having a great time, and many were dressed to the nines. I was marveling, taking it all in, and before I knew it, it was my turn. I approached the wheel feeling a little (okay more than a little) nervous! I gave it a good spin. The clicking sound it made as it rotated reminded me of the sound of a clipped playing card on my childhood banana bike as I rode around the neighborhood.

The writing on the wheel was a blur, the letters gradually coming into focus as the wheel slowed. Click . . . click . . . click. I started reading what was actually written on each segment. Click. . . click. . . click. There was still one word that I couldn't quite make out, and sure enough, that's where the wheel stopped. Once it did, I was finally able to decipher the word, "Punching." No wonder I had trouble reading the word in the first place, but now I was even more confused. "Punching? What?"

I walked over to my station and was met by a stunning woman dressed in an equally stunning, sexy black gown. I introduced myself, and said in a feeble voice, "This is my first experience with anything, I mean anything!" She reassured me that she would go very slowly.

For the readers who are not familiar with this particular activity, punching is not like Rock 'Em Sock 'Em Robots (at least it doesn't have to be). It is a form of impact play, and when done well the punches resonate deeply within the body of the receiver, and there's no stinging sensation on the surface of the skin.

My station mistress began giving me light but firm blows to my upper arms, chest, and back. I closed my eyes and breathed with each rhythmic thud. My body started to sway. I must have been receiving the blows fairly well; she delivered the next one using her entire forearm across my chest. Boom!

And what a boom it was. I felt launched into another dimension, diving into a sensation, an emotion, an overall body experience that I couldn't name. I gasped, wide-eyed, looking deeply into her eyes. She gently asked if I was okay, "Would you like me to continue?" I took in another deep breath and said, "Um, I think I need to take in this in for a moment." I turned to leave and felt her fingers knitting around mine. She said, "Before you go, I want to show you one more thing." I said, "Okay" And stepped back up to her station.

"Bend over," she commanded. I did as I was told and felt her palm plant firmly on my left buttock. "This is your left side." The next blow landed on my right buttock, "Here is your right, but here is your sweet spot." I felt her hand landing firmly and directly right in the center of my butt. An orgasmic jolt shot from my genitals up directly through my head. "Ooooo!!!"

In just three minutes, I went from being a Tantra teacher—who had a narrow definition of how loving partners should act—to being a Tantra teacher who enjoys impact play. Who knew!

Mark's story

I followed Patricia and stepped up to the wheel. I spun, round and round and round it goes, and where it stops . . . caning! Some experienced players were standing around, and they chuckled. Someone said, "You're in trouble," but I was past the point of no return and couldn't back out.

I went to the station, where a petite, slender woman with an array of canes awaited me. She asked me to drop my pants and bend over a sawhorse. She started hitting my buttocks softly with the cane. The blows were not hard, but I could feel the sting.

She alternated between delivering these stinging blows and gently caressing my skin, producing a surprising interplay between the impact of the cane and the soft caresses. I went into an altered state of consciousness, a kind of trance, within the first minute and remained there for the duration. When I got to my feet and pulled up my pants I was a little unsteady, as if mildly intoxicated.

The experience was not a turn-on for me, but I discovered one of the reasons that some forms of BDSM can be so powerful and recognized that BDSM and Tantra have more in common than I imagined. Both approaches are body centered, and both involve inducing altered states of consciousness through physical experience. Contrary to some of my previous misconceptions about BDSM, I saw that, when done consciously, intentionally, and even reverently, the potential for profound exchanges of energy with a partner is always there.

When it comes to BDSM, I am probably more vanilla than Patricia, but after this event, I had to contend with the fact that she enjoys impact play. I grew up with seventies-era feminism, and the idea of hitting a woman was not okay, not ever. But she wanted me to. This was a very, very hard obstacle to overcome. But overcome it I did.

The first step involved getting instruction from skilled practitioners—spanking lessons and a flogging workshop. The next step was mental. Eventually, I was able to tap into the fact that it's pleasurable for her and get turned on by that.

The final step was the most challenging, since it involved a shift in my self-image. My inhibition went deeper than any concerns about consensual hitting. It was hard for me to see myself as dominant or to admit that playing a dominant role is a turn-on. Recognizing and embracing this as part of who I am seems much healthier than trying to pretend otherwise. It makes me more fully human and gives me access to pleasures that I would otherwise have denied myself.

Our experience at Dark Odyssey was inspiring, and the sense of community among the attendees was strong. In the aftermath, we were inspired to do some community building of our own. With that in mind, we co-founded Pleasure Salon, a monthly gathering for sex-positive people in the New York area. The event has been running for over eleven years. Though we've passed the torch to a new generation of organizers, we remain convinced that building sex-positive community and face-to-face social networks is radical and necessary, now more than ever.

SEX IN THE DUNGEON (YES, REALLY)
by Janet W. Hardy

(This article appeared previously at www.leatherati.com.)

My friend P has not had sex with me—just ask him. But I've had sex with him.

No, this isn't one of those "the doctor said, 'I can't operate on this boy—he's my son!'" thought problems. It's just a matter of how you define sex. (For one of us, sticking an electrified dildo into someone's cunt doesn't count; for the other, it does.)

And that's what makes being a sex writer such fun and such a challenge: nobody in the world has come up with what I consider an adequate definition of sex. I sure haven't. The first time I attended a Tantra class and found out that I could orgasm from the right kind of breath with maybe a little eye gazing and nongenital touching, I realized that I don't have the first idea where sex begins or ends.

I've noticed that a fairly reliable marker of a newbie, though, is the claim that "BDSM/leather isn't about sex." It's certainly true that you can attend a great many play parties, particularly in the hetero/pan community, without ever seeing anybody's slippery bits making contact with anyone else's. If your definition of sex is the usual, mundane orifice-and-genital combination with the occasional tricky bit of handwork thrown in, then, yeah, you can probably do kink for a long time, maybe a lifetime, without having sex.

But if you use a grander definition—sex as all the things that rev us up, turn us on, make us hard or wet in anticipation or memory, change our consciousness out of intellect and into primal gimme-that desire—then I contend that it is impossible, or at least a very bad idea, to exclude sex from the dungeon. I've never heard a player with a double-digit number of years in the scene claim that "BDSM/leather isn't about sex" (unless perhaps they're trying to wangle a playdate out of someone who doesn't find them sexually attractive).

Ever gotten yourself off thinking about power or pain or helplessness, then tried to replicate the fantasy during your actual play? Sex. Used flashes of sensation and sight and smell and taste from your last playdate to feed your thoughts during everyday masturbation or penetration? Sex. Touched your partner during play and felt your whole body light up and the top of your head open and a convulsion ripple through your body from the chewy center right out to the fingernails and pinky toes? Sex.

At least as far as I'm concerned.

And I think it's a *terrible* idea to pretend that sex isn't at the heart of what we do. Without sex, kink can all too easily turn into engineering, one step away from Pavlov's experiments or Lego constructions. Sex helps us remember that the individual on the other side of the ropes or paddles or commands is a *person*— a person we care about, a person whose feelings matter, a person to whom we're entrusting our tenderest and most vulnerable feelings.

Because sex is, at its heart, about vulnerability. Not just the physical vulnerability of genital exposure or of penetration, although that's certainly a part of some kinds of sex. Sex is about the vulnerability of being seen at our rawest and least guarded. Arousal divests us of our normal protections, leaves us wide open and terrified. What is scarier than letting ourselves be seen when we're all turned on, and then discovering that the person who turned us on doesn't reciprocate our arousal? Nobody looks, or is, tough at the moment of orgasm: it's the most unprotected state a human can experience during waking consciousness.

I wonder, sometimes, if the "BDSM/leather isn't about sex" falsehood isn't, at its origin, about tops and dominants who are terrified of their own vulnerability—who wear their leathers as armor (against rejection, against criticism, against the possibility of being wrong). By denying the existence of their own soft underbellies, they use kink as a refuge from their insecurities. The resulting scenes are cold and unconnected and unfeeling, but, hey, the doms have gotten through another day without feeling small, and that's what kink is all about, right?

(Note: Bottoms and subs who insist that their tops be impervious, invulnerable, or superhuman—and who withdraw support at the least sign of anything real or flawed—are as much at fault as tops and doms who insist on pretending to be that person. There's more than enough blame to go around here.)

I sought out the kink communities many years ago in search of intensity so profound that, for the duration of play, all normal ego protection was shed like an old dead skin, in favor of something fresher, realer, rawer. Those are the fantasies that got me off for many years before I ever put my hand on the ivory plastic Fuller hairbrush that was the first toy I ever used on a human being. They turned me on more than any mundane friction of mucous membranes ever could. They still do.

Some fifteen or twenty years ago, I walked through the dungeon at a major national conference. It looked like a kinky K-Mart: rows of St. Andrew's Crosses lined up like products on a shelf, more rows of massage tables, more rows of spanking horses—as regimented and cold as a military cemetery. On each cross or table or horse was a human being. Behind them stood rows of other human beings, wielding floggers or canes or singletails, whirring in lines, like a wind farm. And, yeah, I know you can't always tell from the outside what's going on between two people in a scene, but as I walked through that dungeon, I looked in vain for anything that looked like love. Or, failing that, connection. Or, failing that, sex. Hell, I'd have accepted even *bad* sex.

And I didn't see any of it.

And that was the moment—although I didn't realize it at the time—that I began withdrawing from the public scene. As soon as I got home, I let it be known that I was no longer interested in teaching any class that was about physical technique. (Have you ever thought about the fact that the out-of-town speaker who taught that hot flogging workshop you attended probably met their demo model half an hour before the class began? What does that tell you about the value our scene is placing on intimacy and connection?) I began questioning the ego-driven part of my personality, and I blush to tell you that it's not a small one, that was prioritizing showing off for an audience over making connection with my partner. If that was sex, it was an ugly kind of sex and I didn't want to be part of it anymore, and if it wasn't sex, it was even uglier, a way of using my partners and my audience to get my own ego ya-yas off. Yuck.

So when we let the contention that "BDSM/leather isn't about sex" go unchallenged, that's the mentality we promote: that disconnected, inhuman manipulation of nerve endings and cultural memes. And it sure isn't what I came here to get.

We're not stuck with it, though.

Want to fight back? Want to achieve for real those juicy, intimate, raw, terrifying fantasies that you thought were an impossibility? Then quit playing with people you wouldn't fuck. Quit showing off for audiences—this isn't performance art, it's sex. Quit trying to do tricky techniques just because they're cool and weird and something nobody's ever done before—the only judge holding up a scorecard is your partner, and if you and your partner go flying together that scorecard says ten, whether the scene was a hand-spanking or a scrotal inflation. (I personally doubt that anybody's ever gone flying during as baroque and fussy and technique-y a scene as a scrotal inflation, but I'm willing to be wrong on that.) Don't pick up a single clothespin, or let one be applied to your body, unless you're willing to be as transparent and vulnerable and open hearted as you're capable of being.

Because no matter how you play or who you play with, that's your best self. Your realest self. Your sexiest self.

And you, and your partners, and the scene as a whole, deserve nothing less.

INTIMACY AND THE D/S RELATIONSHIP
by Jay Wiseman

When vanilla people and/or newbies ask me about BDSM, I often reply that BDSM has three main subdivisions:

1. Anything having to do with restraint of movement, such as bondage, locking someone is a cage, and so forth;

2. Anything having to do with other-than-common erotic stimulation, such as floggers, clamps, electricity, and so forth;

3. D/s dynamics, such as collars, submissive/slave positions, contracts, and so forth.

No emotional rapport is required to do bondage. For example, I teach a lot of bondage classes, and it is very common for me to tie someone up that I have met for the first time right before the start of the presentation. No emotional rapport is required to administration sensation. I've attended any number of presentations on flogging, whipping, and so forth in which the presenter met their demo bottom for the first time right before the start of the presentation.

As for D/s relationships, I find those very difficult to stay in unless my submissive/slave and I have a really high degree of emotional (and intellectual) rapport. There is a school of thought that says that there should be little to no rapport between a dominant and their submissive, that it's better to keep them at arm's length so as to better preserve the nature of the D/s relationship. I suppose that works for some people (pretty much anything works for at least some people), it certainly doesn't work for me, nor does it seem to work for the overwhelming majority of people in D/s relationships that I have met during my decades in the scene.

I have been in three D/s relationships that lasted two years or longer, and in all three cases we fell in love with each other. It was my repeated experience that such love did not negatively affect our D/s dynamic at all. In fact, it's fair to say that our romantic love enhanced our D/s relationship.

I will note that some submissives/slaves do not want an intimate personal relationship with a deep emotional rapport. They want to be objectified, dehumanized, made less-than, and so forth. For example, one submissive I had wanted to be kept as a pet, and one does not have heart-to-heart conversations with one's pet. While our BDSM play went really well, our non-BDSM time together was very frustrating for both of us. I was looking for a girlfriend and a slave, she was looking for a Master but not a boyfriend. The relationship didn't last long.

I consider D/s to be the most intimate type of BDSM, and if it is attempted without intimacy, great distress can ensue. In his excellent book, *People Skills*, psychologist Robert Bolton observes that "proximity without intimacy is inevitably destructive." My experience in D/s relationships is entirely consistent with his statement.

If one person would act as a dominant toward another person, it is important to make a brutally accurate assessment of oneself to see if one has the emotional strength and stability to be such a dominant. If your own personal life is something of a wreck, then it's likely not a good time for you to take control of a substantial amount of another person's life.

For example, some years back I met a lady at a munch in November and we seemed to have an almost instant rapport. (This is not unusual among people who end up in D/s relationships. I know a woman who said, "I took one look at him and knew that he was my Master"—and she was indeed correct.) However, at the time we met, she was committed to another dominant until February and I was trying to cope with a recent and highly traumatic breakup. No way did I, at that time, have the emotional strength and stability to be a dominant toward anybody. We did, however, keep in touch and by the time February arrived I was feeling much stronger and much more stable. I was once again in a position to be someone's dominant. We entered into a D/s relationship that lasted for years.

In many ways, a D/s relationship is comparable to ice cubes of water in a glass with the submissive being the ice cubes and the dominant being the glass. The implicit, and sometimes explicit, promise of the dominant to the submissive is that it's safe for the submissive to melt from being ice cubes to being liquid water, to surrender some of their boundaries, because the Dominant will contain them within the Dominant's boundaries. The dominant will extend their force field, so to speak, out far enough to contain the submissive within it. The dominant may swirl the melted submissive around a bit, or possibly put a cap on the glass and shake them up, but all of this will take place within the boundaries established by the dominant—the glass.

It can be disastrous to enter into a D/s relationship if both parties are not fully psychologically ready. I've known a number of cases in which a would-be Dominant wanted a submissive to deeply surrender to them, right down to the submissive being told what to wear, what to eat, how to wear their hair, and so forth. When these "dominants" finally got into such a relationship, they found that they were not psychologically ready to assume such a role and bolted from the relationship. The result was that the submissive, to return to the glass/water analogy, splattered all over the floor and was heavily traumatized. To be somebody's dominant is not a trivial thing.

It's essential for the dominant to provide a (forgive the cliché) safe space for the submissive. If the submissive does not feel welcome and safe when they kneel at their dominant's feet, then their D/s relationship needs some serious work. This work may take many forms such as seeing a BDSM-knowledgeable therapist, attending support group meetings for dominants or submissives, taking part in online discussions, and so forth. Let me observe that a responsible dominant in a functional D/s relationship will likely have little to no problem with their submissive attending a support group for submissives. If they do have a problem with that then that is, at the least, a yellow flag regarding the relationship.

There is a D/s discussion group that meets monthly here in San Francisco that is open to both dominants and submissives, and I have attended many, many of their meetings over the years. Highly aware, highly experienced people, many of whom are in quite healthy, very functional relationships attend. There is a very great deal of useful knowledge and wisdom in that group. If something similar does not exist near you, then perhaps you can start one.

The D/s relationship has its emotionally vulnerable aspect, not only is the submissive emotionally vulnerable to the dominant, but the dominant is also emotionally vulnerable to the submissive. Indeed, if a D/s relationship ends badly, the dominant is often more traumatized than the submissive. Because of this vulnerability, it is essential to build and maintain a high level of trust. People who are not trusting pretty much never end up in D/s relationships that last for any significant amount of time. As for building this level of trust, I read a line in a novel one time that contained a level of trust that I really like: Trust is the residue of kept agreements.

If you make an agreement with your D/s partner it is very important that you keep that agreement in both letter and spirit. This particularly applies to dominants who have agreed to refrain from doing or attempting to do certain things. For example, if a dominant agrees to refrain from attempting anal sex with the submissive, and then spontaneously, with no prior discussion or agreement tries to anally penetrate them, then the overall relationship may be heavily damaged, quite possibly to the point of destroying the relationship. Discussions can be, and are, commonly held regarding changing or removing a relationship agreement, but until both parties fully understand and agree that the relationship agreement has been changed or removed, the agreement stands.

In summary, I have been in D/s relationships that had a low degree of intimacy, and I have been in D/s relationships that had a high degree of intimacy. The former were troubled, didn't last long, and often ended badly. The latter were relatively untroubled, tended to last a long time, and while there was some pain when they ended, it was usually a clean pain with no residual trauma on either end. Indeed, I think the essence of an intimate D/s relationship can be summed up with this quote from a former slave of mine: "I love you, Master."

WHEN YOUR EROTIC IDENTITY IS DAMAGED
by Race Bannon

This essay originally appeared on my blog and was so universally well received that I felt inclusion in this book would be useful. Countless readers told me that they related strongly to the situation I found myself in. By not detailing the specifics of my own erotic identity challenges, I believe I allowed the reader to role reverse more fully with me, inserting their own unique challenges in place of mine. Thus, my story became their story. I hope you find it equally helpful because I think whether one is kinky, or simply closely bonded to some form of erotic identity, we all encounter scenarios with our sexualities where our erotic foundations feel threatened. May what you're about to read provide some solace should you find yourself in a similar state.

There is an assumption that there are certain people so confident in their sexuality and erotic identities that nothing can challenge those aspects of their lives. Nothing could be further from the truth. I am living proof.

This isn't easy to talk about. Our society, as well as our sexual and kink subcultures, worship at the altar of confidence and certainty. Most of our kink scene is shrouded in a veneer of iconic bravado and unwavering certainty. Such solidity adds to the fantasy for many because their kink and erotic identity is founded upon such things. In a scene replete with rigid hierarchical rankings and deified roles and positions, it's no wonder that any crack in that armor risks the entire enterprise.

Cracks happen though. The armor of our sexuality is often in truth nothing more than a thin covering easily pierced by something as random as someone's casual negative comment, or as monumental as a life-altering bad experience or situation.

I'm not going to rehash exactly what happened to me. I don't often air my own life's inner workings in public, at least not in print. But please accept as true that a few years ago a series of life happenstance challenged my sexuality and erotic identity to its very core, and those challenges reverberate throughout my life even today. It's been a long slog to recovery and that process is still unfolding as I write this.

Since I was in my early teens, even prior to my fully coming out at the age of seventeen, certain types of sex and power dynamic play formed the foundation of my sexuality to such an extent that it eventually morphed into an identity. What I did erotically not only formed sexual fantasies and practices, but it also formed an identity that has generally served me quite well.

Realizing in my youth that I was an erotic rebel, a sexual maverick, coupled with my then newfound realization I was indeed gay, created for me a bedrock from which the entirety of the rest of my life naturally flowed and flourished. I was a gay leatherman. I was a devoutly kinky adventurer. I had found that version of myself that fit like an outrageously comfortable glove. I had found a set of communities that accepted and celebrated those aspects of me. I had found me and my people.

While my various social interactions and work took me to all walks of life and endeavors, it was my gay kink identity from which I always operated, whether that identity was evident in all situations or not. No matter where I was or what I was doing, inside of me resided a gay leatherman and kinkster who took solace in that self-identification. In short, it made me happy.

Fast-forward from my early teen years to a few years ago. In one fell swoop, a series of unexpected conflicts and between a rock-and-a-hard-place situations occurred and my entire erotic identity crumbled. My sexuality was damaged. I was shattered. I was supremely unhappy. Life sucked because my foundation had given way beneath me and I wasn't sure how to rebuild it.

Did most people know this? No. A few close friends did. A handful of my leather and kink network did. But generally, most people saw the same old me writing, speaking, organizing, advocating, and educating. Few suspected that underneath it all I was suffering badly and feeling like everything was going to shit.

Why am I telling you this?

Perhaps in part this is cathartic. Sometimes opening a window of transparency allows a breeze of relief to wash over us.

Or perhaps my main motivation is to instill in everyone reading this a bit more understanding that even the most apparently solid of people can be shaken and pushed off balance. I see the nasty barbs or accusations thrown around at leather and kink folk on social media and I cringe because I know those words might be crushing someone on the other end of them.

Or perhaps I simply want people to realize that when someone looks "just fine," they might not really be fine. Underneath they might be hurting like hell and covering it all up with a persona of confidence and solidity that belies their hurt but that their friends and audience have come to expect from them.

So, what have a I learned from all this? A lot. About myself. About life. About sex and the sexual subcultures in which I mingle and thrive.

I've learned that, first and foremost, I must be me. My relationships are important. The people around me are important. My communities are important. But ultimately, if I can't be truly me, if I can't fully maintain the identity that brings me strength, then I'm of no good to anyone. Anything I say, do, or advocate for would be coming from a false pretense if said by someone not living up their own sense of optimal and best self. Living a lie is a terrible idea.

I've learned that it doesn't always take much to crush someone mentally or emotionally. It can take just a few words. It can happen in an instant. And that instant can end up forming a life crisis far bigger than might seem possible upon reflection on that brief life-altering moment. I hope people realize this when they say some of the things they say, especially in this era of the social media broadcast effect when harsh words can distribute through the social ether like a strong putrid wind.

I've learned that when your erotic identity is challenged, you deal with it or it will eat away at you and taint everything in your life, sexual and otherwise. To not deal with it is to doom yourself to deep unhappiness, and I say this as I myself am continuing to struggle. But my struggle has gone from daily depression to more of a nagging reminder that if I falter from being myself and living the life I need to lead I will plunge myself into a depth of despair that I do not need to enter. I've become a lot stronger.

Let me wrap up this post by asking something of you.

Please, do some introspection around your own sexuality and erotic identity. Are you living up to the potential that will make you happiest? Are you eschewing outside rules and constructs when they collide with what you know will make you happiest? Are you consciously configuring your life to create a sexuality, an identity, your sense of being as a human, that brings you the greatest joy and satisfaction?

The answers to those questions will hopefully either validate an already strong sexuality and erotic identity or propel you to improve them to align with what makes you happiest.

I ask those questions of myself every day now. My erotic self and indeed every aspect of me is a lot stronger today than it's ever been, but I still tread on a walkway populated by a mine field of doubts and challenges. That is sometimes the human condition. It's only by facing it head on that any of us can improve ourselves and our lives.

Be yourself. Be your authentic self. Be the self, erotically and otherwise, that brings you the greatest happiness because doing any less is short changing yourself in ways you might not even realize.

Be happy. Sexually. Erotically. Every way. Just be happy.

CHAPTER 10
SPIRITUALITY

For many sex positivity is strongly connected to our spiritual selves.

SPIRITUALITY AND SEX
Interview by Jeremy Shub with Kenneth Ray Stubbs

This is a highly edited version of the interview. If you would like to read the full interview go to our website www.sexpositivenow.com)

Maybe you can tell me a bit about yourself and if you have a connection to sex positive or if that expressions means something to you, or just how you see sexuality

Ray--Moving to San Francisco in '73 and started teaching erotic massage in '75 so I got to know a number of people there who were really into open sexuality and exploring. I found a number of people who were doing services out there in the world receiving money which included sexuality, and they were really at home with their sexuality and at home with their spirituality and carrying on with spiritual tradition. And I thought – because my life seemed like, in many ways, it had been about re-integration, spirituality and sexuality – but when I realised that concept to people, it seemed like it was going in one ear and out the other.

I was born in Southern Baptist; the spirit is good of God and the flesh is inherently evil. That is a paradigm, a cultural belief that I grew up with and I had to come to … it was so prevalent, I had to come to the perspective that it doesn't seem right to me and I began to explore a bit more, which is much easier to do in university in the hippie days.

I'd gotten to know a number of people who were doing sexual services for money and were very very spiritual, and so I thought their stories would convey my idea more clearly than my just harping on in an abstract way. So, I got together nine different women that I knew - I chose to focus on women only although there would be men that fit into that category as well - who were doing sexuality-type things for which they were receiving money and they were still so spiritually aware. I asked them to write their stories and what they did, how did they step into doing that and some of their spiritual/religious points of view.

Many of them, when I asked them personally, what had influenced them, a number of them had said the book by Nancy Qualls-Corbet, a Jungian psychologist, a book entitled 'The Sacred Prostitute'. So I read that book … I ended up, that first book, that anthology … of these nine women and it was my introduction to them because I knew each one personally, framing it from the perspective of the goddess literature of the time.

About … go back to the ancient days where the goddess in the temple would do sexual things and it would be a healing process and so forth … so that was how sexuality and what we might now call fertility religions and religions that embrace sexuality were more prevalent before Christianity became such a dominant voice … the male priests in Judaism became the authority over the female and then of course we had Islam come in with such a male focus but before that there was another book, 'When God was a Woman', by artist historian, Merlin Stone.

I frame this perspective of sacred prostitute from the goddess literature which was popular back then, this book came out in 1995. There again I began to feel there was real limitation to some of the concepts in that book. One, popular Goddess literature was a revision of history, in a way that, while it was very good to hear, it was also, I think … too limiting in certain ways and it sort of reversed … the male God was the top and now it was reversed, it was a female Goddess that was on top. We are still stuck and bound in opposition, one or the other, and I thought that was too much limitation which was predominant tone really in Goddess literature of the '80s and '90s.

It came out with this documentary … anyway … the book 'Women of The Light', I subtitled 'The New Sacred Prostitute' because that was the term, a choice of the time, in the literature, in sexological literature and in popular literature as well, pretty much, it's not the only term.

I felt one, that I wanted to step beyond the goddess literature perspectives that I was hearing so strongly and two, because I began to hear from a number of sex workers, they didn't like the term 'Sacred Prostitute' because it implied, they thought, that the sex worker was inferior and the sacred prostitute was superior somehow, that there was this class distinction so to speak.

I want to find some term that did not have an implication of maybe that if you didn't work in the temple that you were not as together or not as meaningful. If you were working at the bar, that was not as good as working at the temple, so to speak.

I wanted to look at that again so I did this documentary called 'The Sacred Prostitute', that was the name of the documentary. In the documentary I started to use this term 'Sexual Shaman' because … what I felt was is what the way that people were believing what the ancient sacred prostitute was able to do, it was not due to just having sex or having sex in a ceremonial way, it was due to whatever extent possible, maybe, that the energetics of the practitioner, in this case The Priestess or a Priest, was able to do energetically, which was …

The concept that made sense to me was, 'The Shaman'. Of course, the Shaman means many different things in different cultures. The word came into my mind, 'sexual shaman', there was the alliteration, sexual shaman, I could now … while later on I found it had been used by a few people, it had never really been established, so not to coin the term but to bring out the term and characterise it in a way that I wanted to could convey what I think is really happening so that to the extent that going to a sexual practitioner maybe more transformative was due to not just to having a few extra oral techniques or anal massage techniques, it was what the practitioner was able to do energetically that was unseen, which is what exactly makes a person a Shaman.

A shaman is still an external form and that's important but over time I began to realise, being in different ceremonies with different traditional shamans, that what made them effective and different than some other healers, was what was being done that was unseen. I could go into a lot of explaining about that would take us beyond the focus of what we are talking about here I think … unless you want me to go into some it …

So, the words, 'Sexual Shaman' just sort of like 'oh yeah, here's a different term, I can characterise it' and I think it really connotes more accurately what was really going on and what people were describing in terms of what they thought was happening with the Sacred Prostitute. I found a term that worked with me ... I eventually came out with second documentary called 'The Path of The Sexual Shaman', which went into the energetics more of Shamanism as well as sexuality.

We're looking at sex positive. I was trying to find language that did not put down anybody, find the concept that began to look at sexuality in a different way and at that point we had in western sexology, we had looking at sexual dysfunction using at certain techniques and the main thing that Masters and Johnson brought in the picture was somatic techniques where before that it was just psychological, psychotherapy techniques.

Masters & Johnson with their 'sensate focus exercises' were finally bringing in the body and then there were people like myself and Joseph Kramer and other people that were going much much more in the body. To teaching erotic massage and his sex body work for example because I think, when it comes to sexuality, that a lot more can be released and opened up if you don't try to go and interpret it and analyse it ... you just go directly to the body, in some cases, much more will be opened up. That's not to say there's no value for talk therapy because there really is, but talk therapy only, in relating to some situations around sexuality, I think is way too limiting.

What I was finding after I had my neck injury in 1991 and became a quadriplegic, I could no longer do somatic and I wasn't a talk therapist, I did seminars but I was definitely not a talk therapist, didn't train to and I didn't want to be one. I began to find through my own meditations and studying different shamanic traditions as well as Buddhism, certain types of Buddhism, not all Buddhism, not all Buddhism, I have to express that certain types of Buddhism are quite sex negative, Theravadas Buddhism is really sex negative ...

I was integrating what I was learning in Shamanism, was happening in western sexology, being in San Francisco with all the sexual freedom and people exploring so much and I began to realise that you can look at sexuality from an energetic point of view.

In Shamanism for example because I had a neck injury I could not go into a sweat lodge because is really hot because it would kill me literally as my body cannot regulate temperature. So what I would do in a sweat lodge ceremony is that I would sit outside the sweat lodge. I was outside the sweat lodge, I mean and listen from the outside and participate as best as I could. So what I was trying to do at that time is energetically to focus my energy on the inside where the energy dynamics of the people were taking place, as well as what was happening with the hot rocks and the heat and the fire and the steam. I had to get my energies, not with a somatic but from farther, exterior from my physical surface of my organism.

Also given the nature of my body function and given I'm up in Arizona and given that we started opening up on Skype and internet connection, 5,000 miles away, it sort of lent itself to started doing energetic connection with people both either physically in the room or at a great deal of distance.

I did a lot of meditation for like guidance I was getting was to every night to go outside for an hour and look into the desert sky and find a star up there then focus on it pretending to be one with any life form and any of the planets in that star that solar system, I don't know if anything happened. It was a practice I did for about an hour or 30 minutes I did for nine months this was a shamanic practice I was doing. I considered it a shamanic practice.

Then I started focusing in on human beings at a distance because sometimes tune into being one with them to vibrate like them, not to do anything to them, not to try to turn them, just to vibrate just as they were vibrating, I would feel this energetic intimacy that I was only used to feeling post-orgasmically lying beside a lover. It was very very similar, oh it's similar.

Over-simplifying a lot of this to give you the idea, I began to realise that it was possible to mate energetically, in a very intimate way so it not need to be sexual or erotic. If it was sexual and erotic it was, but if it wasn't then it wasn't. It felt good, the vibration felt good regardless of whether it was sexual and erotic or not, take what you got and enjoy it. It was feeling it was feeling good. Or going to a power spot and interacting with the earth or a crystal. I had a really powerful experience with a crystal once. It was two feet away from me I wasn't physically touching it, it wasn't near my genitals although I could, that was not the way I was using it. It had a real powerful … it was not erotic but it was on the nature of orgasmic sometimes an explosion and sometimes just a hummmmm

Because of my physicality and what I was doing over a number of years in different context, energetically focusing across space that I began to develop some abilities to vibrate like other people or other physical situations such as an earth being at a power spot or a tree or a rock and getting into that vibration of what I call Oneness which is my language, you would call merging … that given my physicality. It was not easy to do coital sex, being quadriplegic, it was a lot of hassle I won't go into details just a lot of hassle.

I found I could do it energetically even at a distance of 5,000 miles away and it was so much easier and it was different but in some ways just as satisfying, not the same thing satisfying. So after a while, sexuality, spirituality and energy all blended together because it was about being with the whole person not just their clitoris or their penis or their sexual desire.

It all began to evolve that way but if I had not been quadriplegic and had to try to get my energies inside the sweat lodge, that may not ever have happened because the physicality of touching someone. I taught erotic massage so I touched someone and there was an energetically dance going on in there. An energetic dance but still based in the somatic because I still had contact.

My two hands … for me, sex was about lovemaking my hands primarily, the genitals were secondary, except for a few minutes (laughter). I'm over simplifying it but if I can't make love with my hands it wasn't as satisfying. I wasn't interested in just fucking … most of the time. I don't mean to say fucking in the negative way, just moving.

 I could get more satisfaction by tuning into the person energetically and it may take me even further in terms of longer extended orgasms and or orgasmic experiences.

Masters & Johnson did a great service for us by looking at the physiological aspects of orgasms but in the process of doing that threw out a lot of other things that were so relevant to orgasms so a lot of other experiences that are orgasmic was thrown out because it didn't have the pelvic floor contractions. It both deepen our knowledge about sexuality, what Masters & Johnson did with their physiological definition of orgasm, but also limited us in any sort of mystical shamanic energetic aspect of orgasm. I had to open up my definition of orgasm to include physiological but there are other types of orgasm as well that can feel very different, still be very orgasmic. It may not be associated with any sexual activity.

Having sex with nature, for example ... the point is that after a while an energetic connection, for me, it was the energetic connection, that might involve physical contact and might not involve physical contact. Then you have a lot of extrapolation from that. So that where I'm sort of magical blend of Tibetan Buddhism, so to speak and Shamanism, so to speak, Western Sexology, so to speak and Western Tantra, so to speak.

What we call sexuality can be so much more BUT if you do not embrace your sexual nature and your body which is another way of saying, 'sex positive', you're not going to get there or get there occasionally when we have a cosmic orgasm. To have it on an ongoing basis, we have to say, 'well, sexuality is okay, it doesn't look like what I thought sexuality would look like, but this is meaningful, and let's go with it and see where it goes.'

You might end up going back to the old one or two favourite sexual positions with your partner or you may go somewhere entirely different. But unfortunate, I think western tantra is only beginning to touch some of these other aspects of the energetics of earth we could possibly go.

I recently started doing these Earth Energy Project with another person, where we energetically become One with the energies of the land, of the earth. The first one we did was several months ago, he was going to this Radical Faeries Gathering in Gavdos, very small island in the Mediterranean, just south-west of Crete. He kept telling me about this and it sounded very interesting. I kept looking and looking, why don't we do a ceremony there. By the time we got there we did a ceremony.

I didn't know this until later but every one of the men in the ceremony got horny doing this ceremony. I didn't know that, because I wasn't focusing on it as an eco-sexuality point of view and I was just looking at the energy. I began to realise, oh, this is eco-sexuality because what I found was tuning being one with the earth being and I do think there's a consciousness of a being that is different from the type of being that we are, is embodied with this physical planet and that energy is fucking big, I mean BIG. That's what happened in that first ceremony, I just sort of tuned into the energy and said, 'Holy Shit, this is BIG energy'.

It didn't feel like that for me personally, I didn't label it as such, it just felt like BIG energy ... I was not getting it from people or power spots or crystals there was this BIG energy and yeah, it was like making love with the earth being, not just tuning in to it - I don't use a gender when talking about the earth I think it's too limiting to say Mother Earth/Grandmother Earth, so I just use the word Earth Being and realise it's another being.

There's broad definition of spirituality and the energetic connections with these other types of beings, some of which do not embody in a physical organism. Spirituality, sexuality and energy it all becomes an energetic dance that keeps exploding and unfolding. It's pretty far out to be saying, especially for a short interview for a book …

I'm pointing in a direction, that I've been going in for ten or fifteen years and I'm going even further. It was only four months ago I felt this big energy, the earth thing you see, 'Holy Shit!' I had not developed enough to be able to handle it enough, but apparently, I was ready at that time and maybe there's even more to go into. It's lovemaking eco-sexuality but at some point, I just want to drop the labels and say energy, dancing energetically.

Questions, thoughts, reflections, to go further into this. I've said a whole lot of stuff man.

It means a lot to me to have your company and to hear your wisdom and your warmth and your generosity is really magnificent to me, so thank you.

You're most welcome. I love sharing my ideas … They're still unfolding, it's all working hypothesis, all working hypothesis and open to new discoveries, because I keep finding these new discoveries.

Well the two parts my attention hovers around is one, about the expansion you spoke about because I have an interest in neo-tantra and traditional tantra and the difference and about what I call unity which is when we dissolve into the nothing and the everything.

I'd like to hear your thoughts on both your mission or your purpose or your intention, your vision, your goals, why you are doing this? … and then maybe the expansion is another part.

I guess as you're saying I guess the vision as I said a little earlier re-integration spirituality and sexuality.

I just started studying in my adult life, I kept moving in natural reaction. I'd accidentally end up here, or accidentally end up there, walk into the certain places in certain times AND that the term that relates that sums them up would be energy. It's more than energy but that's a way of simply looking at it.

Once I started … I have a program or teaching which is not 20 levels. It started with level one [with this path I was on with this Shaman, a teaching I had about 10 years ago. I'm still on level one and it's 20 levels. By teaching others, what I coming to have a knowingness of, is a way for me to develop myself. If I could hang out with some of the high Lamas, that would be ideal. That's not going to happen.

It's been over a number of years now to develop a course and the next thing you know I have 3 more courses coming down the line. I'm not trying to make them happen, they just come up. We get together every two weeks and do meditation together and things like that and I'm hearing from other people and their points of view and energetically dancing with people who are different from my energetic patterns … knowing this, I've come to have a vibrational knowingness, also attracted people who are interested in this.

I get to grow by interacting with other people who want to move in the same direction even though we don't know what that direction is, necessarily. We'll discover as we go further and we get a sense of 'Oh that was the direction I want to move in and didn't realise'.

A way for maybe for me to grow is by teaching, not so much to learn what I'm teaching but by teaching it, I'm learning about how other people are learning it and perceiving how other people coming to have a knowingness of it and dancing with that… so, it has become a way for me to grow myself, that I might not have done, if I was doing this in total isolation.

Now some of these … I was just watching a documentary on Khyentse Rinpoche, went off to a cave for 13 years by himself pretty much, did meditation every day, from Tibetan Buddhist tradition, this was back in the early 1900s, guess it was in Tibet. That's one way of doing it but I can't do it that way. In our western education system it was never in context.

By being with others it's a way of keeping myself in perspective of looking at it, of furthering, going deeper. I keep doing it and doing it and doing it. I keep doing it because it's satisfying. Where I think of myself now energetically is way way way way beyond any fantasy I ever thought that I could ever be, energetically, way beyond it, just way beyond it. At least, that's how I think of it.

I think that if I had a mission or purpose for life, had to do with that. It started when I teach much about sexuality but when I embrace sexuality. Even though, I've been physically celibate for over 15 years, ooooh baby, do I dance energetically, I'm an energetic slut (laughter) even though I don't think of it that way anymore. (laughter) I used to think of myself that way; 'Oh, Okay I'm an energetic slut, so what?'

I think that really … does that sort of answer your question on that?

Yes, yeah …

In the context of expansion, could you give me a sense of what you know about expansion?

Right back when you started talking … you were talking about … arousal without orgasm and what's happening for me and the intersection between Taoist thoughts and traditional tantra, say and shamanic practices and just my own body, is that … I had been conditioned a lot to see sexuality as the escalator of kissing and then oral sex maybe and then penetrative sex and orgasm or ejaculation.

And that can become more gourmet with better techniques about it but it was basically … that thing and now I'm learning about the expansion without the need to have a goal as you were saying or without the need for orgasm or ejaculation but to stay in an aroused state and not a peak state but just to … move through the states … of arousal but … using my body as a tool or using sexuality as a tool to change my state.

Right, I think I have a sense. First of all, I have to change my whole framework around that to answer that question. You are pretty much describing what I'm going to call a physical body orgasm …

Now if you step over to what I would call a light body orgasm. We're made up of different main energetic structures, twenty of them, from my conceptual frame. I'm not even referring to the physical organism. The organism is what has the ejaculation, male or female ejaculation.

These other energetic structures which are not made up of atoms and molecules and energetic patterns, from my point of view, how I understand ... those energetic patterns, have a structure to them and different structures have different functions, different shapes so to speak, different functions. The physical body energetic structure is the one that's involved in doing this lovemaking, but it's the orgasm that happens in that energetic structure. Ejaculation happens in the organism, the bond for organism, but the orgasm happens in the energetic structure.

What tantra's been teaching about and focusing on, pretty much, is another energetic structure that I call the light body. That's just my terminology. The light body has thousands and thousands of currents going up and down they include the Sushumna meridians. Yogis call the Nadis and the energies move through these currents and these currents are not physical, they're made up of energetic patterns and when you ... and a lot of people who are teaching that type of orgasm talk about breathing in certain ways. (Breathing)

That dynamic breathing is one way of doing it then you contract the pelvic floor muscles, pelvic floor muscles to help that and you can feel and imagine pulling the energy up, that's one of the different patterns. If you do that you will have, what I call, a light body orgasm. Which can occur at the same time as a physical body ejaculation or physical body orgasm. But the Light Body orgasm is not the same kind and for a male to have an extended orgasm ... what, in most cases is what is probably happening is a light body orgasm. One after another, one after another, one after another without ejaculation. You see, when you have ejaculation, here's how I interpret it, I don't know if biologist would agree with me or western sexologist would agree with me. The organism says 'Holy shit, we've lost our supply, for an hour, the main demand. We have to procreate, we have to continue the species, so shut everything down we're going to create more sperm.'

Well, if you develop a light body orgasm, it's explosion after explosion after explosion without ejaculation, the light body orgasm can occur in the abdomen, the pelvis, in the throat, the heart, the head ... the whole total body orgasm from the feet to the top of the head and you may not have an ejaculation. You can have those. I had one point and at one point after about 30 minutes, 40 minutes, we just got to stop, my muscles are too sore. This is the abdominal muscles. This is someone I was talking to someone on the phone, we were meditating together, she was in New York and I was here in Tucson, Arizona, 2,000 miles away. We weren't trying to have orgasm, we were trying to meditate with each other. But then we just took off. After a while I said, 'I have to stop because my muscles are too sore'.

That's very explosive, it can happen quite spontaneously, it can happen in a non-sexual context which I've had them like that ... then there's a third type of ... that I call a Spirit Body orgasm which is very subtle. It feels more like a tasting subtle nectar, it not explosive, but it sure is sweet, oh so sweet. You want to be still.

And the couple of times I had those, it was like this other person who sitting across the room, we weren't being sexual but I begin to feel this bubble around us and I knew stuff was out there beyond it, but it was not important it was what was inside that. Being very meditative and feeling this sweetness. It was like, you know when you go to the ... in the United States we have these county fairs, they take the sugar and they put it through this swirling device, it turns out to be what we call it cotton candy. You don't bite into it, you put it into your mouth and melts in your mouth, like nectar. It was sort of like that but not sugary and you just want to be still. There's no (heavy breathing) there was nothing afterwards really other than this 'aaaahhhh that was nice'.

Then there's something that what I heard, Daisetsu Teitaro Suzuki, the Zen master that brought Zen Buddhism from Japan over to the US before WW2. There was a description of his having somatic experience, I thought 'oh that's what I call a soul body orgasm. Where you feel one with everything, just everything. You might be having sex with a partner or you might be just walking down the beach or something else and this energy comes over you and you feel like 'I am everything in existence'. It's a very mystical experience. Now if you're into western tantra, 'oh I just had an orgasm' but if you're a monk in a monastery, 'I just had a mystical experience'.

When I heard about in the 60s, a story about St. Teresa of Avila, a Spanish nun of 16th century; why she was not put to the flame I don't know. She had these intense energetic experiences doing cartwheels across the floor and she would explain it as having mystical experiences with God and she's looked up to and revered and eventually became a saint, I think. St Teresa ... of Avila. This was back in the hippie days when a person told me this, I said, 'oh she was just having an orgasm.' This was way way way back before the perspective I have now.

She was just happy having Light Body Orgasms. Because of the context you would not call it sex, they're mystical experiences with God. If you were had a western tantra class you would say it was sexual of some kind. It's the context that we bring to the definition of what it was. The point is, that in all four of those situations, we are bringing in more energy ... we're bringing in more energy. But not the type of energy, like a carbohydrate ... the guys roll over after the ejaculation and fall asleep because the body is saying 'we have produce sperm, we have to produce more species, more of the species ... and that's an oversimplification.

There's other energy going on that's really important, which is important if you want to develop yourself - develop the energetic structures that enable you to develop yourself spirituality. I didn't go into a full explanation of how I see the sexual shaman. There are 3 things that happen when you have an orgasm:

1. Bringing in more energy. If you want to be a shaman, you have to be able to bring in more energy to do the transformation in a non-sexual way.

2. What happens in orgasm, you really merge with the other person and you are usually belly to belly or back to back or something like that. You don't even notice it because of the orgasmic experience but you start to vibrate like the other person - this is my observation, over time. I call it merging or Oneness.

For a shaman to do what he or she does, he has to vibrate like the client, the person there for the ceremony, whether it be positive or negative he or she has to be vibrating the same pattern but it does not affect him or her, the shaman, because of his development. He has to go into sync with it. That happens in orgasm too.

3. Come to have a knowingness. Literally, a knowingness of the other person. In a sense, after that experience, you are able to vibrate the like them ... because it becomes a part of your vibrational patterns. But that's not in a negative way, because by the time you are a shaman by my definition, this is all processing, this is all process, it neutralises, it's all good. It's not negative. There's a lot more explanation about how there are energy suckers, but that's a whole different thing that I'm talking about.

All of this can happen with these different types of orgasms, now some of the orgasms are with nature and some orgasms are with other people. I played with the idea of Taoism, of not ejaculating. Well, it was interesting when I finally had the silver mercury amalgams, I think that's the word … came out of my teeth, I could have an orgasm and not lose my energy. Before that I would have orgasms and really lose my energy. I noticed as soon as I had those out I had different energy. There's a whole another physical thing that's going on.

The Taoist approach of not ejaculating or at least doing retrograde ejaculation, which was happening in my case, it was helpful. What I later began to observe is, most Taoist teachers are energy suckers. The idea that the male doesn't ejaculate so he saves his energy, then he has sex with a female and he uses energy from her … one day I thought, 'wait a second, what the fuck is this all about?' I would like to see the female sexuality as being on the same level and the same value as male sexuality and rather than being an energetic 'fill-up station' or a 'gas station'.

I started looking at a lot of the Taoist teachers, not all of them but a lot of them are energy suckers. There's a whole Taoist tradition around sexuality that's teaching people, in effect, somehow, to be energy suckers. They're literally suck the energy of the other person. That is baaaaad – I don't mean it's bad karma, energetically unhealthy for both the sucker as well as the other person that's being the energy is being extracted from. That's a whole another thing to go into.

I now pretty much just threw out that whole Taoist perspective of not ejaculating because if you're going to have full orgasms in other ways and do other things energetically and want them to develop or sort of need ejaculation and not lose the same energy. That does not mean, as a male, you don't need to replenish your sperm. I don't have an answer for that. I think I pretty much throw Taoist, some of the Taoist perspective out into the trash can but that's my point of view, in this point of time. It was useful at one point in my life.

Well have to go soon-ish. I wondered if you had a brief sum up or brief message you would like to share with anyone who is reading this book?

It's always about going inside and trusting where you are.

Because most people think 'Oh, I'm not like other people sexually' when other people have their shadows, they don't share. Like I told you when I finally embraced that it's okay to be sexual with men, really, psychologically, I moved to a different place and suddenly, one day, three different women came back in my door and we ended up having sex, it's like 'Whoa'. I wasn't on some level trying to prove something, it opened the floodgates to being who I was and be willing to say no. Just because someone else wants to be sexual, you don't have to be sexual because your partner says that and maybe the relationship you're in is just not going to serve you or the person, at this point in time.

Keep looking inside and exploring what that is and having the willingness and hopefully, the space to see what that is. Because most of us will have to go through some changes around our sexuality, to get … because life is going to change you.

Where I was at 16, horny, at 16, to where I am now at 73, a quadriplegic and a different hormonal structure. That's a BIG difference. There's going to be some big differences in there.

You got to be open to allowing yourself to be who you are or exploring what you think you might be or where you are. There's got to be a simpler way of saying this. It's like, what's that old saying, 'Be Here Now', (laughter) but that doesn't ... it was sort of like ... there's no absolutely right or wrong around sexuality, there just never is ... well, thinking back, you want consensus, assuming consensuality, assuming consensuality, I guess there's no right or wrong maybe some not so wise actions and you might want to study ahead of time to see; 'is this a really good thing to be doing?'

For example, back when AIDS was coming in with San Francisco I was working, I was doing massage at a medical clinic. A lot of gay men came there and I thought this is GRID, Gay Related Immune Deficiency ... disease. No fucking way this is only going to be for one segment of the population, not for only Gay men, it's going to be everybody. I started using a condom ... even though there were other ways to have birth control, I started using a condom. I'm probably alive today because I did that. That was a choice I made. I don't know what's going on, but not meaning to go boy scout motto ... 'Be Prepared'. (laughter) That was San Francisco, in the days before we'd gone to AIDS, gone Gay, gone GRID - Gay Related Immune Deficiency.

So, that's a whole lot of sum up for people.

Yeah, thank you, there's a whole lot more conversations. Thank you now and I hope we get to speak again. I'd love to hear more about your world and your experiences.

Okay. Thank you very much.

CIRCLES OF LOVE, SEX, AND SPIRIT
by Erfahrungskreis: Verena Neuenschwander and Remigius Wagner

The three of us, Verena, Devamani, and Remy, got to know each other in neo-Tantric practice groups. Our relationship grew into a love affair in 2012, and shortly thereafter we decided to give birth to a common child. Because we are all over fifty years old, we weren't focused on a literal baby, rather, we wanted to become parents to a figurative child and a family, family of a common purpose, a common project, and a community for love, sexuality and spirituality. This baby should sustain and strengthen our relationship, deepen our life experiences, expand our love, integrate mindful sexuality, and become a specific contribution to the world.

Indeed, after a few months our network, Erfahrungskreis, (or, in English, Circles of Awareness, Practice and Evolution—erosCAPE) was born and has thrived steadily since. We brought in our experience and knowledge from some of our previous private and professional activities to help get erosCAPE off the ground. These include background and skills around love, sexuality, spirituality, relationship, communication, healing, mediality, terminal and palliative care, awareness, cultural philosophy, self-awareness, and creativity. We have been exchanging these skills with colleagues and friends, both within our circles and beyond, ever since.

Our relationship of three lovers has expanded flexibly and transparently along with the project. Each involved person can choose the container and form of exchange that feels good and beneficial for him or her. Our exchange in erosCAPE is based neither on client relationships, nor on for-profit teacher-student relationships, or professional successes but on deep encounters with experienced people, at eye level, in a protected, private environment created by us all. This form of mutual exchange is meant to deepen our life experience and to contribute to the evolution of our consciousness. Now we meet in different in-person groups forty days a year and hold twenty-four online meetings annually. Once a year we go for a longer journey to other countries. During these meetings, people can choose to practice and deepen their skills and understanding of love, sexuality, and spirituality. So far, groups of four to fourteen people have attended each event, creating a relatively small and intimate setting where each person gets enough space to play a part.

One of our main projects, Sexual Flow, dives into concrete forms of sexual exchange and intercourse. Remy has organized this project since 2006, and he later brought it into our circles. At our two- to four-day Sexual Flow meetings, participants find a flow [24] as freely as possible, both individually and in the group body. In this way, we express our love, sexuality, and relationships in a group of friends and as a part of the sexual vibration of all beings and of the cosmos. We learn to abandon our feelings of shame, to challenge social taboos, to take courage to feel new sexual desires and forms of its expression, and to recognize established patterns of behavior. By doing this, we learn to expand our sexual self-understanding and repertoire. The participants bring in previous experiences from their sexuality, partnership, or in their professional field (e.g. what they have learned as sex coaches). We practice a variety of methods, from neo-Tantra and sexological bodywork to other schools.

Of course, mindfulness, safe sex, communication rules, and other basic conditions for our safety are obligatory so that the participants feel as safe as possible. With these keystones we create a trustful and intimate atmosphere where growth is possible. Taking enough time to reflect and talk about what we do and how we feel about our work is also central to our efforts. We include methods such as constellation work, deep meditation, breathing work, ritual, performance, etc., depending on the flow to give us the support we need. All of this deepens our sexual competences and the understanding of partnership and therefore it promotes new and free expression in sexuality and relationship.

This process opens us for questions such as what for we want to use our sexuality or sexual energy in the current or next phase of our lives. Some individuals in our circle would like to experience the highest ecstasy, lust, or love

---

[24] We take this term from the research of Dr. Mihaly Csikszentmihalyi, a professor of phycology. Flow, or the full involvement of the total self, refers to the mindful capacity to be fully present with one's partner, one's self, and the interaction without distraction

in sexuality, perhaps a state that exceeds or calms down, fulfills or ends their yearlong striving for a superlative. Others also use sexual flow to integrate and transcend previous difficult experiences with sexuality or even sexual abuse through new and positive experiences. Other people use the practice of sexual flow as a possibility to experience harmony between sexuality and relationship or between desire and fulfillment. Life energy, fulfillment of sexual desire, deep connection, love, a sexual field, etc. probably play a significant role as well.

Different people use sexual flow for different purposes. For Devamani sexual flow is a container in which she learns to perceive her body and its sexual vibration more consciously and to use the flow of sexual energy to find out what she wants as a sexual being. It is important for her to be honest, to feel what really supports her to let go deeply in sexual lust and ecstasy. Here, she can surrender to subtle spaces and states where the delicate and the wild energies nourish one another. Remy, on the other hand, has used sexual flow to bring into reality most of his sexual fantasies from his previous life. For him, in addition to lust, love, and encounter, sexuality becomes a catalyst for deep perceptions, expanded awareness, and creativity as a yogi, writer, performer, and psychic. For Verena sexual flow carries the possibility of deep healing, both individually and transpersonal. Through this setting, she learned that it is possible for her to let go of sexual conditioning to one sex and instead feel the underlying neutral flow of sexual energy. This opens one to a free expression of love in sexuality with both men and women. She came to learn that sexual energy probably is the most powerful expression of life energy and can therefore be used for healing work from the gross to subtle levels of manifestation.

Through this work, the relationship between the three of us widens from relating between us to a bigger context of love in an intimate circle of friends and even further to a love for everything that exists. Such openings are gateways to an expanded and more wholesome understanding of relationship and sexuality, to more flexibility in our expression of life, and at the same time to more commitment to one another, involving relationship work at all levels (e.g., shadow work, coaching).

In 2015, we worked through an online course by Dr. Joseph Kramer, called Yoga of Sex. Since then, members of our cohort meet once a month for an online discussion about our personal development in individual and couple's sexuality, as well as related topics. We talk about our sexual preferences, hopes, problems and desires, our current sexual energy, recent experiences, which toys we use, and which books or media we have consumed. Through this open and trustful exchange we learn from each other and are mirroring each other which, gives us support in our development.

In another group, called Partnership and Intimate Relationship(s) Integrally Reflected, the participants deepen their understanding of relationships, their sexuality, communication, forms of conflict resolution, and other relationship skills. In this group we learn about tools for caring and nurturing living partnerships. We use the knowledge of several special fields, and the integral map by Ken Wilber, as a basis for our work. We hope to build an appreciation for the benefits of traditional couple concepts while opening ourselves to new partnership and relationship models.

Sometimes it feels good to be in groups of one's own gender. For that reason, we run a Tantric women's circle and a men's group. These are in-depth and experimental groups on current men's work and women's emancipation with a neo-tantric background. Each year, both groups hold three of their own weekend meetings with a fourth weekend meeting conducted as a joint event. An upcoming women's group is dedicated to the subject of sex work. They want to look at and feel this huge topic from many different perspectives, from inside and outside, including what it means for them as women socially and for their personal relationships. The men decided to reflect the consumption and production of pornography. As a preparation, each man was invited to create a personal porn consumption CV, and every man did it. It is an invitation to abandon shame, to reflect on mindful porn watching, to share sexual fantasies, and to distinguish which they would like to carry out in real life and which ones they would rather leave in the virtual world. We may look forward to a later summary, and perhaps synthesis, in a joint meeting of women and men.

Looking to the future, we are concerned about how aging will occur in the erosCAPE community. Will nursing homes or places of care exist where our still-unusual and avant-garde sexual expressions can be lived? Shall we someday create some nursing home community circles with like-minded people, where sexuality and sexual energy will be an important aspect of our care and be integrated into the last breath of our lives? We are also concerned about the increasing coverage of and public interest in sexual assaults and abuses, including the #MeToo movement. Is the creation of spaces like erosCAPE enough to contribute to healing of both individuals affected by such attacks and our society as a whole? Or do we need even more or different work, that the social and political reaction do not create new repressions, suppression, and rigidification?

Opening to positive sexuality and a zest for life, overcoming shame, healing old wounds or painful experiences, deepening our encounters and commitment to each other, and learning how to willingly support each other are not only of benefit to us personally. We feel that, as a part of the society, the men and women of Eros are contributing to the growth of love and the evolution of this world. We hope our practice is a useful contribution to, and in resonance with, a healthy sexual vibration within every person, every couple, every group, all societies, our ancestors and other-than-human ones (e.g. spiritual entities), and with the light or sexual vibration that creates the whole cosmos. We are a part of it like you are, diving again into our body and sexual encounters, our lust, creativity, love, and whatever each of us is looking for. It's beautiful that there's such a huge variety of sexual expressions and that it's getting easier to experience as many as we choose.

HAS JUDEO-CHRISTIAN CULTURE EVER BEEN SEX POSITIVE, OR HAS IT ALWAYS BEEN AN INCUBATOR FOR SEXUAL SHAME?

by Tina Schermer Sellers

> I awakened from my trance state and was stunned to find the world I was living in, the world of the present, was no longer a world open to love. And I noticed that all around me I heard testimony that lovelessness had become the order of the day. I feel our nation's turning away from love as intensely as I felt love's abandonment in my girlhood. Turning away we risk moving into a wilderness of spirit so intense we may never find our way home again. I write of love to bear witness both to the danger in this movement, and to call for a return to love. Redeemed and restored, love returns us to the promise of everlasting life. When we love we can let our hearts speak.
>
> —bell hooks, *All about Love*

Thomas is sitting in my office. It's one of those dark, cold days that Seattle specializes in for most of the year, and I'm kind of glad for it, because the weather seems to match his mood. We both drink tea. My heart is breaking with his.

It's been fifteen minutes and he hasn't said a word. The tears fall unceasingly down his beautiful, freckled face. He reminds me of my own son at twenty, innocent, so lovely, so much life ahead. But I can tell he has been carrying silent pain, that there is a story trapped inside of him, that he is trying to figure out if he can tell me, *really* tell me, what he's holding.

In his email he had said that his friend Anna, whom he had grown up with in a small town in Kentucky and who had recently read my book, told him to come chat with me. Finally, quietly, painfully, slowly, through big gasps for air, eyes gazing out my window as he speaks, Thomas tells me he doesn't feel like a boy, that he's never felt like one, not for as long as he can remember. He grew up in a very conservative, Evangelical Christian home, he says during a pause in his tears, and both his father and his grandfather are pastors. In his family, it was understood that human beings are born either a boy or a girl and always straight. There was no other way to understand one's gender identity or sexual orientation. But since arriving at our Christian university, he had felt the freedom to try to understand what was "wrong" with him, exploring his attractions and desires openly for the first time in his life.

He had spent so much of his high school years fantasizing about how to kill himself, and more than once, he had come very close to putting a feasible plan together, stopped only by his persistent belief that "God did not make mistakes." Now, having come out to his friend Anna, Thomas had realized that he needed to talk to someone. As we sit together, I learn that he hasn't been sleeping, and the quality of his schoolwork has suffered. He deeply loves his family, his faith, and his friends—but he honestly can't imagine how anyone could still love him if he were to become honest with those around him about who he really feels like he is. As he speaks, his earnest, loving heart is so apparent to me. This is a dear, dear soul.

I listen as I feel we are both on sacred ground. We, the church and culture, have done a huge disservice to Thomas. We have sexually and spiritually abused him. He has no idea how beloved he is *just as he is*, no idea that he was created perfectly as a transgender human, that we desperately needed him in our community—that we want him to thrive. I know we have a difficult road ahead of us, but I also know that now that the story sits between us in the room, we can each hold the sacred space, honoring its beauty and the path that is revealing itself ahead.

How the church and culture got it wrong

The sexual ethic of the Christian church, rather than flowing from Jesus' ministry of love and justice for all, developed from the mind-body split left over from the Greek philosophers of 300 BCE and the assumptions of patriarchy that have shaped culture for millennia. These things came about primarily through the Roman influence in the third and fourth centuries when Constantine, the Roman emperor who had become a Christian, appointed the church's leaders. The male competition for this leadership and power-positioning took place in a context in which the body and its desires were understood to be evil, always pulling one away from God. Most distrusted of all were the body's desires for sexual connection. Spiritual, rather than physical, pursuits were seen as the only way to the heart of God. Those who could deny the body the best were seen as the most spiritual.

This spiritual and sexual ethic had nothing to do with the ministry of Jesus, who valued the body (Luke 7:36–50) and valued a holistic, nonjudgmental approach to faith development (see, e.g., John 4:4–15; 8:1–11). Instead, the church built a sexual ethic that further bifurcated and defamed the body, rather than seeing it as a pathway to the heart of a living, loving, erotic God, witnessed to in the Hebrew tradition of the Song of Songs.

That legacy of dualistic, body-suspecting thought gave us and our culture (which has built an entire economy on the mind-body split by selling the body) two thousand years of sex-negative ideas, thoughts, fears, mandates, rules, and double messages. We have failed to teach about God's design and intent in the amazing gift that the body is, the beauty of what humans can share with each other and learn about their creator through sexual communion. But when we take a deep dive into the Hebrew Scriptures and Jewish mystic history, we find stories that reveal aspects of how God, over thousands of years of the Judeo-Christian narrative, has tried to help us to see the gift of sexual desire and sexual touch as the healing eros by which the Divine calls us Beloved and invites us to know the power of love here on earth.

For many, the no-sex-before-marriage discourse was further restricted in the early 1990s to include the idea that a person must remain "sexually pure" before marriage. This fear-based message was communicated through the abstinence-only education initiative that began in the early 1980s and ran through roughly 2005, helped along by billions of dollars from the US government. It affected the religious and nonreligious youth of our country, particularly Christian youth, who would hear the abstinence-only message emphasized at church youth group functions, camps, rallies, and retreats. An entire genre of books, released from around the mid-1990s, hit the market, like *I Kissed Dating Goodbye* by Joshua Harris. The teaching in these books was understood to mean that expression of sexual desire, including sexual thoughts, was off-limits. No sexual action was to be entertained (masturbation, kissing, longing, touching, fantasizing, and so on) prior to "biblical" (heterosexual) marriage. The purity movement, which had gained popularity in 1993 with the True Love Waits purity pledge sponsored by LifeWay Christian Resources, was in the background as a generation of Evangelical youth absorbed a culture of body-suspicion and desire-shaming within their own bodies. It didn't help that much of the time, the language about what "purity" meant was vague, which left room for untrammeled condemnation of the self and of others for having or expressing sexual desire. Here is the pledge (my emphasis added to vague terms) that, according to LifeWay, over two million adolescents signed:

> Believing that true love waits, I make a commitment to God, myself, my family, my friends, my future mate, and my future children to a *lifetime of purity* including sexual abstinence from this day until the day I enter a biblical marriage relationship.

There are vague and undefined phrases in this teaching, leaving young adults lost in doubt and confusion. Fearing they would do something wrong, youth condemned themselves after *any* experience of sexual longing. Nonspecific phrases in purity literature were interpreted by youth and youth leaders as a warning against sexual desire. For example: "Understand that purity begins with *what is in your heart and your mind;*" "A lifetime of purity is contingent upon *setting boundaries* and living within them;" "Purity is not contingent on the past. If you have already *given in to physical desire*, pledge today that from this day forward you will remain *physically pure.*"

What is stunning to me, is how this purity message resembles the most extreme ascetic movements of the early Christian church, where to serve God was understood to require renouncing all sexual thoughts, feelings, and actions. Many of my Christian young-adult clients have told me that the message they were given was restrictive and repressive: when they even *desired* someone, whether in reality or in fantasy, they were impurely "lusting" after them and thus "sinning against themselves, the other person, their future mate and God." In fact, I recently stumbled over a quote from a 2010 book on Christianity and sexuality describing the *feeling* of sexual attraction, "even when not aware" of it, as "the very existence of such atmospheric erotic intentionality [that] subtly stains you. It is yet another aspect of our battle with darkness."

This kind of teaching, the kind that fails to differentiate between feelings (which naturally occur outside of our control) and thoughts and actions (which we have choice over), is a weapon of choice for shame, a powerful tool for inflicting wounds on someone's development. Since desire is as natural as breath, teachings like those of the purity movement leave youth hiding what they feel or do inside a dark vault, leading youth of any sexual identity or orientation to condemn themselves until they hate themselves and their desires. The tragedy for many of these earnest young Christians gets even worse when they learn that the self- and church-inflicted assault on their sexual desire doesn't simply disappear when they commit to a partner. As they grow into adulthood, both the guys and the girls, many develop significant sexual dysfunction and chronic low-desire issues that can persist into their twenties, thirties, and beyond. Plus, there's mounting evidence to suggest that purity pledges don't actually work for the purpose of maintaining virginity until marriage. Research on the effect of purity culture (pledges, rings, books, etc.) suggests only a slight delay of the onset of sexual activity (twelve to eighteen months), a reduced use of contraception when they do engage in intercourse, and a significant increase in sexual shame, condemnation, and self-loathing. In her groundbreaking book *Sex and the Soul*, Donna Freitas interviewed over 2,500 students at public, private, Catholic, and fundamentalist Protestant colleges around the United States, asking about their sexual beliefs, attitudes, and behaviors. "Of all the students I interviewed at all four types of institutions," she writes, "the only students who spoke of pregnancy scares and having unprotected sex came from the evangelical colleges" (Frietas, 2008).

I spent some time talking to students who grew up inside the purity movement, to try to better understand what they were taught and experienced. One of the women I talked to, a young woman named Phoebe said this:

> From my personal experience, the message was hardcore. Along with "sexual purity" was "emotional purity" and living within certain boundaries so you didn't give pieces of yourself away by going "too far" physically or even having serious emotional connections, [or] conversations with the opposite sex. You were told to have clear relationship boundaries—but this was never clearly defined and was hard to understand. A lot of the pressure came from my parents, and certain church groups and parachurch organizations. This quote kind of describes the overall idea and concept that was constantly driven home: "Imagine for a moment one of those huge lollipops, the kind that you buy at an amusement park candy store. Take off the wrapper and pass it around to ten people. Allow them to lick as much as they want. The leftover is saved for the husband or wife, the rightful owner of the lollipop. Yuck! Who would want that?!"

Phoebe goes on to say,

> Imagine being told this—so now you feel dirty, unwanted, yucky, and worthless. If I have given anything away even just "emotionally" this is how I feel about myself. Here is a quote from a book I was given as a teen, "When we give away pieces of ourselves emotionally and spiritually ... what is left over for the rightful owner? ... Keeping yourself emotionally pure is a gift that should be left and given to the rightful owner—your spouse."

Added to the vague and unforgiving message of purity is the covert message that one's body is a thing to be owned and pronounced worthy or unworthy by someone else. "The idealization of sexual purity is powerful at evangelical colleges," writes Donna Freitas, "and it exacts demands on students that can be severe, debilitating, and often unrealistic. Because of the stronghold of purity culture, many students learn to practice sexual secrecy, professing chastity in public while keeping their honest feelings and often their actual experiences hidden."

Sexual shame has profound effects on lives well into the future. It affects one's ability to give and receive love, and love is the only element that can heal sexual shame. Nothing is more damaging to the human spirit than sexual shame. I believe the Christian church had no idea it was involved in participating in abusing its youth by causing them shame, but it has. The symptoms are evident and widespread.

Recently, Noel Clark, PhD developed the very first operational definition of sexual shame:

> Sexual shame is a visceral feeling of humiliation and disgust toward one's own body and identity as a sexual being and a belief of being abnormal, inferior, and unworthy. This feeling can be internalized but also manifests in interpersonal relationships having a negative impact on trust, communication, and physical and emotional intimacy. Sexual shame develops across the lifespan in interactions with interpersonal relationships, one's culture and society, and subsequent critical self-appraisal (a continuous feedback loop). There is also a fear and uncertainty related to one's power or right to make decisions, including safety decisions, related to sexual encounters, along with an internalized judgment toward one's own sexual desire. (Clark, 2017)

As you can see, you do not have to have come from a religious home to have acquired sexual shame. Growing up in a country that provides no comprehensive sexual health education and only fantasy-based or violent, erotic, patriarchal media as our sex educator also provides its own platform for sexual shame. This place of secrecy, shame, misinformation, and self- and other-condemnation is far from the abundance God intended in the gift of sexuality, a gift with power and potential for pleasure and loving attachment that extends far beyond the physical responses of the body. Join me as we look into the stories God gave our Hebrew ancestors that illuminate both God's love for us and our potential to share in mysterious manifestations of this love through sacred touch, a touch that invites us into literal "love making" as an act of creation, the very creation that produced the universe.

Song of songs

> My beloved called out to me and he said, "Rise up, my dear mate, my beautiful one, and come to me. Behold, the chill has fled and the rain has ceased and gone on its way. The blossoms have appeared throughout the land. The time for pruning has arrived and the voice of the turtle doves can be heard around our land. The figs have livened up their hue and the vines are bursting with their bouquet. Arise, my dear mate, my beautiful one, come to me. My dove who is nestled is hidden in the crevice of the rock, in the hollow of the steps' ascent, reveal your form unto me and let me hear your voice, for oh, how sweet is your voice."
> (Song of Songs 2:10–14)

Did you know that the Bible has a book dripping with erotic, sensual desire? It's true! I think of the Song of Songs as the best-kept secret of the Judeo-Christian scriptures. In my many years of navigating American Christian culture in all its various colors and textures, by far the most ignored book from the pulpit is this beautiful book. Why? Is it because it's a sensuous text? Is it because it's a tricky subject? Is it because it causes us to confront the connection between God, love, sexual desire, and holiness? These are not areas we know how to assimilate, much less address out loud.

Since the formation of the western Christian church in the second and third centuries, the body has been cast *apart* from the soul, sexual desire *apart* from God, sensuality *apart* from holiness. If you have ever thought sexual pleasure or sexual desire was a perverse part of you, these beliefs (part of a stream of thought we call dualism) are probably why. Given this long-embedded teaching, how are we to confront the spiritual capacities of sex, let alone the sensuality of the Song of Songs? Perhaps Christian churches have largely ignored this incredible piece of Scripture because we've not had a clue how to handle it. If the body is bad, but this text seems to think it's good, then of *course* we'll be confused as to how to approach a book like this.

I must say I love a God who graciously invites us to confront our foolishness. It was the church who, in thought and doctrine, eventually separated these seemingly powerful elements from each other. Yet long before this, it was a loving and wise creator who created us *whole*. We are a beautiful, intended integration of the earth and the spirit, the flesh and the soul, gifts of a loving and wise God. They were never to be understood *apart* from each other. In fact, just the opposite. They were to be understood as conforming each other, whole only in relation to each other. We are to listen fully, embody wholly, and seek wisdom as we revel in God's song of desire.

The Hebrew people did not seem to struggle with the sensuality of the Song of Songs in the same way the Christians eventually would. Rabbi Akiva (50–135 CE), referred to in the Talmud as the Head of all Sages, said, "All of Scripture and its texts are holy, but the Song of Songs is the Holy of Holies." Here we have a highly respected Jewish teacher saying that the Song of Songs was to the Holy Scriptures what the Holy of Holies was to the Jewish Temple. Imagine that! The Song of Songs is thought to be the Holy Place in Scripture where, like the Holy Tabernacle, God seeks to be in intimate communion with us. The Jewish people, through appreciating the central importance of the Song of Songs, were reminded that the central and primary text of Jewish living involved the highly evolved love and sensual awareness of God's presence. They got a glimpse of the love that God felt for His people, a peek at how profound the love between them and the Creator could be, and also how spicy and deep and amazing the relationship between human lover and human beloved could be. Here was an example of sexuality informing spirituality and spirituality informing sexuality.

If the Song of Songs is the most sacred book of Old Testament Scripture, then all other texts and teachings must serve the purpose of the Song of Songs. This text is about experiencing God's presence and essence through a passionate, awe-inspiring, and boundless love. It is an erotic message of union in which two forms of love—ecstatic love and human love—coalesce into an experience of the God of Love. That's a new idea for many Christians, many of whom have not been exposed to a Jewish understanding of the Song of Songs and who have been taught to fear sexuality, sensuality, desire, and eros.

As we work to quell these fears, it's important to remember that the Holy of Holies, the inner sanctum of the Temple, was not an easy place to enter and was full of danger if not approached with careful preparation and specific intent. Only the High Priest entered this sacred place, and only on the Day of Atonement. He had to follow the ritual of preparation with the utmost of care or he would die. It involved the readiness of the heart and of the mind, the cleansing of the body, the wearing of sacred clothes, and the bringing of incense and blood for the atonement of sins. Within a Jewish understanding of God's love for his people is the understanding that while this love was passionate and total, it was also sacred.

In a parallel way, sexual love and sexual expression were understood to model this sacredness and intentionality. Entering the sacred place of lovemaking was understood as the place where love was made and the God of love was encountered. Both partners took deliberate time to prepare the heart, soul, and body for entering this sacred place: time to bathe and adorn the body; time to prepare the room with special lighting, scents, and oils; time to prepare the heart for giving and receiving love; time to prepare to encounter God. Pleasure, awe, and love blended into one. Here again, we see the parallel process between God's love for his people, his desire to be in intimate relationship with them and his desire for them to experience boundless, powerful love in and through the body and the soul—sexuality informing spirituality, spirituality informing sexuality.

"I am my beloved's, and my beloved is mine, Who is delighting himself among the lilies" (Song of Songs 6:3). This is but one of seven Hebrew stories I write about in my book *Sex, God, and the Conservative Church: Erasing Shame from Sexual Intimacy* that are lovely, shocking, and full of proof that it's possible for there to be an erotic God who calls us Beloved, and calls us to enjoy a sacred, powerful sexual life. It was from this place, that I began to encourage Thomas to indulge his imagination in a God who did not make mistakes. From here and along a loving road of conversation, sharing of his story, learning about sexual health, and learning to celebrate his gender identity, Thomas was able to erase sexual shame, and celebrate the healing gift of the God whom the ancient Hebrews knew to empower and inhabit their sexuality!

CHAPTER 11
ECOSEXUALITY

Thanks to Annie Sprinkle, Beth Stephens and Teri Ciacchi, Ecosexualtiy is being celebrated worldwide. It invites people to treat the earth with love rather than see it as an infinite resource to exploit. Ecosexuality uses "ideas from different regions such as India and their idea of seven chakras to get closer to the earth." The idea of Ecosexuality grew from the need to protect the resources of the earth and the need to save it.

ECO SEX

Interview by Jaz Papadopoulos with pioneers Annie Sprinkle and Beth Stephens

Looking around the gallery, my eyes landed on a hand-written sign up sheet: "Wet Dreamers." It was September 2016, at documenta 14 (widely considered to be the best art exhibition in the world) in Athens, Greece. Something in the program had caught my eye: Wet Dreams Water Ritual with Beth Stephens and former sex worker Annie Sprinkle. As the sign up sheet, a request for collaborative from performers, taunted and tempted me, I raised my eyes and saw the couple themselves. Annie was wearing a very cleavage-friendly dress, abundant with feathers and glitter popping out of her hair. Beth was in a dapper silver (p)leather vest. Annie waves, says hi (she really is the most kind person I know), and before I know it we're all out to dinner and I'm teaching them how to say ευχαριστώ.

What is the role of pleasure in your work?

Annie Sprinkle: To experience pleasure is a gift we're given at birth. Beth and I want to make a more pleasure-filled world! So, we like to share our ideas about how to have more pleasure.

Beth Stephens: It's fun! And life affirming.

A: Pleasure can be an antidote to misery, pain and suffering.

Why is sex positivity important to you?

A: I like that sex positivity is creative... and compassionate. Its positive!

B: Rather than judgmental and punitive, it's permissive, it's curious. It's liberatory!

What are your proudest achievements in the world of sex positivity?

A: Being with Beth!

B: Being with Annie! (laughter)

A: My greatest achievement is having a well-balanced relationship with purpose, and love--

B: And ecosex--

A: And ecosex! And joy--

B: Fun--

A: It's living an erotic life, and sharing it with the world around us. For us, sex and creativity are one and the same. I mean there's reproductive sex--

B: We don't do very much of that--

A: Instead we have given birth to tons of cool projects that generate good feelings.

B: And we like to share them with everybody!

A: We're very interested in sex outside the box.

B: We like sex in our boxes too!

A: In our boxes and outside of your boxes.

Working with these two wasn't my first foray into ecosex – I had once had an orgy with three other humans, many trees, and a mountainside – but Beth and Annie are a force like no other. It wasn't always that I made an effort to energetically connect with each tree as I walk down my block. But now, I recognize them: that one is a dancer, that one hates the city, this one loves being next to these other trees. Wherever I am, I look around and I see relationships. I feel my heart reaching beyond my chest and my roots growing into the earth, connecting to every being around me.

How has having an "ecosexual gaze" changed your lives?

B: When I was in an airplane flying into West Virginia during a really bad storm, I thought we were going to crash. I looked out the window and thought, "Well, here are the Appalachian Mountains I've married. Here's the air I'm having intercourse with. If I'm going down, I'm going down in the arms of my lover." It actually gave me a great deal of comfort (even though it was scary as hell). If I had died in those mountains, that would have been a good place to go. That's all I could think, during this really scary landing, and it gave me a lot of solace. When you are an ecosexual, you always have a lover.

A: I didn't appreciate the nonhuman world as much until I started eroticizing it. It's not everybody's way, but imagining the Earth was my lover helped me feel more connected with the nonhuman world. In my twenties and thirties, I had sex with literally thousands of people. Humans were my objects of desire. But now I see erotic potential, sensuality, and sex virtually everywhere! If you're a sex positive person who enjoys sex, once you get your ecosexual gaze on it's just more of a good thing!

What are common misconceptions about sex positivity?

A: People think that "sex positive" means having sex with lots of people and having lots of orgasms, and if you're not, then you're not a sex positive person. That's not what it is at all, and the misconceptions are what make it controversial.

B: Sex is hard to know. To "know something" is to stop it, to be able to examine it, but our work is always on a moving target. So, our sex positivity involves not knowing. And that can be very scary for some people.

A: Sometimes we can be wrong or make mistakes. But we're process-oriented people. Beth recently said I was a pee-oneer!

B: 'Cause Ms. Sprinkle is a pee queen! (laughter)

A: But I think sex positivity truly allows people to be where they're at, and wherever they're at is fine. Personally, I'm metamorphosexual—always in a state of change.

What is a common misconception about ecosexuality?

A: One of the big critiques we get is about consent: How do we know the tree wants to be hugged? Our response is that we try our best to communicate with the tree, to intuit it, and some trees don't want to be hugged and some do!

B: On the other hand, when you fill your car with gas, no one says, "did you ask the Earth to drill into it before you filled your car with gas?" Exploiting the Earth's resources is how corporations and individuals profit under capitalism, and people don't question it in the same way.

A: Give a tree a full body hug and people freak out. Kill it, no problem. That's a classic example of sex negativity. To think hugging trees is unwanted attention? No! It's loving attention.

B: They don't see the forest for the trees.

B: You were in that crazy ass water ritual! Remember that one!?

My memory of the water ritual is this...We start the ritual. I get naked immediately, which I was not planning on doing. Somebody breast feeds me via water balloons. Somehow, blue paint gets all over my back, and then (CLAP!) we wake up! And there are razor blades and puddles all over the floor!

A: Oh my god!

How do you think that ecosex serves people who have felt excluded from the mainstream sex positive movement?

B: It's an expansion of one's imagination about what sex can be. It allows many more types of fantasies. We're engaging conceptual ways of seeing and understanding the world by expanding our limited conceptions of sexuality.

For example, someone who is lonely and doesn't have a human lover, maybe they can look out their window and imagine having sex with a cloud. Some people might think that's really silly, but I think that any kind of sexual fantasy can be an empowering and pleasurable thing. We have so many taboos in our culture about what we can and can't think about. Those taboos even shape what I might say to you right now. But I think ecosex is really freeing, perhaps especially for people who have challenges with their bodies, or who have been abused, or imprisoned, and so on.

A: We like asking the question, "what is sex?!" Personally, I'm leaning towards just about everything is sex. Ecosexuality gives permission to imagine sexual experiences beyond the human, beyond the genitals, and beyond the body. Where do our bodies start and end? Ecosexuality is sex in an ecosystem – it's inter-relatedness. Humans are Earth.

I think your new book, *Explorer's Guide to Planet Orgasm*, does a really good job of suggesting ecosexy activities to help liberate one's sexuality. For example, the instructions for orgasmic breath play: breathing is a universal and accessible activity!

A: Yes, Planet Orgasm is inspired by ecosex principles. We like expanding ideas of what orgasm is. Genital orgasms are great, but there are many more kinds

B: We even say you can have intercourse with the air you breathe! Plus, there are all those microorganisms you breathe in. Someone in our new film, Water Makes Us Wet, said, "This water could be from Cleopatra's bathtub." That's sexy! I would love to be having sex with the water that Cleopatra bathed in.

A: We don't just use water to get off. We go a step further, to make love with water, and to pleasure the water. We are big aquaphiles!

How do you reckon with having an earth-based practice on land that has been settled and colonized?

B: There's a film called "Hunger," by the director Steve McQueen, about the Irish Hunger Strike. It shows how the only thing the Irish hunger strikers had control over was their bodies. It was their tool for protest: the only thing they could do was refuse to eat. I think in some ways, that's what we have. Our bodies. That's the only thing we have any hope of controlling.

A: I love Joanna Macy's idea that loving ourselves exactly as we are is an act of civil disobedience. Being sex positive is an act of civil disobedience. Being ecosexual is an act of civil disobedience.

B: We need to resist colonization, fight it, and have as much pleasure in our bodies as possible. For us, ecosexuality is about breaking down human and nonhuman binaries. Annie and I aren't perfect. We fail a lot. But we try, and we continue to try, and we open up these places for thought and imagination and play. I really think that the human body is the best starting point that we have.

In Kim TallBear's writing about settler sexuality, she connects ecosex to ways of undoing colonial ways of practicing relationships and sexuality. Part of Empire and colonization is controlling people's bodies, and controlling sexuality. I think that ecosexuality and sex positivity both can help us undo these methods of control, which is in service to decolonization.

B: That's what we hope.

Any last words?

A: A pro domme, whose name I sadly can't remember, once said, "The Earth can be a cruel mistress, and there's no safe word." So, proceed with some caution. Ecosex can have an edge

B: I think the Earth's a huge mystery. We don't really know why things happen, and we try to rationalize why things happen. I think that's just ebb and flow of the tides. Sometimes a tree falls on us and we get killed but we're gonna die anyhow. I think that industrialism and capitalism are killing the earth in a very non-consensual way that's only accelerating, in a way that really encourages us to love the Earth more and to work for environmental health and justice.

A: In every grain of sand is an entire erotic universe waiting to be explored.

An incomplete list of the interviewer's ecosexual proclivities:

Swimming nude [25]
Water sports
Saunas
Aquabation
Friction
Breathing
Asphyxiation
Stargasms
Treebedism
Formicophilia

---

[25] From the Sprinkle and Stephens Ecosexual Fetish Chart.

FROM ROOTS TO SHOOTS: THE SEX POSITIVE FOUNDATIONS OF THE ECOSEXUALITY MOVEMENT

by Teri Ciacchi

Welcome, allow me to introduce myself: my name is Teri Dianne Ciacchi and I am the Hierophant of a queer centric, poly-normative sex magick cult focused on Aphrodite and held in Cascadia Bioregion. I am the matrix of Living Love Revolution (LLR) which is a specific type of social change activism; a face to face embodied praxis of love. Living Love Revolution is intentionally generating networks of what Joy Brooke Fairfield calls "Rhizomatic Intimacy" and "Intimacy Politics" through Pleasure Activism. As the matrix of LLR, I am responsible for generating private sessions, events, classes, quarterly retreats and annual gatherings that function as temporary autonomous zones (TAZ). These TAZ's provide a reprieve from the "normal" world of the "fading uber-culture", and create instead an imaginal context where love is central, sex is holy and we actively engage the other than human worlds. Private session work ranges from therapeutic relationship coaching to trance work, ritual and divination. Classes and events include salons, peer counseling and "trauma aware" consent training and conflict mediation. LLR Aphrodite Temples are quarterly educational retreats in which 25 people get to engage each other in sex magick and explore authentic desire as it arises in their bodies using clearly defined and expressed verbal consent. Since 2012 LLR has produced an annual EcoSexual gathering. These gatherings have become a hive of connectivity for the leaders of the movement, and are now spawning offshoots in other bioregions. All of this erotic sex positive activity is embedded in, and thus inseparable from the social activism movements that began in 1960's & 70's and continue to today. Sex Positivity and EcoSexuality are specifically rhizomatic offshoots of the radical outsider communities within Feminist, Neo-Pagan and LGBTQIA+ subcultures and the art/activism/intermedia they produce.

Earth As Lover, Honoring How We Arrived Here

In EcoSexuality we spend a lot of time focusing on feeding the matrix of our lives, or *MotherLoving* as I like to call it. If the ground you are standing on supports you, then it is wise to get down and honor the ground: to give thanks to the earth, to the Ancestors, to the non-humans and also to the elders whose presence are the foundational resources that make our lives and chosen identities possible. Real people visioned the ideological paradigms and built the social infrastructure of the counter-cultural environments that currently exist in Cascadia. When we look at the roots of the current EcoSexuality movement there are a myriad of of sex positive rhizomes to acknowledge, while this essay cannot possibly name them all, I will mention those whose influences are part of my daily life experience. I also wish to acknowledge that the intersectionality oppressive culture that we live in creates a situation wherein the people I am aware of, have socialized with and can point to as influences are predominantly white and working class or middle class. I know there are thousands of unnamed and historically unknown people whose lives made it possible for me to openly proclaim a sex positive

EcoSexual identity in 2017. I do my best to honors these Queer Ancestors of Lineage and Craft in my personal spiritual practices. I have worked diligently to list an adequate number of these influences in the limitations of this essay.I know that my ancestors of blood have obtained resources of land and riches through colonial and imperialist heritages that disadvantaged and/or took the lives of the indigenous cultures and peoples who existed on the lands now called the U.S.A. I partially understand the struggles of my own blood ancestors as they arrived in waves of immigration from Europe and assimilated into the already colonized lands of eastern and Northern U.S.A. I am committed to continuing to research, address and heal the transgressions and oppressions of my personal ancestral history.

Eros & Thanatos: The Legacy of Our Gay brothers

During WWI, the U.S. Military Services began the "blue discharge" practice, releasing known homosexuals in the port cities of SF, Chicago & NY. Which means that working class men who survived military service became the fertile compost that the gay leather biker communities grew from. This practice was still in place during the US participation in the VIetnam War. My Uncle Marc Ciacchi spoke with me at length about his experiences as an ex-marine who served in VietNam and his understanding of military history:

> "In and around WWII, if guys were discovered to be homosexual, the various service branches would just discharge them out. Some guys used it as an excuse to get out. Anyway, most of those guys were ashamed or embarrassed to go back home, (we can agree that it was a far different time), and seeing as how the main discharge point was San Francisco, they just decided to stay there rather than go back home and have to answer awkward questions."

Disenfranchised and disillusioned these men felt estranged from "normal" life and turning to each other, began socializing in "Outlaw" motorcycle clubs and wearing leather. As my uncle continued to explain his post service experience to me, I saw the similarity between his internal sense of having survived something important (in this case war) that permanently changed his identity and made it difficult to reintegrate into mainstream society, and the Outsider identities of people who started the alternative cultures that became sex positive subcultures.

> " I became enthralled with the biker culture soon after I got out of the Marines. After serving in the military, many guys felt alienated from society. Mainly because of the things they had seen and done and the constant need for the adrenaline rush that comes from dancing at death's door. They could not relate to their friends and loved ones because, for one thing, they did not want to visit that shit on family"

Men who already identified as outlaws; who did not care much for "civilians" opinions of them, found solace in each other's company bonded by the existential dread of their encounters during war and the neurodivergence of their now PTSD altered bodies. They frequently felt more at home on the move in leather on the back of a fast moving bike and also then, in the back rooms of bars; the alley ways that became the dungeons and sex clubs of the 80's 90's and aughts.

The heteronormative sex positive movement known as Swinging also has its origins in male post war bonding and death. Swinging originated in the U.S. Air force's legacy of enlisted men promising to take care of each others' wives if they were killed.

My friend Ganymede, who is featured in the movie *Last Men Standing* is a founding member of the BDSM focused group Black Leather Wings (BLW). BLW was responsible for bringing leather practices and identities into Radical Faerie events in the early 80's. In his personal narratives, Ganymede confirmed that leather culture arose from people leaving the military and choosing to stay in "the City". It would be an error not to mention the impact of the plague of AIDS & HIV and how dramatically it altered all our lives. In the queer sex positive community I helped create in my 20's & 30's, using gloves and condoms and other barriers during sexual activities was an act of loving, respectful fidelity to erotic life force. It was a commitment to social justice; a way to destigmatize sex with HIV positive beloveds in group play spaces.

It is also notable that the protest activism of groups like Act Up!, that arose in response to the advent of the AIDS crisis, intentionally included art and performative elements specific to *"gay"* culture, (incorporating camp, drag and spectacle) in their direct actions. As Ben Shepard shows in "The Use of Joyfulness As A Community Organizing Strategy" :

> "A cornerstone of this approach is a rejection of the hair shirt, anti-pleasure Left. The result is a new generation of activist groups struggling to oppose war and corporate influence while offering a compelling image of a democracy which honors difference in its countless forms. A respect for the interrelations of joy, justice, pleasure, and the use of culture as an organizing tool is at the core of this approach".

These postmodern approaches to social change activism: the use of humor, the building of alternative cultures and the treatment of protests as an opportunity for performative theater and carnival are a foundation of the EcoSexuality movement. For many of us the knowledge that Eros and Thanatos are deeply entwined is part of our respect for pleasure.

The pioneers of Feminist Body Art were sex positive and saw their bodies as primary sites of activism, ecology and ritual. In 1964, Carolee Schneemann created, produced and documented three performances of *"Meat Joy"* : a group of adults in underwear who rolled around on plastic sheeting with wet paint, plastic, rope and raw fish, chickens, and sausages. Annenberg Learner teaching site describes *"Meat Joy"* as "a celebration of the flesh that verged on ecstatic ritual". Fluxus member Yoko Ono staged her performance of "Cut Piece" in Carnegie Hall in which audience members came up to her still and meditative body to use scissors to cut off her clothing. Marina Abramovic, Mary Beth Edelson, Ana Mendieta are my favorite Feminist Body Artists, inventing and producing public displays of female agency and body autonomy.

New York Radical Women (NYRW) was founded in 1967 by Shulamith Firestone & Pam Allen who were joined by Carol Hanisch, Anne Forer, Robin Morgan and Kathie Sarachild among many others. NYRW started consciousness raising groups in which cis women gathered in small groups and used group dynamics tools to equalize how the time and attention of the group members were shared as they discussed their personal experiences and connected them to systemic social oppressions. In her essay "The Personal Is Political" Carol Hanisch explained that the focus of the group was not therapy but political action. By 1969 NYRW split ideologically over strategies, some members stayed focused on consciousness raising and inner work and the "politicos" like Robin Morgan, formed the Women's International Terrorist Conspiracy From Hell (W.I.T.C.H.). W.I.T.C.H. groups sprung up across the country changing the acronyms meaning to fit the specific protest focus, but found the women participating consistently dressed in all black with iconic pointed hats. Margot Adler, an NPR journalist who archived the NeoPagan movement in her book *Drawing Down The Moon*, identifies these activists as influential to the later formation of female separatist Dianic Wicca

Women began to hold separatist rituals and events, women writers and artists began researching Goddess cultures, looking for evidence of matrifocal cultures and using the phrase "The Burning Times". Women were excited to gather together; they began unearthing and honoring pre-Christian traditions. The term "women-identified-women" and new spellings like wymyn and wimmin and wombmoon were coined and used in my friendship circles. Some wimmin disowned the names of their father's bloodlines and took the last names of their mother's mothers'.

The idea that God could be female was incredibly radical in the 70's, (and unfortunately is still seen as radical today by those enthralled with the fading uber culture). The idea of female divinity was so foreign that we had to invent new words in order to speak about it. Feminist theology is the study of God from a feminist perspective but Thealogy, coined in 1976, is the study and reflection upon the feminine divine from a feminist perspective. Here is a short list of some of the Thealogist authors whose works revealed the Goddess to me : Merlin Stone, Anne Kent Rush, Mary Daly, Carol Christ, Barbara G. Walker, Judy Grahn, Diane diPrima.

Feminist Culture began to be generated during this second wave of feminism and as women's experiences became a legitimate part of the discourse of academia, the formerly separate worlds of Art, Sociology, Ecology, and Psychology began to merge and/or be seen from non-dualist lense or a female centric position. The personification of the earth as female and the earth as Mother was one result of paying attention to women and non-white indigenous cultures, and the merging of feminism with ecology and psychology.

Women's studies, Gender studies, Jungian Psychology, Transpersonal Psychology, Ecofeminism and EcoPsychology all of these fields affected sex positivity and began in the late 70's and early 80's in academic settings.

The Goddess Gives Birth to herself: Neopaganism, Polyamory, Reclaiming

The term polyamory originated in the science fiction geek fandom and pagan inclinations of the **Church of All Worlds** whose members founded the first Pagan church in the USA. Incorporated in 1968, and recognized by the IRS in 1970, CAW was an attempt to embody the fantasy cult of Heinlein's Stranger in a Strange Land. Oberon Zell Ravenheart made significant contributions to what were to become sex positive and EcoSexual cultures. He shared the vision of his personal gnosis; Theagenesis, a paradigm that proclaimed that the Earth was a living entity. He used the structure of the church to inspire others to form CAW nests. He invented the terms Neopagan and Polyamory. The CAW community also wrote and published a powerful organizing tool **The Green Egg magazine** in which High Priestess Morning Glory Zell debuted the first article that used the term Polyamory: "A Bouquet of Lovers"(1990) and outlined how to create polyfidelitous fluid bonding circles. Morning Glory was partnered with Oberon Zell and several others. When I attended a C.A.W. Litha ritual in 1997 their polycule family had adopted the last name Ravenheart and were living collectively on rural land in Laytonville CA. Sex Positivity is written into CAW's values statement.

> "While CAW members express a broad spectrum of personal magicks and beliefs, what brings us together is a shared set of values: immanent divinity (expressed as "Thou art God/dess"); self-knowledge and personal responsibility; deep friendship and tribal intimacy; *__positive sexuality__*; living in harmony with the natural world; and appreciation of the diverse nature of human beings." (emphasis mine)

Starhawk's book *The Spiral Dance* was published in 1979 and another branch of witchcraft emerged, this time focused on social change activism. My friends and I huddled around our copies of the book from 1981 onward and began crafting our own rituals and protests. Reclaiming magick and the classes and Witch camps, that grew as the movement spread, became a central part of my life. I do not know if Starhawk herself is polyamorous but her fiction novel *The Fifth Sacred Thing* is full of EcoSexual content including The Declaration of Four Sacred Things which reads like a precursor to the EcoSex Manifesto,. *The Fifth Sacred Thing* also features a genderqueer group sex scene which whetted my imagination. Her Thealogical creation myth comes from the Faery tradition of Victor and Cora Anderson. The Star Goddess falls in love with herself, makes love to herself and gives birth to herself. I still use this liturgy in my Aphrodite Temple work and have used versions of it when teaching self-pleasuring workshops.

Radical Fay are Spiritually Gay

The Spiritual Conference for Radical Fairies was held on Labor Day 1979 and was attended by about 220 men. The Radical Faeries were founded by Harry Hay, Don Kilhefner and Mitch Walker. "The term "Radical" was chosen to reflect both political extremity and the idea of "root" or "essence", while the term "Faerie" was chosen in reference both to the immortal animistic spirits of European folklore and to the fact that "fairy" had become a pejorative slang term for gay men."

Harry Hay's influence is what I am most familiar with and three things in particular impressed me and impacted the culture around me 1) his Marxist economic ideas, 2) his ideas about subject to subject relating and 3) his assertions that gay men were set apart from hetero men because of their spirituality. Harry Hay's life was full of activism and he was a co-founder of the Mattachine Society and the Gay Liberation Front in LA.

The second radical faerie gathering was in August 1980 in Colorado and their work was influential enough that I met my first self identified radical faery while dancing in a nightclub in Columbia, Mo in 1981. What I noticed most about my radical faery friends is that they deeply loved nature and loved to fuck in the outdoors. They worshipped "The Old Gods" like Pan and Dionysus. They were genderqueer men who wore dresses and skirts and cried and had feelings. I was taught how to tend bees, how to drink the nectar of flowers and how to grow and tend orchids and bromeliads by my radical faerie brothers. They struggled to be self sustaining, and to have what we now call small "carbon footprints". They pooled their money, bought land and lived collectively. They lent me a copy of the now rare and out of print book *Witchcraft and the Gay Counter Culture"* by Arthur Evans Taking a non-assimilationist position, they embraced the marginalized identity of faggot and built their own cultures around it.

I enjoy listening to personal stories of my Radical Faerie friends. Ganymede's stories of attending events at the Wolf Creek Sanctuary broaden my understanding of my own history. His presence at Radical Faerie sanctuaries merged Evans's Wiccan worship of the old Queer Gods, with a skillful immersion in BDSM sacred sexual practices. The experiences Ganymede and his friends facilitated allowed a TAZ where personal gnosis combated societally induced shame. For the majority of it's history Radical faerie culture was largely a gay separatist culture. When I understood in 2013 that the Wolf Creek Sanctuary was now open to all genders, I attended my first Beltane there. I felt honored to be on the land that held Harry Hay's ashes.

Pleasure and Danger from 1980's- Aughts: Feminist Sex Radicals

I attended Stephens College; a small private women's college in the Midwest, from 1980-1983 and got a degree in Human Ecology. Two big feminist news stories hotly debated on campus in 1982 were 1) the National Organization of Women's (N.O.W.) resolution of lesbian politics, which refused to support: "pederasty, pornography, sado-masochism and public sex as Lesbian rights issues" and 2) The Scholar and The Feminist IX Conference held at Barnard and the subsequent deep divisions and horizontal hostility that erupted in the women's movement that are now referred to as the "Feminist Sex Wars"Gayle Rubin, Dorothy Allison and Carol Vance were publically targeted for their private sexual behaviors. I began researching their works and reading them.

I found myself on "the side" of the sex radicals. As a person who has survived multiple sexual traumas and healed and integrated from them, I believe that even within a patriarchal culture it is possible to create places and spaces, (those Temporary Autonomous Zones TAZ again) where I have sexual agency. I choose to openly identify as a polyamorous kinky queer sex radical. I make this choice from a risk aware place of informed consent. The outlaw status of my own identity is a way for me to respect the elders who mentor me and honor the lives of people with less privilege and social power who paved the path before me. I take responsibility for being a role model and mentor to the youngers in my community who wish to have sexual freedom and agency.

Feminist peoples and the communities they inhabit have ways, (the traumatic PTSD dances and entanglements of all oppressed groups), of rehearsing distress, projecting shadow and dividing themselves along the faultlines of horizontal hostility and lateral violence. I have participated in and survived several of these social implosions and I'll save you the details. Suffice it to say that cultural evolution is messy and as soon as one marginalized group gets a foothold we discover others who had been "invisible" to us who need compassion, recognition, advocacy and support to become centralized.

There are many other sex radicals who did (and continue to do), the difficult work of confronting the sex negative prejudices and misogynist oppressions of mainstream culture. Every day these people bravely champion authentic sexual self-expression. They stood up and came out in the 80's and they are doing so now. Daily exposing themselves to the slut shaming and inherent marginalization of revealing that their personal sexual preferences, and autonomously chosen sexual practices made them (Oh horror of horrors!) anti-establishment. Crafting my own identities in my 20-40's, I devoured the intermedia (art, music, performances, magazines, films, pornography), they were producing and vowed to follow in their footsteps. Susie Bright, Patrick Califia, Betty Dodson, Deborah Sundahl, Carol Queen & Annie Sprinkle, showed me what Feminist Sex Radicals looked like. I co-created a 5 woman punk band called *The Art Sluts*, held group "sensation parties", sent mail art, swapped cassette tapes with other self produced musicians read and wrote Zines and made art.

Magickal Cascadia

I got an MSW, got married to a genderqueer male sociologist and moved to Eugene OR in 1989. I opened a women's cultural center disguised as a coffeehouse called Baba Yaga's Dream: *A Place for Wild Women and their Friends*. This was my "saturn return" project. I went into business with my friend Dawn Lamp who had a small amount of capital. What I had was a lot of gumption, ambition, a belief in hard work and a love of radical feminism. From 1993-1995 we rattled the women's community by loving people of every gender, showing women created porn, selling sex toys, celebrating Pagan holidays, teaching radical topics, holding and participating in women centered sexually explicit events like the "Leather and Lace show". Our small feminist community divided over responses to these events and once again the focus was on the danger of women owning their own desires. It began to become clear to me that people who did not own or explore their own sexual shadows were not able to imagine the existence of an autonomy they did not possess. I spent the rest of the decade making TerraFire Art: ceramic images of goddesses and occult icons. I built pagan community by holding public Wiccan ritual events through Cauldron of Changes, attending the local OTO lodge, hanging out with the CAW proto nest members and learning sex magick techniques. I began to travel outside of Eugene to sell my pagan art and explore other people's magical events. My circles grew wider, my travels went further. By the end of the decade I had a Cascadia wide network of pagan peers and many of them were talking about this place in Seattle called the Wetspot. Members of outsider groups like us, (Witches, Queers, sex radicals and artists), who don't thrive in the fading uber culture, tend to run in circles of friends and lovers that overlap. We question dualities and false dichotomies, we have shadow projected at us so frequently that we tend to explore it deeply and voluntarily. We worship dark Goddesses like Erishkigal, Lilith, Hekate and Lady Death herself, all of whom make great archetypes for dominatrixes. If we want to have a play space big enough for our events, we know we have to share. The number of kinky queer poly pagans in Eugene was smaller than I wanted it to be. I got divorced, I moved to Seattle and the Wetspot became the center of my new social life.

Defining Sex Positive Culture: Consent, Autonomy & Collaboration

Who gets to say what sex positive culture is? Who gets to define consent?77 Let's take a look at two kinky queer polyamorous women who created sex positive cultural centers to find out. The Center for Sex & Culture was founded by Dr. Carol Queen & Dr. Robert Morgan Lawrence in San Francisco in 1997 and became a non profit in 2001. Allena Gabosch was hired to be the director of the Center for Sex Positive Culture in Seattle in 1999.

Like my role models; Carol Queen & Allena Gabosch, I see consent as central to sex positive culture. I define sex positive culture as any gathering of adults which acknowledges the sexual autonomy of its individual membership and operates under the guidelines of that group's clearly defined and embodied understanding of consent.

In fact, I assert, that while some people may refer to themselves sex positive or run organizations that include the phrase sex positive in their name, if those individuals do not:

1): use some form of "safe, sane and consensual" (SSC) practices and/or engage in risk aware consensual kink (RACK) as guidelines for their events and include safer sex supplies

2): express and embody body-positive, fat-positive, kink-positive, shame free inclusive attitudes and

3): show some awareness of accessibility issues for the vast variety of accommodations needed by people with varied abilities to actually be inclusive then...

they are not honoring and adhering to the cultural norms created by the sex radical outsider Queer elders whose emotional labor and intermedia made it possible to center the term sex-positive.

While they are using the now successful brand of the term "sex positive" to position their work/sell their products, they are not re-creating radical egalitarian inclusive sex positive culture. There is no sense of autonomy or agency available to me (as a fat, queer, kinky, witch elder) at such events. When I attend expecting a TAZ where I can experience sexual autonomy, instead a looks-ist commodified haze, catering to the male gaze fills the space and the awkward social anxiety of "hoping to be chosen" is present. If I express discomfort or begin to explain why I disagree with the gender essentialism or ableism or looks-ism present in the space, I am accused of being angry and unreasonable. Alternatively, I am accused of being hostile to men or having other "character deficits". In other words, I am told that my experience is an internally generated psychological experience; a personal problem. I am told that I am "reading too much into" the social context. I personally find this "apolitical stance" problematic.

In the sex positive cultural centers that formed around the leadership of queer sex radical pioneers Carol Queen and Allena Gabosch: Outlaw/Outsider identities are centered and sexual autonomy is fostered. A new umbrella identity called "Sex Positive" created a sense of unity across our different kinks and unique sexual proclivities. Having reliable and legitimized venues increased our resource base. The equipment access was fantastic, (I never could have gotten that St. Andrew's cross into my apartment and the back room had huge swing harnesses in it). Having regular access to sexual play in a space without stigma or shame was liberating, thrilling and deeply healing. The opportunity to repeatedly choose to attend a smorgasbord of sexual opportunities with both friends and strangers broadened and deepened my life. I began to perceive/experience my own sense of sexual autonomy. I understood somatically that adults have sexual self development processes (why is this not taught in psychology?) and that those processes require a variety of self exploration and group experiences. When we are obligated by socioeconomic resource limitation to link our sexual partners to only those sexual partners who will support us financially and "love us forever" well, it's like the Meatloaf song "Paradise by the Dashboard Light".

It is critical, (and because of economic inequality this is especially true for queer, trans and cis women), that there be spaces of sexual liberation where we can try out a variety of sexual experiences and partnerings and have sexual agency that is not tied to (or in any way threatening to), our financial resource base. Every adult deserves the opportunity to experience sexual autonomy. Without the space to develop our individual autonomy/sovereignty we have trouble extending it to other people. Sex Positive Culture is an essential component of creating the conditions/context that allows sexual sovereignty to arise.

Allena Gabosch is a "Grand Mistress of Collaboration", I say this because the CSPC was a place for every kind of sex positive adult. There were swingers nights, Goth dance nights, polyamory potlucks, rope bondage nights, blood sports nights, age play events, leather women, leather men and genderqueer nights. Allena Gabosch welcomed everyone and was masterful at anticipating people's needs and then providing for them accessibility and inclusivity.

In March 2000, I became member 1934 of CSPC which means there were 1,933 people who identified as part of Seattle's sex positive community before I did. I dove in, attending events at least once a week. Witches and Outlaws were everywhere and I was no longer "the biggest freak in the freak pile". The Women's welcoming committee felt like a consciousness raising group and was, well, welcoming. The group dynamics had been carefully tended: there were Dungeon Masters' to oversee the events, Ambassadors to chat up new members and introduce them to old timers. Volunteers received excellent training and handled everything from the front door to the library, to trash and take down. There was an education committee for a few years and Allena encouraged and supported me when I wanted to create a class called Clitoral Revelations, which I taught with various teams from 2002-2012. I was part of the Seattle Slam poetry scene and by 2004 I was running a monthly Red Hot Words sexually explicit event at CSPC with guest poets. For several years I was the 'camp counselor' for the outdoor fundraising event *Wetspot in Paradise*. In CSPC, I had a great venue for teaching Sacred Sexuality for the 1st time in 2005. The Seattle Erotic Art Festival developed and in 2006, I had an opportunity to do my breast tray performance. The CSPC space was a truly democratic, actually diverse and egalitarian space held in common by the Executive Director, the board and the volunteers. I had some of the most amazing experiences of my life there. I was given the gift of a nurturing community where I could hone the craft of my Living Love Revolution teachings and sow the seeds of my own sex positive subculture.

The Shoots: New Growth, New Directions

The EcoSexuality that I envision and long for starts with co-committing to a holistic web of relatedness that honors the sexual autonomy of every person involved. An extended rhizome of diverse polyfidelitous queer outlaws who consensually negotiate the terms of their resource sharing, the co-tending of their homes and the balancing of their skill sets. The understanding and experience of sovereignty begins inside each human member of the polycule. Sharing resources and skills and having the consistent experience of "enough", their sexual experiences move back and forth through recreation and into communion. Their secure and resonant sense of Self naturally extends the concept of personhood and sovereignty to the animals and land around them. Gaia is related to as an animate living being, with whom we are in reciprocal erotic energetic communal relationship.

My theory of adult sexual self development includes three phases of meaning/ purpose for adult sexuality: Procreation, recreation and communion. This theory is more thoroughly outlined in my essay *What's Sexuality Got to Do With Ecology?*

I quite neatly stopped using sex for procreation in my 20's. I had the privilege of using my social time at the CSPC to focus on sex as recreation and along the way got a lot of healing done. I realized that sometimes sex provided me with a sense of communion: ego dissolving, ecstatic experiences became very interesting to me. The Aphrodite Temple system I created is a form of group Sacred Sex Magick that consistently gives me and other participants, a deep sense of communion. The Temple itself and the people who become my students and join the priestess body have evolved together. In the process of doing quarterly temples together for 3-5 years as a group we come to understand and experience that providing pleasure for each other is an act of Transpersonal love. The sacredness of this relatedness is generated because we are agreeing to hold space for each other's autonomy and facilitate each other's sexual development without trying to possess each other's bodies or extract guarantees of safety and comfort. My ability to imagine this kind of relatedness was a direct result of my experiences at CSPC.

Starting about 7 years ago, Aphrodite Temples programming had a magickal focal point on Saturday night, (other witches would call this a cone of power). Participants were asked to send out a wish, intention or desire that they wanted to see manifested in the material world. This is pretty standard fare for sex magick. As I, myself, and the other consistent travelers of my temple system continue to evolve, the magick and the intentions of the cones of power have evolved too. We began by asking for our own needs and desires to be met, we attended to our own healing. As we became whole and found long term partners and extended our polycules and found "enough" we began to ask for the needs of our friends and families and those not present at temple to be met. We prayed on other people's behalfs, for their desires, for their healing and with their consent. Then we began to include the well-being of non human persons in our cones of power, we sent energy toward the healing of social harms, for the dying of other species, to bees, and to the land and those who had lived on the land before us. Now we send energy to all of these beings and to our Ancestors. We send prayers to our descendants. We ask that all beings be well. As an interdependent group of naked sexing humans, we focus the power of our orgasmic pleasure on the task of deepening our connection with the non-human worlds. We intend that humanity wake up, become emotionally and sexually mature and become present to the splendor and magnificence of their lives and their lover Gaia.

And so the sex positive desire to merge with, be in communion with, and extend loving erotic attention to, other humans; evolved into a desire to celebrate erotic life force with its source: Nature and all of her parts. Thus my ecosexuality was born.

Aphrodite enticed me away from my beloved Emerald City; Seattle and toward the City of Roses (Portland,OR); by setting up a series of synchronicities that were too juicy to resist. A timeline of opportunities unfolded with lightning speed and a sense of inevitability. In February, I was invited to hold monthly evenings of Sensual Magicks dedicated to Aphrodite. Gabriella Cordova invited me to co-create a PDX EcoSex Symposium 2012. By March we were holding organizing meetings in order to create an event inspired by the EcoSex Symposiums created by SexEcologists Beth Stephens and Annie Sprinkle. In April Annie Sprinkle came to Portland for a series of appearances including a "Finding Your E-Spot walking tour". I was honored to chauffeur, her to the next stop on her Cascadian tour: (Evergreen University in Olympia, WA). We discussed ecosex theory and philosophy and our metamour Gaia. In May, I produced and taught "Viva La Vulva!" weekend that included Deborah Sundahl teaching female ejaculation and the LLR team providing Clitoral Revelations & Vulvic Explorations. During the weekend, our venue host showed me an affordable rental house he had available in the neighborhood. In June I co-produced PDX EcoSex Symposium 2012 and met Lindsay Hagamen who attended as a presenter. In July, I moved Living Love Revolution to Portland. Lindsay and I began meeting weekly in September to build relatedness around our shared vision of creating a yearly event where Ecosexuals could network. "Surrender: the EcoSex Convergence" was held yearly from June 2013 -2017 and successfully gathered between 100-200 people each year. In 2018, I moved the event to Orcas Island changing its name to "Celebrating Lover Earth". There are plans to have an event in Boulder, CO; called Eco Eros: An Earth Love Retreat in 2019, and I will likely lead a more intimate camping event on the first weekend in July.

The Mycelial Mat: EcoSexual Intermedia & Cross-pollination

Let's take a moment to praise Beth Stephens and Annie Sprinkle; the sex radical feminist couple who are the queer theory and performance art matrix of EcoSexuality & SexEcology. They wrote the EcoSex Manifesto as well as coming up with the metaphoric shift from "Earth as Mother" to "Earth as Lover". They brought their *Here Come the EcoSexuals!* Experience to Surrender: the EcoSex Convergence in 2016 including the fabulous pollination pod and the E.A.R.T.H. lab. They made it a point to have morning coffee, make media and share conversations with Lindsay and I about our mutual culture making works.

It was wonderful to spend more time with Annie Sprinkle whose sex work, performance art, pleasure activism and sex magick rituals shaped my younger selves and continue to inspire and encourage me. It was deeply supportive to have the opportunity to converge and cross-pollinate with these pollen-amourous queens from another bioregion.

Beth Stephens teaches art at UC Santa Cruz and set up the Environmental Art Research Theory and Happenings lab there. When I asked whose work inspired her own, I learned about Joseph Beuys 95 the german Fluxus movement member. Beuys also taught in a University setting and like EcoSexuals, he focused on: the power and necessity of direct experience; honoring the soul force in non-humans and dissolving the false separation between art and life. Beth also shared with me her admiration for the works of her friends Donna Haraway and Linda mary Montana and how it influences Sex Ecology. Having seen and promoted her first movie *GoodBye Gauley Mountain: An EcoSexual Love Story* I already understood Beth's deep attachment to her Appalachian homeland and her compassion for her working class origins. We talked about how their weddings through the chakras evolved into EcoSexual weddings and our concerns about the drought in California. Their new movie "Water Makes Us Wet" will begin distribution in 2018. What I appreciate the most about Beth and Annie is how pleasurable their work is and how loving and accessible they are as people. I hope to attend the EcoSex Symposium V in Europe. In the meantime I will keep looking for other opportunities to build rhizomatic intimacy with ecosexuals from other Bioregions. I am committed to creating a yearly TAZ where we can converge and cross-pollinate and dream new ways of being into realities. Long live Gaia! May her lovers thrive and prosper as they find ever increasing ways to commit to her and take care of her. May we all continue to commit to life on Gaia until, (As the EcoSex Manifesto says) Death brings us closer together forever.

CHAPTER 12
POLITICS AND COMMUNITY

Even the sex-positive world isn't immune to politics.

POLYAMORY AND THE BLACK FEMINIST
by Ruby Johnson

"It's your thing, do what you wanna do, I can't tell you, who to sock it to." —The Isley Brothers

The Isley Brothers have been a part of my life since early childhood. I have hummed and car danced to "It's Your Thing" for decades. Suddenly, a few years ago, I gleaned an awareness of what the lyrics really meant. The singer is saying, "It's your pussy, and you got pussy control." The lyrics tell a story of NO ownership, NO exclusivity, and NO control of the other person in the relationship. This song came out in 1969 which was in the middle of the Black Arts Movement. Black people were exploring the taboo.

I would love to say that I came into this enlightenment by way of a spontaneous combustion of introspective work. The truth is that my world view on beliefs like, "Who I am in a relationship with?" "How many people I am in a relationship with?" and "When can I be in relationships?" has socially and culturally shifted. In *Rewriting the Rules*, Meg-John Barker speaks to the political, popular, and psychological discourses that tend to present monogamous coupledom as the only natural and/or morally correct form of human relating. The ultimate goal, in this view, is to be married, and if you are bonded with that one person, then you are complete. That one is the only one for you, EVER. I chased that dream for years. The longer the dream was unfulfilled, the more desperate I became. The more desperate I became, the more of me that I was willing to compromise. So, it was no longer a choice but a means to sustain my existence. polyamory introduced me to new perspectives, new ways of viewing relationships, and a new understanding of where the sustenance of life came from. This helped me rewrite the rules and way of thinking in my life.

Today, my shift is, conceptually and behaviorally, constructed with choice, autonomy, and agency. The painful and difficult deconstruction of my blackness, my womanhood, and my sexuality have liberated my parameters of existing.

> "Black feminist thought can be highly empowering because they provide alternatives to the way things are supposed to be."
>
> —Patricia Collins

Untruths

Monogamy is an institution. The institution stands on values and beliefs that dictate socially acceptable relationship structures and how those relationships behave. As long as the prescribed parameters of the institution are complied with, they promise an inevitable "happily ever after." If you do not achieve this "happily ever after," you are doing something wrong. I had thirty-five years of existing on a foundation of dichotomies: normal/abnormal, ladylike/whoreish, man's role/woman's role. Life's matters were clearly delineated. Faithful/cheating was included in those dichotomies. These de facto institutions predetermined the course of my life. I did not know that there was an alternative those options.

The parameters

During my journey into polyamory, I learned to appreciate Audre Lorde, bell hooks, Patricia Collins, James Baldwin, Maya Angelou, and others. Black feminist thought can be highly empowering because it provides alternatives to the way things are. First, empowerment is gaining the critical consciousness to unpack hegemonic ideologies. Second, the follow-up to critical consciousness consists of constructing new knowledge.

My womanhood, My Sexuality

"I began writing about power because I had so little." —Octavia Butler

Black woman devalued. The narrative of my life was that being somebody's someone is all you need. What I'm speaking of is the belief that I am nothing, an empty shell, unless somebody loves me. I became complicit in my own oppression and marginalization. I oppressed my possibilities and marginalized my wants, needs, and desires. I created rules on top of rules on top of rules to protect that narrative. Lies, justifications, and accepting what is unacceptable was a daily practice.

Does that sound like liberation?

Moving out of relationships that were stifled by my desperation for finding The One was the first taste of sweet freedom. I do not have to excuse, explain away, or deny who the person sitting in front of me is. Polyamory is more than a relationship dynamic. It shatters constraints and arbitrary benchmarks set for successful relationships in our society. It allows room for authenticity to develop without the pressure of "where is this going?" or "what's next?" It allows room for infinite possibilities. Polyamory is many loves. The loves are friendships, groups, family, chosen family, lovers, and so much more.

Blackness and sexuality

"We don't see things as they are, we see things as we are." —Anais Nin

I can write ad nauseum about my perceptions versus reality. I perceived myself as ugly and black, set against the background of a beautiful world that I didn't belong to. I fantasized that I was everyone else but me. I did not have the admiration, fondness, affection for my skin that I do today. Throughout this journey, my new relationship with my skin has illuminated my sexuality. I am no longer in the closet. My community has given me much affirmation and acceptance. I did not have to be, and they did not ask me to be, anyone else. Ruby is pretty cool to them. My black is beautiful, and my sexuality is my own.

Polyamory means many loves, my first love had to be me.

LOOKING AHEAD: JUSTICE AND THE FUTURE OF SEX POSITIVITY
by Dawn Serra

When you think about sex positivity, what comes to mind? Some people think it means you love sex and nothing more. By now, thanks to this book and the work of so many amazing sex educators, you probably know that sex positivity actually means an embrace of pleasure and joy and a returning to your body on your own terms, whatever that might look like.

At its core, sex positivity is a response to sex negativity.[26] In other words, we saw what we did not like, what was causing pain and shame, and responded to that need by saying pain and shame do not belong in our sexuality or in the ways we love each other (kink aside). For me, finding sex-positive community, educators, and language felt like a breath of fresh air. There are people reclaiming words like slut, queer, and pervert. Communities rich with people uniting around common interests such as BDSM, public sex, queerness, asexuality, and porn. This is a space that asks, if you could be anything, do anything, and experience anything you desired, consensually, what would you dare to try? Who would you feel safe to be?

I've found tremendous relief and solidarity within sex-positive spaces. As a trauma survivor, as someone in a fat body, as a woman, as a queer person, I've had a chance to ask new questions and feel seen in ways I never would have dreamed in mainstream spaces that are still struggling with sex negativity and shame.

The first time I attended a play party, I was terrified. As a rape survivor, being in sexual spaces can be challenging for me. My anxiety remained high until the facilitators started walking us through the rules of how we would respect each other and care for ourselves. Their explicit permission to say no was thrilling, especially as a woman in a culture that often devalues my no.

That evening I had a chance to watch delicious scenes unfold, and my partner and I settled into a corner for some deeply connecting moments. Being in a space that welcomed setting boundaries, self-expression, and asking for what you want felt new and important.

Imagine if we all had space to safely explore our desires and voices while being held by a skilled facilitator.

As I've stretched into these spaces more and more, I've also started encountering its edges. Who are we leaving out? Who is consistently being left behind? For instance, that first play party I attended wasn't accessible to anyone with a mobility disability as the space was up multiple sets of stairs and the floor was covered in mattresses. Other than my partner, there were no people of color. There were no trans people, and I was the only person in a fat body. It was also at a location far from public transportation, which made it inaccessible to people without a car or who were on a tight budget.

---

[26] Conner Habib introduced this idea to me

Again and again, I've seen this play out in workshops, dungeons, play parties, and conferences. An endless sea of white bodies, of thin bodies, of sexualized bodies, of able bodies, of kinky interests. It's left me wondering can sex positivity actually be radical if it's standing on a foundation of oppression?

Sex positivity, in theory, is a philosophy of unapologetic acceptance and individual self-expression. And yet, sex positivity exists within a world build on frameworks like racism, sexism, patriarchy, cisnormativity/transphobia, ableism, fatphobia, whorephobia, classism, ageism, colonialism, and performativity.

When trans, disabled, asexual, traumatized, older, fat, and BIPOC people are treated as an afterthought, as a diversity checkmark, as a nice-to-have, we must conclude that we are not actually creating something radical. This is where we find ourselves within the sex-positive community today. In order to work toward sexual liberation, we must also be fundamentally committed to complete liberation from all oppression—not only when it's convenient or visible to others. A great many activists and educators are doing this work already. They have challenged me, and continue to challenge me, to question my own assumptions, privileges, and narratives.

These ideas are not my own, but rather the culmination of the oft-unrecognized work of so many others who are living these theories out in their own flesh.[27] Because of them, I have learned that sexual pleasure is a privilege and a luxury. Enthusiastic consent is a privilege and a luxury. Access to workshops, sex toys, porn, and sexual partners is a privilege and a luxury.

We need a sexuality community that is freeing people from the current thought model while also looking ahead to what is beyond oppression. We need educators fighting to reduce stigma, shame, and harm and who have a deep, unyielding commitment to embracing anti-racism, anti-transphobia, anti-classism, anti-colonialism, anti-ageism, anti-fatphobia, anti-cissexism, and anti-ableism work.[28] [29]

Sex positivity is a powerful step in the right direction, but it is only the beginning of what we need to do collectively to rise up and embrace what's possible.

We need to start by listening. We need to acknowledge that a lot of work has been done in these spaces, especially by marginalized people, and we need to lift those voices up. We need new questions. It's not sufficient to simply ask what we want for ourselves or what it means to be in a body without sexual shame. We must ask: what do we need, collectively, to heal and reimagine? Because sexuality is at once both utterly individual and communal. It is how we relate with ourselves and with the culture at large.

So, how do we, as a community committed to pleasure and human connection, embrace the decolonization of our thought models and language when it comes to sex, gender, love, and relationship?

---

[27] [28] I borrow Cherríe Moraga's phrase, "theory in the flesh" to acknowledge the lived experiences survival and faith of marginalized people within oppressive systems.

[29] Continuing and developing my perspective this space is also a result of work I've done with anti-diet culture speaker Melissa Toler, as well as writings by Chela Sandoval and Angela Davis.

What might we need to let go of around our stories of gender, binaries, and pleasure? Instead of prescribing certain kinds of pleasure experiences (such as orgasm), imagine a movement that instead teaches self-inquiry and reflection so that each person and community can begin to find the language for their unique and communal understandings of joy, connection, and ecstasy.

The more time I spend deconstructing the systems that are keeping us all trapped in harmful patterns of oppression, the more I realize that sex positivity is not the answer, but it is the beginning of a powerful question that could lead to liberation. Sex positivity brought me here, and what comes next is up to all of us—in who we choose to listen to, in how we choose to challenge the stories we've been given, and in what we do with that knowledge.

I'd like to specifically name the people who have been doing this work for far longer than I have and whose wisdom and labor informs me. Please note that all of these individuals are people of color that exist at multiple intersections of oppression.

CHAPTER 13
OUR SEX-POSITIVE FUTURE

Where are we headed? What is the future of sex positivity?
What happens if we live in a sex-positive world? Freedom!

HOW DEATH TAUGHT ME THAT GREAT SEX CAN CHANGE THE WORLD
by Dr. Liz Powell

I'd been flirting with E for the year and a half that I had known him, and he had never seemed that interested in me. Then, on June 17, 2017, I went to brunch with friends, and when E walked into the restaurant, he kissed me on the lips instead of the cheek—and I felt lightning coursing through my veins as excitement and passion radiated from where his lips touched mine until they filled my every cell. Over the course of the meal, we went from playfully bumping each other's shoulders to him biting the back of my neck. We were smitten, instantly and fully. Less than two weeks before that brunch I had made a decision to put all of my current relationships on hold. I was in a state of overwhelm and discontent deeper than I'd known before. I was traveling for work almost half the time, I wasn't sleeping well, and I felt like neither my personal nor professional life were successful. When I would see a date scheduled in my calendar, I would feel dread and obligation. I was noticing myself becoming more critical and short tempered with the amazing humans I was seeing. I knew that it wasn't fair to keep seeing people just because I felt like they would be upset or because I owed it to them. I cancelled all my dates. I was determined to spend some time being very seriously single and utterly selfish with my time. My commitment to myself was that I would not schedule any dates or hook-ups in my calendar until at least October.

Deciding to not date was something that surprised most people who knew me. I identify as queer, switchy, solo poly, megasexual, and a slut. This means that I interact sexually and romantically with people of all genders and enjoy BDSM in both top and bottom roles. I conduct my relationships in such a way that values autonomy most, and I am someone who has difficulty forming romantic connections without a sexual connection. Finally, I am "sexually extroverted," so I like experiencing and getting to know people in sexual ways. I've always dated, generally multiple people at once, and have had few periods of purposeful singleness in my life.

I worked to reconcile what it meant to be a slut who's not interested in scheduling dates or even sex. And yet, no matter how much I thought about it, the decision felt like it was exactly what I needed.

Given this context, the way my body and my heart caught on fire when E's lips touched mine can offer some idea of how complicated the start of this relationship was for me. We spent about twenty-eight hours together that first day and night, and every touch and word and breath and moment found me falling. He looked at me like I was the most entrancing person he'd ever met and asked, "Where did you come from?" over and over. He bought me popsicles, cooked me breakfast, washed me, and gave me a toothbrush. He gave me caring in ways I would have never even thought to ask for.

Every friend I spoke to about E ascribed the start of this relationship a significant meaning. Some friends believed I had cleared away what wasn't serving me and had made space for someone amazing. To them, E was my gift from the universe for doing the hard work on myself. Other friends, however, saw in E a cosmic test: the universe was challenging me to see if I would fall back into old patterns or if I would hold strong to my commitment to make time and space for myself. I struggled with these two perspectives—was E a gift I had finally made space for, or was he something shiny distracting me from my real work?

We saw each other one more time before I left on my next work trip. He insisted on spending the night with me and waking up early to take me to the airport so that he could get some last kisses before I flew away for two weeks. As we parted, he promised he would be there waiting for me when I got home. We continued texting every day, sending pictures back and forth and sharing the mundane details of our day-to-day lives. Everyone I knew heard about this new man who I was so excited about, and who had upended my careful plans. I began to let myself hope that maybe I had found someone who could give me the kind of relationship that would nourish me deeply. I couldn't wait to get home to see him and continue building what we had started.

On June 25th, E told me that he was feeling "rough" and he was going to take a nap. He sent me a selfie of him sitting on his couch with both his cats on his chest. I kept texting him about the group sex and rough sex classes I was taking that day. I noticed that he hadn't been texting back since midday but figured he was busy. The next day, I flew to another city on my tour and taught a class at a local shop. After the class, I went out to dinner with my dear friends. We laughed, we ate, we drank, and it was beautiful. As the meal ended, I checked my phone and had a message from my former roommate—E was dead. Gone during his nap. Heart failure.

I cried so hard that I couldn't breathe, couldn't see, couldn't talk. Knowing that there would be memorial services during the upcoming weekend, I changed my flight and cut my trip short. I returned home and faced the reality of the death of my new lover, surrounded by friends, many of whom didn't know we'd been dating.

When you think about it, in some ways sex represents the opposite of death. Although orgasms have been called "the little death," the act of sex is the act of creation. Sex can tap into our vibrancy, our life force, lighting up neural pathways and building sensation to peaks and crests. Sex is where many babies come from and sex is what our closest primate relatives, bonobos, use to settle conflict and cement social bonds. As social creatures, humans tend to experience greater levels of vulnerability through touch and sex automatically, as though physical closeness encourages emotional openness. I knew I needed Great Sex so that I could process my pain.

It was like the axis of the globe shifted suddenly and I didn't know which way was up. My emotions were so strong, and I am such a guarded person, that I didn't know who I could trust to see me in that space. So I called up a good friend and lover of mine, R, and asked him if he could help me by fucking away some of my grief.

When I asked this lover for sex, what I was asking for was not just regular sex. I was asking for Great Sex.

What is great sex?

Great Sex is what happens when we bring our most authentic and most skillful selves to the sexual arena. Several elements differentiate Great Sex from normal sex.

Great Sex starts with great communication. While it's possible we could have Great Sex without ever asking for what we need or telling a lover which spots feel great, it's not particularly likely. To have Great Sex then, we must know ourselves, know what works for us, and be willing to ask for it. This necessitates vulnerability: the next element to Great Sex. If I'm not letting someone see the real me, it's hard to have Great Sex—I need to let the real me meet the real you. Great Sex is also something that happens when we feel as good about saying no as we do about saying yes. We cannot have Great Sex if we're enduring things we don't enjoy or if we're too afraid of what will happen if we say no.

Furthermore, Great Sex requires us to take a chance. Whether that chance is on connecting deeply, asking for something we've never asked for before, saying no to something we don't want, or trying out something a partner wants, we must be willing to take a chance for Great Sex to happen; as the saying goes, all the good stuff happens outside of your comfort zone. In Great Sex, we also must give ourselves permission to enjoy and indulge. For those of us in the United States and Canada, many of our cultural ideas are rooted in Protestant ethics around working hard and denying ourselves pleasure. We cannot have Great Sex if we are unwilling to enjoy the moments we are experiencing; if we are judging or distancing ourselves, our pleasure will be necessarily reduced. Finally, in Great Sex we must hold space for things that may seem in opposition to what we expect. For instance, pain might be pleasure, pleasure might bring out sorrow, joy and sadness may coexist. In Great Sex, we make space for the richness and complexity of human experience.

Great (grief) sex with R

When I arrived at R's house, he immediately wrapped me in a big hug. He looked me in the eyes and then kissed me deeply. He asked me whether I wanted food or a drink or to just go upstairs. He asked me questions and listened. I told him what I did want and what I didn't, both of us continually checking in throughout our afternoon. No matter what state I was in—laughing, crying, pleasure—he saw me in that space and let me have my experience. Where some folks might see tears during sex and become anxious or uncomfortable, he kissed them from my cheeks. His ability to be fully present with me through all of my emotions allowed me to enjoy the pleasure when he touched me and the grief as it ebbed and flowed. I let him see me in my mess and I could feel him loving me the whole way. When I wanted to tell stories about E and our time together, he encouraged me to say even more and talked about how sad he was that he never met E. Even though I cried so much I couldn't see, I can honestly say I still enjoyed my experience with R that day because of how fully alive I was in those moments.

Both R and I brought our Great Sex skills to this afternoon. Because we were both communicative, present, vulnerable, and open to the richness and complexity of the experience, I walked away from those few hours together feeling much better. Grief is a burden that lightens when we are witnessed. Through pleasure and caring, I was able to open up the swirling ball of emotions that I had been keeping packed away and, in so doing, watched as it started the process of shrinking. Now I won't claim that one afternoon of sex completely cured my grief; that would be a ridiculous assertion and unrealistic to expect. However, I can say that I couldn't have found a more pleasant or effective way to begin the process of allowing the grief to move through me and to follow its own natural course.

How can great sex change the world?

In that afternoon, I got a visceral experience of just how Great Sex can change the world. I'm not saying that the world would be better if everyone were having more sex, but I do think that the world would be better if everyone got to have the sex they wanted (as much or as little, whatever kinds, with whatever folks). Plus, the skills people need for Great Sex are the same skills we need to be great people.

How much better would the world be if people were able to ask for what they want using skillful communication? Imagine living in communities where people only say yes when they really mean it and no when it's appropriate, therefore preventing resentment from forming. Wouldn't it be lovely to have friends and partners who were able to receive your no with grace and kindness, making it easier for you to give honest answers? In a time when scientists are finding that people tend to have fewer and fewer close friends, increased vulnerability and a willingness to see each other in our pain and our happiness all at the same time could make a real difference. If more people were empowered to take chances and enjoy themselves we would all be able to benefit from the increased pleasure and authenticity.

Great Sex skills are the skills we need for great living. They are the skills that help us be authentic, set and maintain boundaries, embrace joy, and create empowerment.

How did my great sex skills help me cope?

Great Sex with R allowed me to begin the process of healing. I was able to experience and embody my grief while also experiencing pleasure and unite the force that gives life with my feelings on death. I had to be able to ask for what I wanted to get it, and I had to take a chance on letting someone see me fall apart so that I could start putting myself back together. I told my stories and was heard and walked away from that afternoon filled with love and caring. So, while before E's death I thought I understood how powerful Great Sex could be, my experience with grief helped me see much more clearly how important Great Sex can be.

In the end, I think that E was a gift in my life. He showed a type of love that I didn't know was possible, helped me tap into a strength I had forgotten, and helped me learn deeply how important Great Sex is for all of us.

SEX POSITIVITY, EH?
by Jaz Papadopoulos

Two women in a bar. It's a first date. They're intoxicated and have snuck into the bathroom together (same stall, to the annoyance of everyone else in line). They're flirting, taking turns on the toilet, and then...the blonde does the unthinkable. She poops in front of her date. It's like an out-of-body experience, she watches herself doing it, horrified, wishing she were someone else (or at least a little less drunk). The brunette cowers in the corner, hiding from the stink. The next day, the brown-haired one texts the blonde one to come over for a booty call.

Two clowns meet. One is a recent clown school graduate, the other a junior, starting the courses the following week. The one with the wire rimmed glasses is sad, the one with the thick rimmed glasses endeavors to make ol' Wirey feel better. Thick-Rim takes Wirey out dancing, encouraging them to dance only while standing on stools, never the floor. They order in twos, whiskey and a beer back, tequila and a radler, fries and more fries. One bites the other all over, leaving dark bruises. Other asks what One is flagging with their purple bandana: "Bruising top." It's a joke; the kind that's also true. The American asks the Canadian, do you not have *The Simpson*s in Canada? The Canadian laughs a lot and then realizes it was not a sincere question, but people ask Canadians all kinds of crazy things so it gets hard to tell. Later that night, they fuck on the futon in their mutual friends' basement while other friends sleep on the floor nearby.

It's Portland, so really, I'm not surprised. Portland: home of the femme sex coven,[30] as well as the couch where I squirted for the first time. Portland, the Berlin of the Americas (both share a history of border segregation as well, who've thunk). Being here makes me contemplate how it's different than my birth country, what one local queer refers to as "America's Tuque."[31]

Ok, now I'm at a sex party, thrown in a women-run venue (an anarchist warehouse) in the northern prairies of Turtle Island (Winnipeg, Canada). The party is collectively hosted by a group of friends. The room is divided into designated areas, offering diverse options for participation: a porn-watching lounge; a sterile corner with a sharps container and waterproof covers on the floor; a few public beds, tents and private beds; a quiet no-sex zone; and a lap dance station. People brought items and created the areas that they wanted, and they came to initiate and fulfill their desires. This truly feels like a community space, and my mind is spinning: "Wow so hot...look at all these babes...what do I want? Why am I here?"

I look over at the lap dance station. I know the woman giving lap dances. She's gorgeous, a classic bombshell, and queer AF. She had volunteered to set up and tend to the station. As I watch, someone approaches. They greet each other, all smiles and nodding heads, and here we go...but wait, why does she look so bored? She looks SO bored. And the person getting a lap dance has noticed and

---

[30] "Community, Care, and a Femme Sex Coven," Autostraddle. Posted March 23, 2018. https://www.autostraddle.com/femme-sex-coven-372876/.

[31] Aka, Canada.

looks super bored too...limp hands on thighs, eyes fixed on the ceiling. I'm just watching and I'm wishing that the song would end because oh my god how is this so boring and awkward? Why would you volunteer to host lap dances for your friends if you didn't actually want to give them? Aren't we supposed to come here knowing what we want while feeling enthusiastic about it?!

People always joke that Canadians are polite. "Mild-mannered Canadians," our beliefs, and the effects of our behavior have even been the subject of academic studies.[32] Inevitably, cultural norms affect other aspects of culture, including social movements such as the sex-positivity movement. Similarly to how scientific studies show bias by mainly studying males, modern theoretical discourses are based out of—and critiqued within the bubble of—American culture and then presumed universal in their outcomes. A better understanding of the Canadian context—specifically, Canada's culture of politeness—will shed light on how the sex-positive movement has landed in the country.

It must be emphasized that this is a narrow exploration. I am discussing the sex-positive worlds in Canada and elsewhere but not any country or culture as a whole. I am not even providing a thorough analysis of Canada's sex-positive world; I am describing my own experiences as a queer, sex-positive feminist who lives in a mid-sized Canadian city. (Unlike Americans, most Canadians do not live in large urban centers—only six Canadian cities exceed one million people.)[33]

When asked about the top misconception of sex positivity, people reference the idea that being sex positive is about having lots of sex, lots of orgasms, having kinky sex, etc. Indeed, this is a gross misinterpretation[34] Sex positivity is not about doing things. It's not about who's done the kinkiest shit or who has sex most frequently. It's about doing the things that you want to do (and, if those things include other people, they must want to do it too).

Thinking about sex positivity in Canada reminds me of something an old anthropology prof used to say: "Liberalism is fascism in slow motion." If the new normal is to be sexually liberated,[35] well, what does that even mean? In my experience, it means that there are people feeling social pressure to conform to a radical approach to sexuality that they don't necessarily understand or have the social support to uphold in a healthy way. When I think back to watching that lap dance, I am reminded of my own difficulties in knowing what I want, my willingness to offer things that I don't actually want to offer, and my lack of confidence in how to ask for my desires: internalized, self-imposed obligations and judgments. Indeed, research has found that Canadians are more responsive to authority compared to Americans[36], and Canadian political leaders have been

---

[32] Tamara Palmer Seiler, "Melting Pot and Mosaic: Images and Realities," in Canada and the United States: Differences that Count (Second Edition), ed. David M. Thomas (Peterborough, ON: Broadview Press, 2000), 97.

[33] "Population of census metropolitan areas," Statistics Canada, March 3, 2017, http://www.statcan.gc.ca/tables-tableaux/sum-som/l01/cst01/demo05a-eng.htm.

[34] Annie Sprinkle in discussion with the author, August 2017.

[35] Melissa A. Fabello, "3 Reasons Why Sex Positivity without Critical Analysis Is Harmful," everyday feminism, May 14, 2014, http://everydayfeminism.com/2014/05/sex-positivity-critical-analysis/.

[36] Tamara Palmer Seiler, "Melting Pot and Mosaic: Images and Realities," in *Canada and the United States: Differences that Count (Second Edition)*, ed. David M. Thomas (Peterborough, ON: Broadview Press, 2000).

described as indecisive, not knowing (or not willing to communicate) what they want.[37] For those raised in a culture of politeness,[38] of soft yeses and softer noes, a cultural shift needs to occur before a yes-means-yes model will actually succeed.

I'm in Athens, Greece, in what I would call a warehouse party, but it's happening on the top floor of this small building in the middle of the city. One thing about Greece, especially in the post-financial crisis years: nobody really cares what you do, and all the cops are always dispatched to the anarchist end of town anyways. I was at this party because I met this lesbian online, and she invited me dancing. We had been dancing all night, it's six AM and I had been trying to get up the nerve to flirt with her for probably four hours. Finally, I'm psyched up enough to make my first move: I ask her, "Can I flirt with you?" (imagine the whole party coming to an unenthusiastic pause). She looks at me like I'm alien, REALLY alien. She is so unimpressed. "Why are you asking?" she looks uncomfortable. Okay, I just have to go for it I guess. "Can I kiss you?" "Why are you asking?!" Okay, they don't do consent culture here. Do I even know what I want anyways? Has consent culture broken me? Really, I'm concerned.   In reflection, I was hoping her yes/no would tell me whether I was a yes or a no, too.

So, what is the effect of this diplomatic approach to sex positivity? Engaging in a specific act—for example, a lap dance or a dance-floor kiss—is not in and of itself revolutionary. In some ways, participating in acts that one does not actually want to do is more sex negative than it is positive.[39] Suddenly becoming kinky, poly, or anything else that's trending, does not imply heightened sexual subjectivity—it is just acquiescing to a shifted, albeit liberal, normativity.

In the end, this acquiescence does not make us more liberated. Research shows that despite Canada's public face as a welcoming, diverse nation, the country's promotion of liberalism actually acts to preserve hegemony.[40] It's a veil, a facade. In fact, Canada's liberalism is associated with more measurable perpetuation of inequality,[41] if you can believe it. Canada's narrative about multiculturalism is a perfect example: the country's reputation as an ethnocultural mosaic is "a corrective to the rigidity of the ethnic, cultural, and racial hierarchy which had been built into its institutions and its practices."[42] It's a cover up for a history of institutionalized racism, colonialism, residential schools, indentured workers, and white guilt.

It's certainly an enticing facade, yet in the end, *liberal* and *liberated* are not synonyms. Saying we're sex positive, and going through the motions, is meaningless (and harmful!) without building the self-knowledge and skills to practice sex positivity with integrity.

---

[37] Randall Denley, "Denley: Trudeau's troubling inconsistency," *Ottawa Citizen*, September 30, 2015, http://ottawacitizen.com/news/politics/denley-trudeaus-troubling-inconsistency.

[38] In thinking about Canadian diplomacy, I can't help but think about Justin Trudeau's timid responses to Donald Trump. For example, Trudeau's official Twitter statement after Trump withdrew from the Paris Accord was that he was "disappointed."

[39] Carisa R. Showden, "Theorizing Maybe," *Feminist Theory* 13, no. 1 (2012).

[40] Seiler, "Melting Pot and Mosaic: Images and Realities."

[41] Ibid, 100; specifically, this study was referring to the economic status of immigrants in Canada's cultural mosaic compared to the US's melting pot.

[42] Ibid, 102.

The truth about sex positivity is that it requires you to want something. Certainly, that something can be nothing, or not right now, or anything that includes consent, but the idea is that you need to want it. Mild-mannered, diplomatic Canadians struggle with this. Sex positivity is "a movement that arose from a need for us to accept and value sexuality without guilt, shame, and hurt."[43] What happens when people are too polite (read: guilty) to say no? To say what they actually want? Helloooooo Canada! We need to peel back the mild-mannered facade of liberal diversity and ask ourselves, what do we WANT?!

In my journey toward becoming fully-developed sex-positive being, I have encountered some moments of hope. One of these moments came from a project titled The Hermit Project, created by Tessa Wills.[44] Wills would consistently ask participants, regardless of what they were doing, "What would make this better for you right now?" It must be true that there is always room to improve. This is a new framing, one that doesn't rely on responses—yeses and noes—but instead asks individuals to constantly scan for pleasure and desire and supports moment-to-moment movement toward increased enjoyment. This is my new experiment, as I fuck a new friend or an old partner, as I share dinner with my parents, as I struggle to make decisions at work. I ask myself, "What would make this better for me right now?" and I invite my peers to do the same.

What would make this better for you right now?

---

[43] Fabello, Melissa A. "3 Reasons Why Sex Positivity without Critical Analysis Is Harmful." everyday feminism. May 14, 2014. http://everydayfeminism.com/2014/05/sex-positivity-critical-analysis/.

[44] Elizabeth J. Cooper, private conversation with author, May 2017; Learn more about Wills' work at tessawills.com.

HOW I CAME TO BE SEX POSITIVE AS AN ASIAN WOMAN WHO IS ALSO A SEXOLOGIST, AND HOW YOU CAN TOO
by Martha Lee

As the first sexologist in Singapore with a doctorate in human sexuality, I consider myself privileged to support and witness my clients as they reclaim their sexuality and transform their (sexual) lives as individuals and often also as couples. Frequently, they come with questions of what's "normal," "common," "average," and "right," and it falls to me to inform, educate, advocate, and coach without taking away their sovereignty and freedom of choice. At times, I am the first person they have ever spoken to about the sex or confided to about their sexual problem(s).

It is easy to see the link between how our perceived and actual negative sexual experiences lead to negative emotions such as fear, anxiety, guilt, shame, shyness, embarrassment, and numbness. Yet it is also our thoughts, beliefs, attitudes around sex and sexuality that label our sexual experiences as good or bad, and even positive or negative. While one person might shrug off an encounter as a one-off, another individual could be seen having their equilibrium shaken to the core. What makes a person supposedly more sexually resilient?

I believe it is their sexual attitude—which is linked to their access to sex education. One can only be sex positive if they have a positive sexual attitude. The lack of sex ed contributes to a negative sexual attitude and is the culprit of much of the suffering we experience—increased teenage pregnancy, sexually transmitted infection rates, sexual inhibitions, and so on. In Singapore, some parents still insist that sexuality education encourages "promiscuity," and the government has announced that ours is a more abstinence-based sexuality education program. This does a gross disservice to our youth but is better than the sex ed many of my clients and I had growing up—which was little or none!

Putting political, religious, societal, cultural, and familial challenges and barriers aside, how do we as individuals take charge of our lives and take responsibility to replace a negative sexual attitude with a more affirming one? The keyword here is *replace*. We need positive sexual stories and positive sexual experiences to heal and replace the old ones! What can we replace ignorance with? Education. How do we as adults heal our relationship with our sexuality?

Take me, for instance. How did somebody who had little sexuality education growing up become a sex-positive sexologist? To begin with, my relationship with my sexuality wasn't as negative as my peers' (note that I didn't say positive). I had a distinct sense from occasional interactions with my mom around sex that sex wasn't bad and that it was something I could look forward to when I grew up. That thought fed a belief that sex must then be fun, wonderful, and amazing. My initial partnered sexual experiences were empowering and affirming, which strengthened my positive beliefs and attitudes around sex. Because I was interested in learning how to be better at sex, I took it upon myself to learn what I could of sex, inadequate and futile as my efforts were (this was before Facebook and YouTube).

I thought I knew a lot about sex before embarking on my sexuality studies but, of course, learned over the course of my studies that sex was more than sex. At sex school (Institute of Advanced Study in Human Sexuality), I filled in gaps in my knowledge (including learning the names of different parts of our sexual anatomy), understanding (kink and relationship choices), and healing (shame and upper-limit beliefs around pleasure). Through the training received, I can converse about sex with a straight face, educate with factual accuracy, and support with compassion—all the while adding my unique dose of light-heartedness around sex. I have been repeatedly told that what I teach (content) is less important than who I am (my being). Because they had previously lacked sex role models, I became an example of what could be (for an Asian)—a sex heroine!

Now, let's bring this back to you! Here's how I believe one can become more sex positive:

1. Let go of any political, religious, societal, cultural, and familial blame – To blame is to point fingers at what something and somebody could and should have done. This doesn't contribute or add anything toward the quality of your life other than make you an angry or bitter person. Kids do that, and you're not a kid anymore. Let all that rubbish go.

2. Claim your sexuality – Your sexuality is not anybody's (including your partner) but yours. Sure, you can have political, religious, or cultural views and beliefs that influence your sexuality, but ultimately what you decide to do with your sexuality is your choice. Your sexuality is undeniably yours to feel, enjoy, express, and share—if you wish to.

3. Take care of your relationship with sexuality – When something is yours, you take care of it, e.g. your career, studies, finances, and belongings. Your sexuality is no exception. Beyond making sure it is okay, perhaps you would like to nurture, invest in, or cultivate it?

4. Decide what you want to do – It's not enough to claim your sexuality (plant a flag on it) and take care of it (maintenance mode). What else is there to your sexuality? What would make you happy as a sexual person? You can choose to do nothing (hopefully for a short time only) or something but be conscious that it's your choice and you cannot blame anybody for your choices, including yourself.

5. Learn more than what you think you think – Do you want to learn by reading articles or books, listening to lectures or podcasts, talking to people you trust, or attending events and workshops? There are many free resources and content out there! Our sexuality involves more than the physical act of sex. There's sensuality, intimacy and relationships, gender/ sexual identity, and sexual health. You will discover which aspects of your sexuality need more attention when you begin to learn more about it.

6. Heal and forgive – Many sexually functional people don't see how they might need or could benefit from sexual healing, since they can have sex. Healing and forgiving around our sexuality could extend to things like being born a woman/man subjected to sexualization and discrimination, reconciling their feminine or masculine side, releasing their negative emotions around masturbation or sex with the same or opposite gender, or more. Heal all shadow aspects of sex including memories of nonconsensual touch or painful sex, and you will feel freer and stronger. We all need sexual healing, and you are no exception. You might benefit from the support of a sex-positive practitioner as you engage in this process.

7. Practice and experiment – If we approached sex with childlike curiosity and wonder, we wouldn't be afraid to ask questions in order to get feedback, conduct pleasure/pain experiments, and practice techniques so that we might get better at it. Sure, our partner might say or do things that hurt us, but if we owned tools to heal ourselves, we'd be less afraid of not being able to take it. If we had the communication tools to assert ourselves, negotiate, compromise, and navigate through difficult conversations, we wouldn't be scared to raise what might be a sensitive subject. People who try can get better as opposed to those who don't bother.

8. Let go of judgments – When we are hard on ourselves and label ourselves as a loser or never good enough, these negative thoughts lead us to feeling bad and start to shape our reality. Sex-positive people ease up on the self-labeling and labeling other people. We don't have to identify as a LGBTTIQQ2SA (Lesbian, Gay, Bisexual, Transsexual, Transgender, Intersexual, Queer, Questioning, Two-Spirited, and Asexual) to be sex positive. Sex-positive people get that our LGBTTIQQ2SA friends, like everybody else, just want to be safe and happy. Sure, some aren't looking for a love, relationship or marriage. Maybe they're just looking for fun or seeking new experiences. Sex-positive people don't judge.

I hope this piece has been useful to you, and I would like to invite you to reflect on my definition of sex positivity:

Sex positive is an adjective often used to describe people who are comfortable with their own sexuality and sexuality in general. It is not about having unfulfilling, guilt-ridden, and downright bad sex void of pleasure —nor about judging the sex lives of others and making anybody feel bad (including you) for what you do or do not choose to do. Being sex positive is being sex affirmative.

What is your definition of sex positive? What could you do to further your relationship with your sexuality so that you can be more sex positive? More importantly, what are you willing to do and what are you going to do—for you?

SEX IS BORING IN PARTS
by Captain Snowden

One
Yes
Kinkier than thou
Polyier than thou
More Tantra than thou
Not helpful
It's called play for a reason
Noes are essential to trust yeses
Boundaries are sexy
Some walls
Some crepe paper caked with glitter

Two
No Failing and failing is sex positive
& let's circle back & repair & apologize & breathe
Re-member that each one of us is the person someone else is being patient with
What if there is no re-pair or re-member nothing to go back to that can hold us all in the silence we really need to under-stand each other.
Let's create new culture together caring for each other its a verb right, thanks bell

Three
Maybe The Eros is a trickster
Following looping spirals with trapdoors working at pleasure
Pleasure for work
For pleasure work do it long enough & you've done it long enough

Four
Convive Bodies change over time
Not having desire is sex positive- period
Genders are galaxies triple folded on each other like that note I sent you in 6th grade
Desire changes
Bop it down and it comes up like a whack-a-mole. Again and again- sometimes It also naps
That thing that I yucked I have been thinking about so much that now I am wondering where I can find someone to do it with Where did I put that number?

WRITERS BIOGRAPHIES

Allena Gabosch

Executive Director of both the Center For Sex Positive Culture and Foundation for Sex Positive Culture from their creation until retiring January 1, 2015, has been active in the sex positive movement practically from its inception; producing educational and social events for the sex-positive community since 1990. She is a frequent speaker on many sexuality related subjects at colleges and conferences around the US and Canada and Europe, with an emphasis on Sexuality, Relationships, BDSM and Polyamory. She is working on two books. Her personal mission statement is to bring joy to sexuality and to make a difference in the world.

Andrew Gurza

Andrew Gurza is a Disability Awareness Consultant and Cripple Content Creator whose written work has been featured in Huffington Post, The Advocate, Everyday Feminism, Mashable, and Out.com, as well as several anthologies. He is also the host of the *DisabilityAfterDark Podcast: The Premiere Podcast Shining Light on Sex and Disability* available on all podcast platforms.

Andrew resides in Toronto, Canada. You can find out more about his work at **www.andrewgurza.com** or connect with him on **Twitter @andrewgurza.**

Annie Sprinkle & Beth Stephens

Beth Stephens & Annie Sprinkle have been partners and collaborators fifteen fertile years. Their Ecosex Manifesto launched a movement and officially added the E to GLBTQIE. Their award winning documentary film about coal mining in Beth's home state West Virginia, Goodbye Gauley Mountain—*An Ecosexual Love Story* is available on Netflix & iTunes. They just finished a new documentary, *Water Makes Us Wet—An Ecosexual Adventure*. If they weren't busy enough, they've also just released a book, *Explorer's Guide to Planet Orgasm*. Beth is a professor and chair of the Art Department at UCSC and Annie is an artist and college lecturer. In 2017, their work was exhibited in the prestigious art exhibition, documenta 14, in Germany.

Beau Korvin Black

Beau Korvin Black is Ojibwa (Chippewa), French, Scottish, and a sprinkling of English. They are Two-Spirit, Masculine-of-Center (MoC), Leather Daddy, and a bdsm switch. Beau is a new face to writing in published works, but an old hat at unpublished poetry writing. They began writing poetry as an angsty teen and early twenty-something. They are embarking on a new adventure as a life coach and public speaker. This is a dream and a calling for them. Beau lives in Seattle, Washington with their amazing roommate, two spunky cats, and a very handsome little dog. When not bent over a pad of paper, or in front of a computer screen, writing deep thoughts, they can be found sitting on their balcony sipping hot coffee, and enjoying the misty rain of the Pacific Northwest.

Betty Dodson

Betty Dodson, artist, author, and PhD sexologist has been one of the principal voices for women's sexual pleasure and health for over four decades. Her first book, *Liberating Masturbation: A Meditation on Selflove* ('74) became a feminist classic. *Sex for One* ('87) sold over a million copies and is an international best-selling book. *Orgasms for Two* ('02) embraced partner sex. Most recently, she released *Sex By Design* that details her experiences with America's Sexual Revolution, the women's movement and her feminist sexual activism.

In 2011, Betty received the public service award from SSSS (Society for the Scientific Study of Sexuality) and the MASTERS AND JOHNSON AWARD presented by SSTAR (Society for Sex Therapy and Research). Betty was recently named one of the top ten sexual revolutionaries by Cosmopolitan magazine and number 43 of the 100 most important people in sex by Playboy Magazine.

Tina Schermer Sellers, PhD

Tina has had a distinguished career as a marriage and family therapist, medical family therapist, and certified sex therapist. As professor, researcher, author, and speaker, she has won numerous awards and been featured on radio, TV, podcasts and documentaries. She is the founder and Medical Director of the Northwest Institute on Intimacy which provides sexual health and sexual dysfunction treatment training to clinicians and clergy not otherwise provided in their graduate training. Her award winning book, *Sex, God, and the Conservative Church – Erasing Shame from Sexual Intimacy* reveals the devastation caused by sexual shame in the wake of the purity and abstinence only movements, and reveals the path to healing for both clinician and client. Check out the website **ThankGodForSex.org** to find videos of people who were affected by abstinence education and who have found healing through therapy and other forms of emotional and sexual healing. **www.TinaSchermerSellers.com** and **www.InstituteOnIntimacy.com**

Dawn Celeste McGregor

Dawn Celeste McGregor is a cis-woman, queer, sex-positive activist and advocate for consent and a shame-free society. She is a LGBTQAI and Woman's Rights activist, Expansion Coach, Mysticism and Relationship Expert and Professional Writer who teaches about equity, authenticity, expansion of the self and society, personal freedom, responsibility, connection and opening to the flow of the Universal Force. Her writing about has been published in The Advocate, Unite Magazine, Seattle Gay News and The Seattle Lesbian. She has a monthly column in The Seattle Lesbian called *Queer Relationships*. **Facebook@Expansive Living and coaching and writing** website is, **expansiveconnections.com**.

Buck Angel

Buck was born female on June 5,1962. He never felt female and struggled through life until he had the life-changing opportunity to transition from female to male and finally live life authentically. He had many obstacles during his transition mostly due to no information for transitioning for FTM transsexuals. But with the help of compassionate doctors, he lives his truth and now can help to educate the world with his story. His mission is to inspire people to redefine gender and to foster a new generation as they discover the fluidity of sexuality and navigate gender politics. His message "It's not what between your legs that defines you" has sparked many a conversation and opened minds to the important message that gender is what you say it is for you, and that self-acceptance is not only what makes a person happy, it's how others come to understand you. Angel travels the world spreading his message of self-love, compassion and exploring how to live authentically in your own body.

Charlie Glickman PhD

Charlie Glickman PhD is a sex & relationship coach, a sexuality educator, a sexological bodyworker, and an internationally-acclaimed speaker. He's been working in this field for over 25 years, and some of his areas of focus include sex & shame, sex-positivity, queer issues, masculinity & gender, communities of erotic affiliation, and many sexual & relationship practices. Charlie is also the co-author of The Ultimate Guide to Prostate Pleasure: Erotic Exploration for Men and Their Partners. Find out more about him on his website **charlieglickman.com** or on **Twitter @charlieglickman** and **Facebook @charlie.glickman**. For Charlie's sex coaching and sexological bodywork services, visit **MakeSexEasy.com**.

Cunning Minx

Cunning Minx is the sultry-voiced producer and host of the *Polyamory Weekly* podcast, now with over 300 episodes. The podcast shares tales from the front of responsible non-monogamy from a pansexual, kink-friendly point of view. A kinky boobiesexual, Minx founded the show as a resource for the poly and poly-curious to form a community, share experiences and help guide each other on their journeys of poly and kinky exploration. Minx has been a submissive, bottom and otherwise generally non-dominant type for the past ten years.

Minx has spoken on poly, kinky and Web 2.0 community-building topics at ShibariCon, Geek Girl Con, MomentumCon, Atlanta Poly Weekend, Sex 2.0, Leather Leadership Conference, Dragon*Con, GD2, Heartland Polyamory Conference, New York Poly Pride and Poly Living. The Poly Weekly podcast is the winner of the 2007 Erotic Award for Best Podcast and has received accolades from ErosZine, Fleshbot and the Chicago Sun-Times.

D J Williams

D J Williams is the Director of Research for the Center for Positive Sexuality and a social / behavioral scientist at Idaho State University. His scholarship intersects sexology, leisure science, and criminology. D J is a leading expert on deviant leisure, thus he is sometimes affectionately known as "Dr. Deviant." His research has been published in numerous academic journals and books, and his work has been featured in media outlets worldwide.

Dawn Serra

Sex is a social skill. Dawn Serra speaks it, writes it, teaches it, and she helps you learn how to develop it. She is the creator and host of the weekly podcast, Sex Gets Real, and of the annual sexuality summit, Explore More. She also lectures at colleges and universities on sex and relationships and works one-on-one with clients who need to get unstuck around their pleasure and desire. Dawn identities as a white, cis, queer, fat, trauma survivor and uses pronouns she/her/hers.

Deej Juventin

Deej is a leader in the field of embodied therapy and somatic sex education. His work focuses on supporting people to mobilize the body's innate capacities for growth, learning and change. He has helped pioneer somatic education, teaching professional trainings in sexological bodywork, somatic sex education and embodied counselling in Australia and internationally.

He is the founding president of the Somatic Sex Educators' Association of Australasia, and co-director of the Institute of Somatic Sexology. Deej holds qualifications in psychology, sociology, counselling, adult education, bodywork, somatic sex education and professional supervision. He has a Masters in Somatic and Spiritual Psychology, and was awarded Somatic Sex Educator of the Year at the Sexual Freedom Awards in London in 2016.

He believes in radical acceptance as part of the process of change.

Dr Liz Powell

Dr. Liz believes that great sex can change the world. She is on a mission to help you have more meaningful, pleasurable relationships in life and work, as well as the bedroom. She's a coach and licensed psychologist (CA 27871) helping couples and singles develop self-confidence and authenticity in their relationships, whether conventional or non-traditional. Dr. Liz has made multiple media appearances, including as a co-host as on the Life on the Swingset podcast and on the Canadian Broadcasting Corporation radio show Ideas. As a sex educator, Dr. Liz has spoken on many stages internationally including the American Association of Sexuality Educators, Counselors, and Therapists Annual Conference, the Guelph Sexuality Conference, and the Woodhull Sexual Freedom Summit. Dr Liz believes that being confident in who you are is the gateway to great relationships and great sex - and great sex, according to Dr. Liz, can change the world. Learn more about Dr. Liz at **sexpositivepsych.com**.

Emily E. Prior

Emily E. Prior is the Executive Director for the Center for Positive Sexuality and a Social Scientist. Her research focuses on the intersections of identity, deviance, and feminism. Emily has studied human sexuality and gender topics from a variety of perspectives, including Psychology, Sociology, and Anthropology and won the Vern Bullough Award for research. Her work with the Center allows her to incorporate her love of educating and research within a positive sexuality framework.

Verena Neuenschwander

Her main interests are human relationships, sexuality, love, spirituality which are practiced with an integral frame that include body, mind, soul and spirit. Spiritual ground is mainly tantra and yoga, both traditional and contemporary, coming together in an integral life practice.

Aside she works as an osteopath and shiatsu therapist in her own practice for over 30 years, where she accompanies and supports people on their way of healing.

Remigius (Remy) Wagner

Remigius (Remy) Wagner works with several groups who deepen consciousness with meditation, bodywork, love and integral life practice. He holds a MA in Art History, Linguistics and Computer Science and diplomas as teacher, trainer and coach. He is mainly active as a cultural historian, coordinator and editor.

Eva Sless

Eva Sless is an award-winning Australian writer who specialises in sex with a focus on education and pleasure. For twenty years Eva has been entertaining, educating, and amusing audiences with her unique style, her tongue-in-cheek humour, and solid advice.

Her recently published sex education book titled "A Teen Girls Guide To Getting Off" is essential reading for young women and parents of young women with the aim of changing the world, one sex-positive conversation at a time.

From sex toy reviews and personal anecdotes, to researched advice and education for women, Eva is often referred to as the Indiana Jones of sex: Wild and exploratory and a little bit silly... With a classroom element.

Gloria Brame

A former English professor, Gloria Brame first became interested in the study of human sexuality when she got personally involved in the BDSM world, circa 1985. In 1991, she began work on her classic textbook of kink and fetish, Different Loving. Her research into the history and social anthropology of sex transformed her life. She became obsessed with a simple question: who gets to decide what's normal sex? She saw that most theories of masturbation, sexual performance, BDSM/fetish, gender and all non-heteronormative sex and gender expressions were tainted by social prejudices, and has made it her mission to shine a more truthful light on these subjects. Gloria completed her Ph.D. in Human Sexuality specializing in BDSM/fetish in 2000. In the 10 sex books she's published since then, Gloria has devoted herself to studying the evidence on sex and gender diversity and the psychobiology of sex. Her work has made her a leader in the study of sex, with an international reputation as a pioneer in the field.

IM Jae

IM Jae is an internationally recognized sex educator and coach. She has been actively involved with alternative sexual lifestyle communities for many years, both attending events as well as in leadership positions, including holding the title of Ms World Leather 2006. IM Jae produces a variety of events such as education retreats, classes, sex trivia, play parties, etc. She has a sex education podcast called Size Queen Love, as well as a blog and live meetup event that are all about men with large penises and the people who want them. In her personal life, she is the "mother" of a very sassy parrot. The Washington DC area is where she currently makes her home. You can find her in on **Instagram @IMJCoach** and her websites are **imjcoach.com** and **sizequeenlove.com**.

Janet Hardy

Janet W. Hardy is the author or coauthor of twelve groundbreaking books about relationships and sexuality, including *The Ethical Slut* (more than 200,000 copies sold to date, including the third edition published in 2017 by Ten Speed Press).

Janet has traveled the world as a speaker and teacher on topics ranging from ethical multipartner relationships to erotic spanking and beyond. She has appeared in documentary films (Slut, Beyond Vanilla, Vice and Consent, BDSM: It's Not What You Think), television shows (SexTV, The Dr. Susan Block Show), and more radio shows and podcasts than she can count.

Janet serves as Editorial Director for Greenery Press, the firm she founded in 1992, as well as for Down There Press. She also runs The Active Voice, which offers editorial, event and promotional consulting.

She often fantasizes about being handcuffed to Stephen Sondheim's piano.

Jay Wiseman

Jay Wiseman has over 40 years of experience in BDSM and was one of the early pioneers and builders of the BDSM community in the San Francisco area. Jay is the author of the frequently recommended book "SM 101: A Realistic Introduction" and the founder of the publishing company that later became Greenery Press. His book, "Jay Wiseman's Erotic Bondage Handbook" is widely hailed as the book that sets the standard of fundamental knowledge for this practice. His instructional videos on rope bondage are excellent resources for both beginners and experienced bondage practitioners. His book "The Toybag Guide to Dungeon Emergencies and Supplies" provides crucial information to both players and dungeon monitors. He is currently working on a number of books and videos.

Jay holds a first-degree black belt in Tae Kwon Do, is an on-again, off-again member of Mensa, and lived in San Francisco's Haight-Ashbury district during the Sixties. A former ambulance crewman with years of experience, and recipient of the highest Red Cross commendation for emergency action, Jay now teaches classes in basic and advanced emergency medical care for BDSM clubs and other groups. After receiving his law degree in 2005 and passing the California bar exam in 2006, he sometimes works as a part-time law school professor. He is also a certified mediator. His areas of special legal interest include providing legal support for alternative communities, teaching bar exam preparation, search and seizure law, and conflict resolution.

His website is, predictably, **www.jaywiseman.com.**

Jaz Papadopoulos

Jaz is an interdisciplinary artist and writer of Greece, Turkish and Ukrainian descent. They work in experimental poetry, installation, video and performance. As an edge-walker, they explore the in-between – that which is overlooked by language and other social and cultural powers. They are interested in diaspora, gender, bodies, place, memory, grief, and ritual, and work with a practice informed by feminism, and spirituality, and embodiment. In 2016, Jaz completed a residency at the Cartae Open School in Winnipeg, Canada, and performed at documentary

14 in Athens, Greece alongside Annie Sprinkle and Beth Stephens. Currently, they are a recipient of the New Artist in Media Art Production Fund at Video Pool in Winnipeg; are the Arts and Culture editor for an alternative newspaper, The Uniter; and are a collaborator with the alternative theatre company Happy/ Accidents. Their video works can be found on their vimeo page, at **vimeo.com/ jazpapadopoulos**. Born on Treaty 1 territory, Jaz now splits their time between Winnipeg and the west coast of Turtle Island. They revel in reading through their colourful book collection, eating fruit off the tree, and cackling around a table with other witches.

Jimanekia Eborn

Jimanekia Eborn is a sex educator as well as a trauma specialist. She is someone that has had trauma in her life. Being someone born intro trauma, having her mother murdered at a young age. That has led her to want to help others that have been assaulted, others that need a safe healing space. She has been working in the field of mental health since she was 22 years of age. There is where she found her passion for helping those that have experienced sexual trauma. Through her work, she has connected with teenagers and adults around the world. Jimanekia is striving to provide support for those that have struggled after sexual assault. She wants to assist you with reconnecting with your sexuality and spirituality. Whatever, that means to you. As well as providing sexual education to the world.

SEWJim.com
MorethanNo.org (I am the Director of Education for this non profit)
www.morethansex-ed.org (I am a facilitator and teach 4th-12th grade comprehensive sexual education)

Joel Davis

A series of grueling aptitude tests 40 years ago revealed that, despite having a little interest in a lot of things, Joel had no great interest in anything in particular. Armed with that insight, Joel has spent the past 30 years as a freelance American Sign Language interpreter, mostly in the Seattle area, where he makes his home with his husband, Shawn, and their not-at-all-spoiled dog, Bandit. When not volunteering as a peer support group facilitator as he has for the past 20 years, Joel thrives on a decades' long stint with the Seattle Men's Chorus and, as the founding Archivist for the Gay And Lesbian Association [GALA] of Choruses, has written extensively on the history of the organization and the LGBT Choral Movement.

Joel has been HIV-Positive for more than half his entire life and is proud to assert that he is among the first cohort of long-term, HIV-Positive Gay Men to stand on the precipice of retirement.

Jordan Bouray

A polyamorous Seattleite born with both a body and brain that didn't exactly meet factory specs, Roundfoot teaches on kink and sexuality from an unusual perspective: a seated one.

Karen Lucas

Karen 'Kaz' Lucas is an established leader in the Kenyan arts and culture ecosystem. Having begun her career in the early 2000s as a singer, she has gone on to win awards and run creative ventures and projects cutting across the performing arts, media production, digital marketing and innovative events that shape the industrial standard. Notably, her web-series project Kenyan Woman provided a new perspective on what it means to be a successful woman in Kenya, therefore uplifting young women by demonstrating that women can define themselves beyond stereotypical boundaries. Kaz has had a lifelong passion for changing the way sex education is taught to young people. Driven by this passion and enabled by her media experience, she started The Spread Podcast, a sex positive podcast that creates a safe space for people to understand their sexuality and learn to live confidently in awareness of their sexual identity.

Kevin Patterson

Kevin Patterson is an active member of the Philadelphia polyamory community. He's been practicing ethical nonmonogamy since August of 2002 after opening up a relationship that eventually became his marriage. In April of 2015, Kevin was inspired to start Poly Role Models, an interview series for people describing their experiences with polyamory. Poly Role Models is part of a drive and a desire to change the way our lives and communities are viewed. It is a platform for the diversity of our relationship structures and the people within them to shine through.

Kevin's work can be found and supported on **Facebook @PolyRoleModels** on Tumblr, Twitter, & Instagram, and at **www.patreon.com/PolyRoleModels**

Kim Loliya

Kim Loliya is a coach, bodyworker and consultant specialising in women's sexuality and empowerment. Kim's practitioner work at The Pleasure Institute includes working with trauma, pelvic pain, orgasm difficulties, scar tissue, relationship difficulties and much more. Through body-based, practical tools, Kim creates a gentle healing space for women, non-binary people and couples and offers new avenues for intimacy, joy and healing. Outside of her clinic, Kim works as a facilitator and curator in the U.K and internationally and is the co-creator of sex+, a sex positive magazine that shares real stories and rewrites narratives

Kris Lovestone

Kris Lovestone is a relationship coach & sex educator from Costa Rica who helps people to get what they really want out of their relationships and sex-lives so that there are fewer broken hearts and homes in the world. By teaching emotional intelligence, communication tools and the anatomy of arousal, he facilitates people finding their true authentic desires, boundaries & preferences and assists them to put them into action and manifest them safely in their lives.

He holds a degree in health science, is a masterful facilitator & mediator and is extensively trained in communication protocols, relational technologies and consent best-practices. He is a proud father and a devoted partner in a prosperous long-term open relationship and works as a teacher and speaker. He is the author of Conscious Cock and the Nutella Proposal and is the creator of the *Conscious Cock Boot Camp for men*. Follow him online at **consciouscock.com**

Lasara Firefox Allen

Lasara Firefox Allen is an activist, advocate, and is the author of four books including Jailbreaking the Goddess (Llewellyn, 2016). She works in the field of social work. Mother to two amazing young people and married to the love of her life, Lasara lives with her family in the wilds of Northern California.

Captain Snowdon

Captain Snowdon - captain lives uninvited on the territory of the Lekwungen and WSÁNEĆ peoples on Vancouver Island. Their background is in social justice, harm reduction outreach, sexological bodywork, performance art and poetry. Captain runs the Sex Positive Art and Recreation Centre in Victoria and co-creates the Somatic Sex Educator Professional Training **www.somaticsexeducator.com** Currently, captain uses the pronoun they/them, identifies as a genderqueer-queer radical faery- faggot witch and is in love with the ocean and facilitation for liberation still loving it 30 years and counting..

This is about learnings so far... about how the work of sex positivity is deep and vast. How being with the ebb and flow of desire, eros and community requires us to reimagine again and again the kind of world we want to live in and live in it like we are already there.. here on the ground in practice and fuck up together.

Linda Kirkman

Dr Linda Kirkman PhD is a sexologist, sex therapist and sex educator. She has a background in education and public health, and broad experience in public speaking, lecturing, writing and counselling as well as delivering workshops and seminars. Her work is a flexible combination of counselling or sex therapy, preparing and delivering workshops, seminars and professional development on diverse aspects of sexuality and relationships to audiences ranging from primary age children to health professionals.

Mac McGregor

Mac McGregor is a dedicated, heartfelt activist and educator who focuses every part of his existence on creating a world where people can feel free to be true to themselves. Mac is a bringer of Unity through Community Empowerment and will always find a way to build a bridge instead of a wall. Mac was appointed by the Mayor as a Seattle City Commissioner in 2011 and he served until 2016. Mac is the transgender and gender non-conforming outreach director for Social Outreach Seattle and a former board member for Seattle Counseling Center. He is on the Seattle Police Department LGBT advisory board. And continuously speaks on panels and solo at numerous colleges, non-profit groups and state and city government on gender & sexuality. Mac recently worked on a small team to help Seattle Police Department develop policy and training around working with the transgender community. Mac donates his time as the head instructor for Social Outreach Seattle's Self-Defense Academy, teaching self-defense to empower all people, regardless of income. Mac is also a diversity educator focusing on gender and sexuality. Mac's experience prior to transition was that of a successful female athlete and business owner. This experience led him to be a champion for women's rights, attempting to close the pay gap and achieve equal opportunity for women and folks that are gender variant.

Maggie McNeill

Maggie McNeill was a librarian in suburban New Orleans, but after an acrimonious divorce economic necessity inspired her to take up sex work; from 1997 to 2006 she worked first as a stripper, then as a call girl and madam. She eventually married her favorite client and retired to a ranch in Oklahoma, but began escorting part-time again in 2010 and full-time again early in 2015 after another divorce (this time amicable). She has been a sex worker rights activist since 2004, and since 2010 has written a daily blog called "The Honest Courtesan" **maggiemcneill.wordpress.com** which examines the realities, myths, history, lore, science, philosophy, art, and every other aspect of prostitution; she also reports sex work news, critiques the way her profession is treated in the media and by governments, and is frequently consulted by academics and journalists as an expert on the subject.

Martha Tara Lee

Surrounded by friends who were sexually inhibited and struck by dire lack of positive conversations around sex and sexuality in Singapore, Dr. Martha Tara Lee decided to take it upon herself to be an advocate for positive sexuality by embarking on her doctorate in human sexuality then launching Eros Coaching in Singapore in 2009. Since 2011, she has been the only sexuality educator certified by the American Association of Sexuality Educators, Counselors and Therapists (AASECT) in Singapore. Often cited in the media, Dr. Lee is the appointed sex expert for Men's Health Singapore, and Men's Health Malaysia journals. She is also the host of weekly radio show *Eros Evolution* for OMTimes Radio. She was recognised as one of the 'Top 50 Inspiring Women under 40' by Her World in July 2010, and one of 'Top 100 Inspiring Women' by CozyCot in March 2011. She continues to provide in-person and Skype sexuality and relationship coaching, conduct workshops, and speak at events. She is the author of *Love, Sex and Everything In-Between*; *Orgasmic Yoga: Masturbation, Meditation and Everything In-Between*; and most recently, *From Queen to Princess: Heartbreaks, Heartgasms and Everything In-Between*. **www.ErosCoaching.com**

Dr. Meg-John Barker

Dr. Meg-John Barker is a writer, therapist and activist-academic specialising in sex, gender and relationships. Meg-John is a senior lecturer in psychology at the Open University and has published many academic books and papers on topics including non-monogamous relationships, sadomasochism, counselling, and mindfulness, as well as co-founding the journal Psychology & Sexuality. They were the lead author of The Bisexuality Report and they are involved in running many public events on sexuality and relationships, including Critical Sexology. Meg-John is also a UKCP accredited therapist working with gender, sex, and relationship diverse (GSRD) clients. In addition to their many academic books, they have now written several books for the general public including Rewriting the Rules (Routledge, 2013), Queer: A Graphic History (Icon Books, 2016), Enjoy Sex (How, When and IF You Want To) (Icon, 2017), How to Understand Your Gender (Jessica Kingsley, 2017) and The Secrets of Enduring Love (Penguin, 2016). They are frequently mentioned in the media, and they blog about sex and relationships on **rewriting-the-rules.com. Twitter: @megjohnbarker.**

Justin Hancock

Justin Hancock is a sex and relationships educator, trainer and practitioner working with young people and adults in this field since 1999, and co-author of Enjoy Sex (How, When and IF You Want To) (Icon, 2017). His website BISHuk.com is one of the leading sex and relationships advice websites for all those over fourteen and is sponsored by Durex UK. The accompanying book to the website, Sex Explained: A real and relevant guide to sex, relationships and you was self-published in 2013 which was very well received by activists in sex, sexuality and sexual health work such as Brooke Magnanti, Buck Angel and Dr Ranj Singh. In addition to this Justin works with practitioners in sex and relationships education and sexual health services providing training and resources. He was involved in writing teaching resources for the DO SRE for Schools project. He has made a number of media appearances on television, radio and has written several pieces for newspapers and blogs. **Twitter: @bishtraining.**

Nekole Shapiro

Nekole Shapiro helps you dive into your body to find your own best expert for your own best life. She combines a lifetime of body-work experience with her Columbia University pre-medical and cultural anthropology studies. As a second-generation grassroots organizer, educator and body worker, she is a go to person for parents, birth pros, sex educators, activists and countless others searching to bring the human back to humanity. Her "almost indescribable" approach is catching on and changing lives!

Mark A. Michaels and Patricia Johnson

Mark A. Michaels and Patricia Johnson, co-authors of Designer Relationships, are a devoted married couple. They have been creative collaborators since 1999, and their critically acclaimed titles have garnered numerous awards. Michaels and Johnson are the authors of Partners in Passion, Great Sex Made Simple, Tantra for Erotic Empowerment, and The Essence of Tantric Sexuality. They are co-founders of the Pleasure Salon, a monthly gathering in New York City that brings together sex-positive people and pleasure activists from a variety of communities. **www.MichaelsandJohnson.com**

Race Bannon

Race Bannon has been an organizer, writer, educator, speaker and activist in the LGBT, leather/kink, polyamory and HIV/STI prevention realms since 1973. He's authored two books, been published extensively, spoken to hundreds of audiences, created the world's largest kink-friendly psychotherapist and medical referral service, was a leader of The DSM Project that led to a beneficial change in the way psychotherapy views BDSM, founded a groundbreaking alternative sexuality publishing company, been an internet radio sex talk show host, received national and local awards, appeared in numerous documentaries, and currently writes for the Bay Area Reporter (ebar.com). His sexuality and relationships blog is **bannon.com** and some of his other work can be found at **racebannon.com**.

Kenneth Ray Stubbs, Ph.D.

In 1975 Ray began teaching erotic massage to people of all sexual orientations in San Francisco. His 1989 Erotic Massage — the Touch of Love book was the first instructional book to illustrate genital massage and has sold over a million copies worldwide.

He has taught many somatic modalities and has written/created over a dozen books and DVDs on sacred sexuality including Women of the Light: The New Sacred Prostitute, Sacred Orgasms, and The Essential Tantra. He also co-created the 90-minute documentary The Sacred Prostitute and a recent documentary, Path of the Sexual Shaman: Teachings on Energy, Orgasm, and Wisdom. Ray is the former vice-president of the Association of Sexual Energy Professionals.

On a shamanic path for over two decades, Ray is a 13-year SunDancer and has been greatly influenced by Tibetan Buddhism. His latest creation is the Shaman Cards: Ceremonies for Energy and Wisdom. Via Skype and the phone, he now gives individual sessions and trainings on energy, sexuality, shamanism, and transformation. **www.SexualShaman.com**

More here if interested: **www.whisperedspaces.com/kenneth-ray-stubbs/**

Ron Richardson

Ron Richardson, also known as Lustyguy on Polyweekly, has been around the sex positive movement since the late 1980s. He worked for about five years at Seattle's Lusty Lady, ran an adult video production company that filmed only people in actual relationships, and for the past five years has been a regular co-host and co-producer on *Polyamory Weekly*, Cunning Minx's podcast on polyamory, sexuality, and communications.

Ruby Bouie Johnson

Ruby Bouie Johnson is a clinical social worker and sex therapist who has 14 years of experience in a variety of behavioral health settings. Currently, she is private practice in Plano, Texas. Over the last 4 years, Ruby has been specializing in kinky, polyamorous, and open relationships as well as sexually- and gender-fluid clients. Ruby has a strong family and group theoretical and intervention skill set. She is able to work with triads, quads, and polycules with power dynamics and communication problems. Ruby has published in various journals and in the African American Encyclopedia on Criminology, she has presented at Kinky Kollege, Consent Summit, Association of Black Sexologists and Clinicians, American Association of Sex Educators, Counselors, and Therapists, and her proposal was recently accepted by National Sex Education Conference. Ms. Johnson is a contributor for Huffington Post, is on faculty for the Kink Knowledgeable Program, and serves on the board for the National Coalition for Sexual Freedom. Ruby is the CEO, Founder, and organizer for PolyDallas Millennium LLC.

Ruby has a hub of information at **www.blacksexgeek.net** or **www.facebook.com/blacksexgeek**

Sara Blaze

Sara Blaze is a lifestyle Fem Domme, a Professional Dominatrix, a community leader, a partner and a parent.

Sara is the President of MVK Alternative Lifestyle Society, BC's largest BDSM not for profit organization focused on outreach and education and has held this position for over six years. Sara is also the Producer of Westcoast Bound, MVK's premier annual event focused on BDSM education. With her leadership, Westcoast Bound has grown exponentially from 100 attendees to nearly 500.

As an educator, Sara teaches both locally and internationally and has been interviewed on several occasions.

Shay McCombs

Shay McCombs is a young writer and activist, as well as an incoming freshman at the University of Washington. They are asexual, polyamorous, and nonbinary; they support social justice publicly but heavily criticize it among its advocates. Shay is an enthusiastic research geek, particularly for queer history, effective altruism, medieval music, and cognitive science. Through the local pagan church, Our Lady Of The Earth And Sky, they help lead a small group of second-generation queer pagans that works to foster youth, asexual, and non-binary inclusion in pagan spaces.

Sui Yao

With a visual communication design background and six years of professional experience in the advertising industry, I decided to become an entrepreneur by becoming an independent creator in one of the most exciting ad markets in the world.

I aim to use my art and thirst for experimentation to create work that pushes the edge in this increasingly globalized and commercial world. I aim to transform the social implications of media into intriguing experiences to help all groups, with an emphasis on female cohorts in China.

Born, raised and educated in China and then working in innovative advertising agencies has allowed me to act as the conduit between Eastern and Western value systems. Long-term, I see myself as a vanguard of Chinese culture by bringing China to the world. I endeavor to look at contemporary truths in Chinese culture and try to communicate these to third parties through my work.

Susie Bright

Best-selling author Susie Bright, the country's preeminent feminist sex writer, is one of the world's most respected voices on sexual politics, as well as an award-winning author and editor who's produced and published thousands of the finest writers and journalists working in American literature and progressive activism today.

Tai Fenix Kulystin

Tai Fenix Kulystin provides therapeutic trauma coaching, somatic sex education, tarot and astrology readings, ritual design, writing, and workshops for transformation, liberation, and social change. They strive for authentic, compassionate connection in their work and life, and hope to bring others to a greater sense of sovereignty, self-understanding, and wholeness. Tai is a trans genderqueer, polyamorous, white, professional middle class, queer witch dedicated to anti-oppressive trauma healing work utilizing empathy, embodiment, and pleasure. Their professional coaching work is called Conscious Pleasure and they are based in Seattle, Washington. For more information about Tai's work, please visit **www.TaiKulystin.com**

Tamara Pincus

Tamara Pincus is a licensed clinical social worker and AASECT certified sex therapist who runs a private practice in the Washington DC area. She specializes in working with kinky, poly and LGBTQ clients. Tamara has been active in alternative sexuality communities since 1998. Tamara completed her Bachelors in Psychology at Smith College and her Masters in Social Work at Catholic University of America. She has spoken around the country on issues related to ethics in sex therapy, consent culture, polyamory and BDSM. She has published articles and pamphlets including What Professionals Need to Know about BDSM (through NCSF) and What is Polyamory and Why Do Social Workers Need to Know About it (through GWSCSW). She is one of the authors of the book "Its Called Polyamory: coming out about your non-monogamous relationships." She is a mother of two who lives in a multi partner polyamorous household.

Taryn de Vere

Taryn de Vere is a sex-positive parent, a mother of 5, a writer and parenting adviser.

Teri Ciacchi

Reverend Teri D. Ciacchi, MSW Teri is the relational matrix of the Living Love Revolution, a holistic sex educator, a Priestess of Aphrodite, a leader of the EcoSexuality movement, and an EcoMagicks practitioner. She has been generating Cascadia Holistic Peer Counseling system since 1997, holding Aphrodite Temples since 2000 and co-creating Surrender:The EcoSex Convergence since 2013. In July 2017 she started Interdependence and Autonomy LLC, a for profit business that builds consent culture by healing conflict through education, mediation and facilitation and creating "consent - centric" events. Her newest endeavor is Ecosex Celebrating Lover Earth, held on Orcas Island Summer Solstice 2018.

Reverend Ciacchi looks to Nature for guidance and wisdom. She translates the teachings she receives from mycelium (mushrooms), bees and stardust into useable social skills for human beings. She leads collaborative workshops and events that honor the innate connections between humans and the Living Earth. You can find her works at the following websites:

www.LivingLoveRevolution.org, www.iandaspace.com www.AphroditeTemple.com www.ecosexportland.org and **www.ecosexorcasisland.org.**

Uma Ayelet Furman

Uma is one of Australasia's leading somatic sex educators, with many years of experience working with individuals, people in relationships, and groups. Uma has innovated somatic sex education through her groundbreaking work in client-centred practice. Based in Brisbane, Australia, Uma works internationally, specializing in supporting people to work somatically through sexual issues and concerns. She is a Certified Somatic Sex Educator and a founding member of the Somatic Sex Educators' Association of Australasia (SSEAA).

Veronica Monet

Veronica Monet, ACS is an internationally acclaimed sexual empowerment change agent. CNN, FOX, Politically Incorrect, Yale, Stanford and UC Berkeley are just a few of the numerous news and educational institutions that have hosted Veronica for her forward thinking insights and expertise.

Veronica helps individuals and couples heal shame and live fully. As a Relationship Coach, Sexologist and Anger Specialist, she combines her extensive education with deep empathy. Personally overcoming incest, rape, violence and abuse she is committed to helping others own their personal and erotic empowerment in the most loving and honorable lifestyle tailored to them.

Veronica invites you to join her in *The Shame Free Zone*™. Here you will discover her game-changing *Exquisite Partnership Formula* ™, a program designed to turn conflict into connection and sex that gets better with each passing year.

Yuri Kotke

Yuri Kotke is a Certified Sexological Bodyworker, Sex Educator and Therapist resident in São Paulo, Brazil. Since a very young age, Yuri has tried to understand the mysteries of the body and sexual pleasure. Going first through Performance Art as a Theatre Bachelor, Yuri discovered Sexological Bodywork and traveled to the other hemisphere to take the training in Canada.

Yuri believes sexual pleasure and connection is our birthright, our shared heritage, and something we all can access with the right tools. He, together with Paula Fernanda Andreazza, helms the Latin American Institute for Somatic Sexology, a business with the intention to assist the sexual awakening of Latin America through body-based practices and loving, nonjudgmental support for all bodies, orientations and identities.

Jing Jing Wang

Jing Jing Wang is a queer, intersectional feminist, and Chinese American. They spend their time making all forms of art, building community, and loving. **Instagram@jingshiwang01**

www.ingramcontent.com/pod-product-compliance
Lightning Source LLC
Chambersburg PA
CBHW071905290426
44110CB00013B/1283